Donors

City of Falls Church

Falls Church Tricentennial Committee

Virginia Power

Sponsors

Don Beyer Volvo

The Village Preservation and Improvement Society

Ben and Nancy Birindelli

Bob and Meredith Morrison

Jim and Mary Slattery

Dave and Edie Snyder

Ed Strait

Ric and Trudy Terman

Jim and Olga Trollinger

Tom and Mary Margaret Whipple

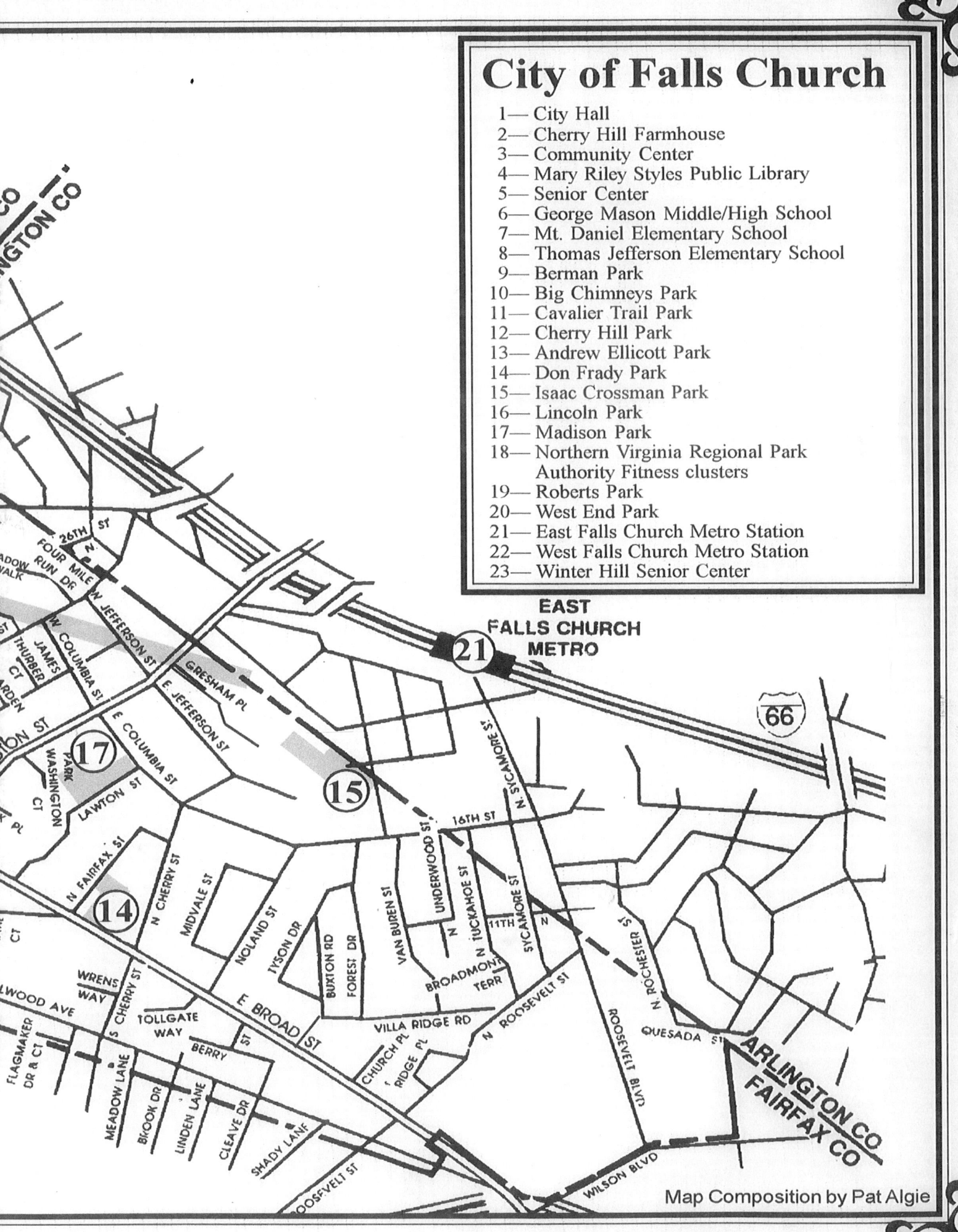

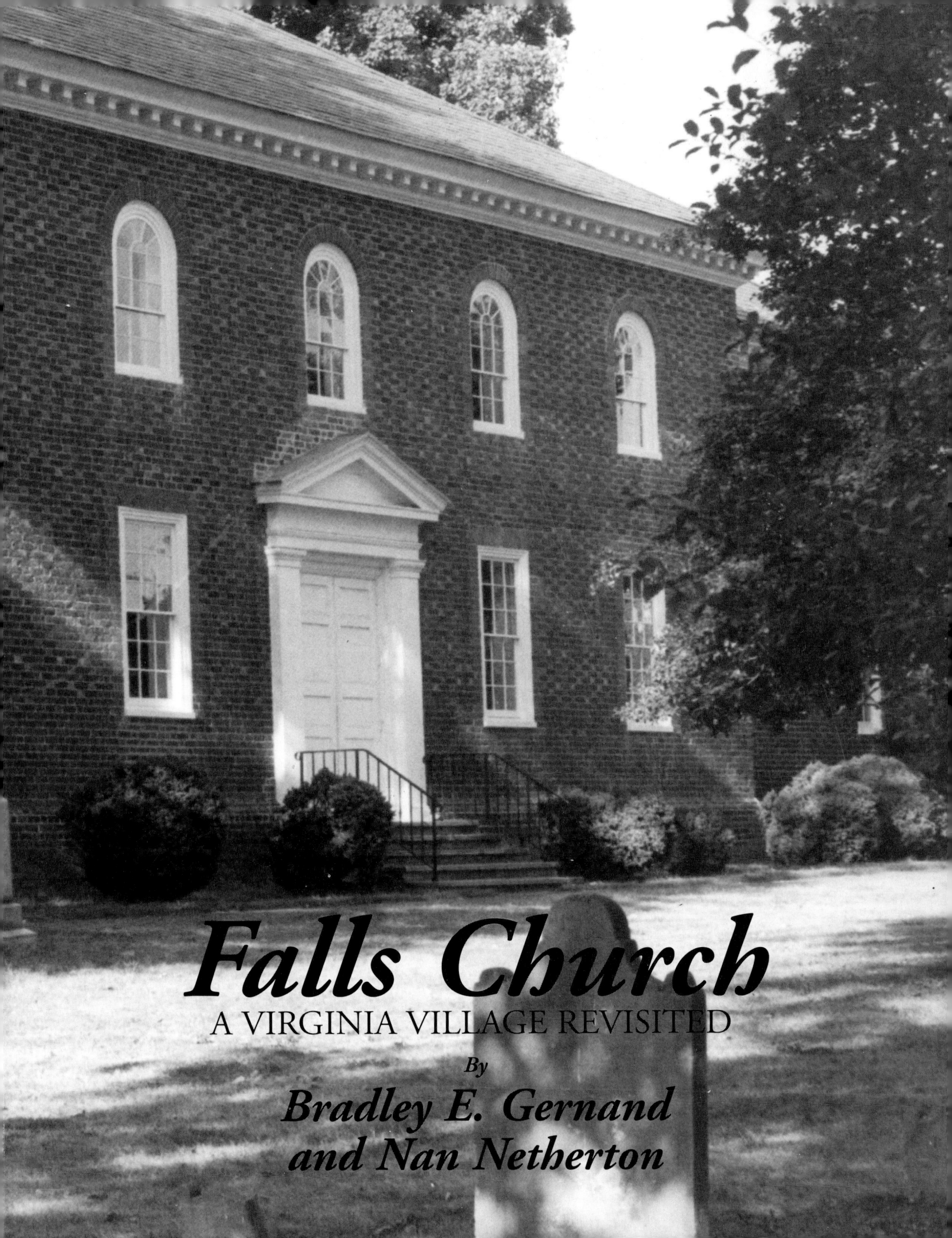

Falls Church
A VIRGINIA VILLAGE REVISITED

By
Bradley E. Gernand
and Nan Netherton

City of Falls Church
Mayor David F. Snyder

Council Members

Mary Ann Capria	Daniel E. Gardner	Steven A. Rogers
Merni Fitzgerald	Samuel A. Mabry	Kathie Winckler

City Manager
Daniel E. McKeever

Falls Church City Tricentennial Committee
Ben Birindelli, Chair

Joyce Cory	David Eckert	Rosemary Hayes Jones
Barbara Cram	Merni Fitzgerald	John Rodock
Ron Crouch	Edna Frady	Kieran Sharpe
Susan Earman		Maurice Terman

Staff Liaison: Nancy Birindelli, Deane Dierksen, Diane Morse
Representatives: Patsy Mitchell, USPS; Marie Yochim and Doris Katz, DAR
Deane Dierksen, 100th Anniversary Library
Nancy Birindelli, 50th Anniversary of Schools

Falls Church Historical Commission
Maurice J. Terman, Chair

Ronald Anzalone	Deborah H. Green	Shari Marie Maloney
Sarah T. Bridges	Edwin B. Henderson II	Edward B. Strait
Brian Gradle		Adelaide Wang

School Board
John Durham, Chair

Jerome Barrett	William Buckingham	Rosemarie Hunziker
Ruth Brock	Jay Grusin	Kieran Sharpe

School Superintendent: Mary Ellen Shaw

Library Board
Ruel Pile, Chair

Nancy Bentrup	Ronald Crouch	Bradley Gernand
Donald Camp	Chester DeLong	Edward Rose

Library Director: Mary McMahon
Former Library Director: Deane Dierksen

Copyright © 2000 by City of Falls Church

All rights reserved, including the right to reproduce this work in any form whatsoever without permission in writing from the publisher, except for brief passages in connection with a review. For information, write:

The Donning Company/Publishers
184 Business Park Drive, Suite 106
Virginia Beach, VA 23462

Steve Mull, General Manager	Sally C. Davis, Editor
B. L. Walton Jr., Project Director	Scott Rule, Senior Marketing Coordinator
Lora Riley, Graphic Designer	Patricia Peterson, Marketing Designer/Customer Service
Dawn V. Kofroth, Assistant General Manager	John Harrell, Imaging Artist

Library of Congress Cataloging-in-Publication Data

Available Upon Request

Contents

Foreword 6

Preface 7

Acknowledgments 8

Introduction 9

Chapters
- I   Buffalo Trails, Indian Paths and Warehouses 13
- II   A Church "At the Cross Roads Near Michael Reagan's" ... 21
- III   A War for Independence 27
- IV   A Federal Seat of Government 31
- V   The War of 1812: Gunpowder and Refugees 35
- V   Internal Improvements 39
- VII   Balloons and Minié Balls: The Civil War 45
- VIII   A Sense of Community 59
- IX   The Summer Soldiers of 1898: Falls Church and Camp Alger ... 75
- X   Domestic Tranquility 83
- XI   The Great War 99
- XII   The Great Depression and Inter-War Years 103
- XIII   Mobilization and a Second World War 117
- XIV   Unparalleled Growth and Prosperity 123
- XV   Reconfirming Village Roots 143
- XVI   Of, By and For the People: Local Government 157
- XVII   The Falls Church Tricentennial Celebration 169
- XVIII   The Way We Were; The Way We Are 179

Appendices
- A   Mayors and Councilmen Since 1875 193
- B   Postmasters Since 1849 195
- C   Chiefs of Police 196
- D   City Managers 196
- E   Boards and Commissions 197
- F   Village Preservation and Improvement Society Presidents .. 198
- G   Friends of Cherry Hill Foundation Presidents 198

Endnotes 199

A Selected Bibliography 203

Index 207

About the Authors 212

Foreword

We are standing at a crossroads in time and in history. We give thanks for living in a peaceful, free, and prosperous City. We know that it takes everyone to make a little City such as Falls Church work—there are no divisions between the government, the people, and business—we are all part of the same civic ecosystem. It works because we work together to make it work.

The "we" are our citizens—all of us—men and women of many races, nationalities and religions. The "we" are their elected, employed, and volunteer civil servants. The "we" are our businesses who not only serve their customers but who also freely put so much back into our community. The "we" are the people about whom this book is written.

In Falls Church at the threshold of the new millennium, we celebrate a particularly rich heritage. Native Americans roamed the area, followed by European settlers who moved here in 1699 and were the outermost edge of Western civilization. Soon they built The Falls Church. Later, troops marched through here on Braddock's Expedition.

Our local leaders, including George Washington and George Mason, made a revolution and established the framework for the most free nation on earth. One of the corner stones—the Declaration of Independence—was first read in the area at The Falls Church. And it was to here that the leaders of the country fled when invaders occupied Washington, D.C., during the War of 1812.

Later, the great commanders of the Civil War were here, as were thousands of Federal and Confederate troops who moved through or were based in Falls Church and in the forts on the surrounding hills. During the Spanish-American War we were again a major base of operations.

Some of our local citizens were leaders in the fight for equal rights early in this century. During World War II, Dwight Eisenhower lived here as he planned the war effort. Before and since, our veterans and public servants have sacrificed to carry on this heritage. The story of these events told in this book is not just the history of Falls Church but of America.

Now, we are part of the most diverse, educated, economically successful, technologically advanced, compassionate, free and influential region in the world. That is a lot to celebrate and a lot to dedicate ourselves to maintaining in the future. This book will help us do both.

David F. Snyder, Mayor
City of Falls Church

Preface

"The mirror with a memory" is how a much impressed Oliver Wendell Holmes described photography in 1859. Our mirror with a memory begins in about 1855 with the earliest-known photograph of a Falls Church resident. But our mirror may also be said to begin much earlier, with Captain John Smith's map of the Potomac River basin of 1608. A glance at Smith's map reveals a world much different from our own in which a different civilization, with different villages, towns, and place names occupied our region.

Pictures never lie, goes the old saying, but they alone do not illustrate history. Falls Church is uniquely blessed to have excellent cartographic coverage, and we have included several of the most useful maps here. Gifted artists with brush and pen have created depictions of people, places, and local events especially prior to the advent of photography. Selections from such works are included.

Falls Church's photographic history reflects that of the medium. Early Falls Church inhabitants appear grim: limited technology required lengthy exposures in which the subjects remained absolutely still. Smiles were difficult to hold and teeth were often unsightly (smiling in photographs is a twentieth-century convention).

Indoor photos became common in Falls Church after the invention of magnesium flash lighting in 1878. George Eastman revolutionized photography in 1888 by marketing his Kodak camera, which made "snapshots," or casual photography, the realm of the common man. Photography in Falls Church grew by leaps and bounds after this date.

Bradley E. Gernand
Nan Netherton

Acknowledgments

We thank the mayor, David Snyder, for his enthusiastic support for the history book project and the loan of Civil War letters never before published. The Falls Church Historical Commission, Maurice Terman, chair, and members also provided guidance when requested by the authors.

Tricentennial Committee Chair Ben Birindelli and committee members were encouraging to the authors and asked good questions which led to helpful research and answers. Many answers came from the Virginia Room staffs at Fairfax and Arlington Public Libraries. Staff of the Local History Room of the Mary Riley Styles Public Library of Falls Church also remained cheerful, willing, and resourceful in repeated searches for different reference materials and graphics. Janet Daeger-Walden, Beverly Rausch, and Brenda Crowley are pleasant people with whom to work. Deane Dierksen, former library director, gave the authors the benefit of her knowledge, loan of computers, and constructive comments after a careful reading of the manuscript draft. Additional readers included Benson and Nancy Birindelli, Janet Daeger-Walden, Carol DeLong, Jane Dexter, David Eckert, Edna Frady, Edwin Henderson II, John Maier, Diane Morse, Ross Netherton, David Snyder, Maurice Terman, Keith Thurston, Adelaide Wang, and Harry Wells.

When a pictorial publication is involved, good photographs are a vital part of the plan and in addition to the fine professional work of William Edmund Barrett and Quentin Porter and the extensive Falls Church library photo collection, we had help from Barry Buschow, Dr. Frank D'Aquila, Maureen Budetti, Howard Herman, John Maier, Scott Boatright, and many others whose credits are shown with their photos. Tony Chaves supplied some early Falls Church images from his extensive postcard collection.

City staff members who assisted us in various ways were City Attorney Roy B. Thorpe, Jr., City Clerks Elizabeth-Anne Shawen and Kathleen Buschow, Environmental Services Manager Son H. Nguyen, former City Manager Harry E. Wells, Patsy Mitchell, staff, Falls Church Post Office; and Communications Director Sheila Graham assisted with their specialties.

Many writing projects would not be successfully completed without the people who take care of the all-important mechanics of getting through the publication process. Bernie Walton was the representative for publisher Donning in Virginia Beach and worked as coordinator of the project with the authors and the Tricentennial Committee in Falls Church. Matthew B. Gilmore and Margaretha Backers-Netherton did yeoman service assisting with the proofreading of thousands of words. Carol and David Dunlap did much of the preparation of the computer disks for splicing the different parts of the work together. Finally to Richard Colvin for his help with the indexing.

Bradley E. Gernand
Nan Netherton

Introduction

The formation and evolution of Falls Church as a community is firmly rooted in its location, its geology, its native plants and animals, and the early settlers, who have long been forgotten. To understand the community of Falls Church, those exploring its history must first understand those forming elements.

Falls Church is located in the Northern Virginia Piedmont region. The underlying intensely folded rocks of the area were formed over 500 million years ago. They were forcibly intruded by molten rock between 250–400 million years ago. The ground level was later uplifted and then eroded by wind and water when Falls Church was a flat alluvial terrace under a wide, shallow river draining from the western mountain range. River rock was deposited on the ground that is now between 400–450 feet above sea level. Following the demise of the river, continued erosion formed winding, narrow, flat-bottomed valleys, punctuated by river rock and gravel-capped hills. These hills and valleys continue to exist today. Until recent decades, these valleys were referred to as "hollows."

Two main streams, Tripps Run and Four Mile Run, have spring-fed sources just outside of the City of Falls Church boundaries. The streams flow toward the southeast into the Potomac River. They are separated by a ridge that rises to 350–450 feet above sea level, extending from Mount Daniel to Taylor Hill. Tripps Run is bordered by a second higher ridge, to the southwest locally known as Prout Hill, and also known as "Horseshoe Hill."

By the end of the Ice Age, this attractive landscape was characterized by deep weathering and fertile black soil covered by game-rich forests and fish-filled streams.[1]

While there is little left in Falls Church to remind us of the game-rich forest and fish-filled streams, a very small woods on Taylor Hill next to Oakwood Cemetery at Seven Corners prevails. The woods provide a diversity of naturally-occurring native Virginia trees, shrubs, and vines, growing in soil undisturbed for over 140 years. The central portion of the woods is the last undisturbed area in Falls Church that has not been infested by exotic, invasive plants which crowd out the native understory plants critical to the survival of our native songbirds, butterflies, and other wildlife that have evolved in this area over thousands of years.[2]

Based on archaeological discoveries, at least 8,000 years ago Native Americans would gather with their families in small groups beside local streams and establish winter camps from which the men and boys would go on hunting expeditions. Several projectile points, used for spears or arrows, have been found in recent times beside Tripps Run near Sisler's quarry and on Four Mile Run, near the East Falls Church Metro station.[3]

Captain John Smith was the first European explorer who left a written record of flora, fauna, and the native people when he explored the Chesapeake Bay area and the Potomac River in 1608. His book on the subject was published in 1624.

Prince Charles of England, later Charles II, granted to loyal followers in 1649 over 5,000,000 acres of land between the Rappahannock and Potomac Rivers and designated it as the Northern Neck Proprietary. This included territory later to become Fairfax County and still later, Falls Church.

As English settlement of the area began in the late 1600s, county governments were gradually created along with Anglican parishes to administer civic and religious life under the established Church of England. Before Fairfax County was created, Truro Parish was established in what was then Prince William County. The parish vestry ordered at a meeting on March 26, 1733, the construction of The Falls Church, later named after the nearby Little Falls of the Potomac River. It was a wooden frame building completed "at the Cross Roads near Michael Reagans" in 1734.[4]

Fairfax County was established in 1742, but it was more than 100 years later that the Falls Church postal village was designated. This resulted from the growth of the settlement which included the immigration of northerners. The road system between Leesburg and Alexandria had been improved when the Middle Turnpike, now Leesburg Pike, was completed in 1839.

Following the Civil War, railroads, which had been built by 1860, electric trolleys, telegraph, telephones, electric power service, and other transportation and communication improvements made Falls Church a desirable place in which to live.

Village leaders eventually requested a town charter from the General Assembly. This was approved in 1875. Shortly thereafter a large public school was built to educate the children of the community. At the beginning of the twentieth century, in 1900, the population of the town was 1,007. By 1990, the city's population was 9,522. Proximity to the Federal Government and the growth of the nation's capital in Washington, D.C. had profound influences on the growth of Falls Church, which became a city of the second class in 1948.

Falls Church is located in the northeastern corner of Virginia in the Tidewater-Piedmont transition zone of the Potomac River watershed. It is seven miles southeast of and across the Potomac River from Washington, D.C.

The climate is moderate with an average annual temperature of 57.8 degrees Fahrenheit. The average temperature in January is 35.2 degrees and the average temperature in July is 78.9 degrees. The annual precipitation is 47 inches, eight inches of snow and 39 inches of rainfall.

The frost-free season lasts about 200 days each year, long enough for the growth of a wide variety of garden vegetables, fruits, flowering trees, deciduous and coniferous trees, shrubs, and plants. In winter, the ground is generally frozen only to a shallow depth. There are several types of soils and topographical details with gently rolling hills and pleasant stream valleys.

Responsive local government, citizen involvement, an excellent public school system, tree preservation and planting, and historic preservation are major concerns of the Falls Church residents of today.

Maurice Bentley DePutron demonstrating enlightened farm-management technique, undated photo. Courtesy Kay Speakman.

Native American projectiles, including spear points, unearthed from throughout the Falls Church area. Courtesy Michael Johnson, 1999.

CHAPTER I

Buffalo Trails, Indian Paths, and Warehouses

When English adventurers including Captain John Smith arrived in the Virginia colony in 1607 and settled at Jamestown, they found themselves among a politically complex group of semi-sedentary Algonquian-speaking Powhatan Indians. These Native Americans were living in more than thirty small chiefdoms or districts within a regional district called Chicacoan in the Potomac River valley.[1]

The earliest known written account of the Indians of Northern Virginia, their customs and the local flora and fauna was recorded by Captain Smith, who with fourteen other Englishmen left Jamestown in 1608 to explore and map the Chesapeake Bay and its tributaries. These streams included the Potomac River, on which they steered their two-ton open barge to where the boat could go no farther upstream to the Little Falls, referred to as "the head of navigation."[2]

Smith and others have recorded names of eleven different Indian nations or groups living along the lower Potomac from its falls to its mouth on the bay. On the left bank or eastern shore, the Maryland side of the river, were the Nacotchtanks, Piscataways, Pamunkeys, Nanjemoys, Potapacos, and Yaocomacos. On the Virginia shore were the Tauxenents, Patawomekes, Matchotics, Chicacoans, and Wicocomocos.[3] These different native peoples occupied the area and hunted, farmed, fished, and fought in the region at European contact time.[4]

At the head of navigation, where Pimmit Run flows into the Potomac River, trader Henry Fleet exchanged goods with the Iroquois Indians from the north about 1630. He recorded not only having observed the plentiful supply of sturgeon which the natives caught at the Little Falls but also noted that "as for deer, buffaloes, bears and turkeys, the woods do swarm with them and the soil is extremely fertile. . . ."[5]

As permanent settlement by European landowners began, large plantations were first established at choice locations along the main rivers and navigable tributary streams. Yeoman farmers obtained long-term leases from the Northern Neck Proprietary which had been first granted in 1649 by Charles II of England. They grew tobacco, corn, and other crops on their small farms.[6]

One of these humble farmers perhaps built a log house with large brick chimneys at the future site of Falls Church. No early deed or other documentation for that land exists nor is a surname known. A cherished local tradition holds that a large stone set in one of two large chimneys was engraved with the number "1699." The "Big Chimneys" house, near the current site of the Falls Church Post Office, was demolished between 1908 and 1914. It is on this legend of the first establishment of a dwelling in the community in 1699 that the observance of the 300th anniversary is based.[7]

Three well-traversed game and Indian trails gradually became main north-south thoroughfares, one the Sugarlands Rolling Road (now Route 193, the Georgetown Pike), the second, the Falls Rolling Road (now Route 120, Glebe Road and Little Falls Road), and third, what was later called the Alexandria Road by Vestal's Gap in the Blue Ridge. The early road westward and south followed a natural drainage ridge to Difficult Run and was chosen as an avenue of immigration by the first English settlers, also becoming a rolling road in 1732 when the Hunting Creek warehouse was built.[8]

By 1730, Governor Sir William Gooch had already reported that although tobacco was Virginia's largest cash crop, export of wheat from the colony was between 10,000 and 20,000 bushels per year and that the greatest part of that was exchanged for rum, sugar, salt, and molasses brought to Virginia by ships from New England and Bermuda.[9]

Two powerful colonial landed gentlemen, Robert "King" Carter and Thomas Lee, planned to establish a tobacco warehouse at the Little Falls as early as 1728. However, the warehouse was not built until 1742.[10]

Powhatan, ruler of the Indian chiefdom in which the site of Falls Church was located, 1607. Powhatan, attended by his court, is depicted inside his longhouse, or dwelling. He is shown sparing the life of Captain John Smith, who is lying prostrate. Smith, Generall Historie, *1624.*

A tobacco warehouse was built in 1732 on Simon Pearson's land on the upper side of Hunting Creek in what was then Prince William County. The land and warehouse lay within new boundaries when Fairfax County was organized ten years later, in 1742. It was at the site of this warehouse that the Town of Alexandria was established in 1749, the first town in Fairfax County. Tobacco rolling roads were so called because tobacco leaves were tightly packed into round wooden casks or hogsheads and rolled to the marketplace. These early roads were established from western and northern inland farms to towns built on the navigable rivers. One such early thoroughfare from Leesburg east, later known as the Middle or Leesburg Turnpike, passed through the center of the Falls Church community on its way to Alexandria.[11]

Map showing the stream valleys and most prominent hills of Falls Church. Commissioned for this work by the Village Preservation and Improvement Society, 1998.

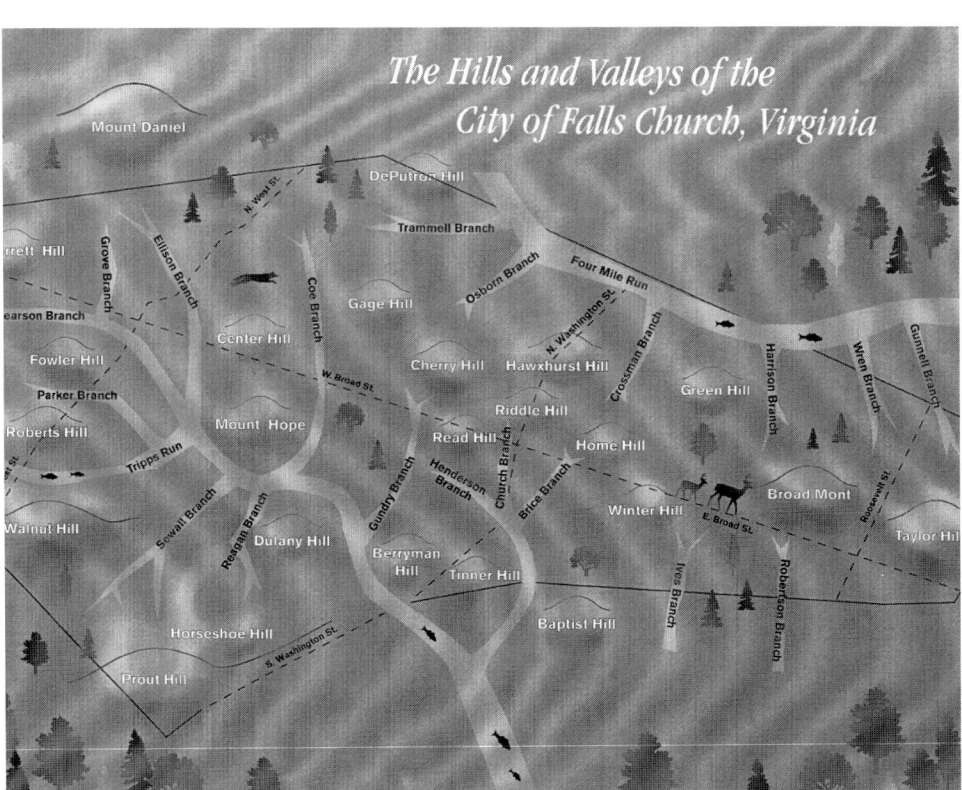

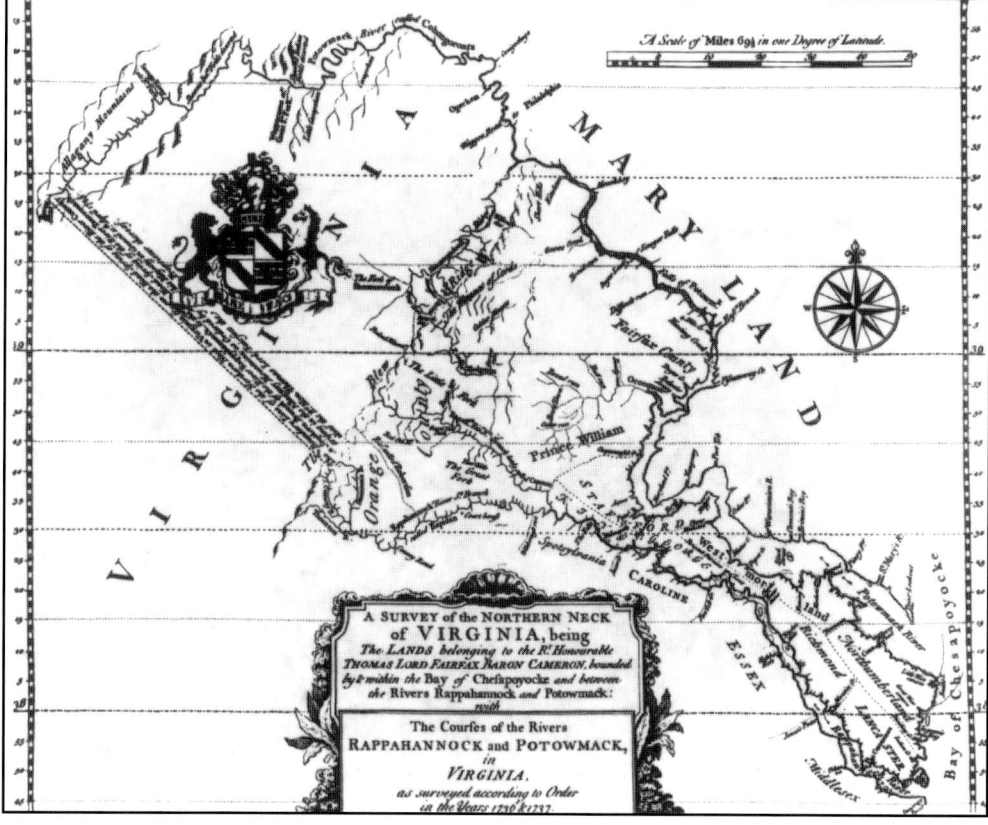

Engraving, Potomac River below Little Falls, circa 1800. The falls of the Potomac River were considered by the colonists and native Americans which preceded them to be the region's most important and defining characteristic. The falls soon lent the first public institution in the area its name—"the church at the falls," eventually shortened to "the falls church," formalized finally as The Falls Church. Courtesy National Archives.

A map of the Fairfax family's Northern Neck Proprietary holdings in Virginia, 1737. The first Falls Church was built three years earlier. The Fairfax family is today headed by Nicholas, 14th Lord Fairfax in Great Britain. John Warner, 1737. Courtesy Library of Congress, Geography and Map Division.

"Land Travelers in Virginia," from an engraving published in 1894. Falls Church was settled by colonists such as these, shown fording a creek in the wilds of Virginia. One settler carries an implement used for hacking a trail. Rivers and creeks, traversed with ships and canoes, offered the easiest transportation. Four Mile Run, Hunting Creek, and the Occoquan and Potomac Rivers were the waterways navigable closest to Falls Church. Lossing, Our Country.

A tobacco-rolling road. Colonial settlers in the Falls Church region used most of the previous Indian foot trails as the basis for their transportation system. Two such trails intersected in Falls Church just west of The Falls Church: later the Leesburg-Alexandria road and the road to the Little Falls of the Potomac. By the 1740s they were important routes for the shipment of tobacco to market. Since tobacco was shipped, or rolled, in large cylindrical casks or hogsheads, such roads came to be called rolling roads. Painting by Carl Rakeman, courtesy Federal Highway Administration.

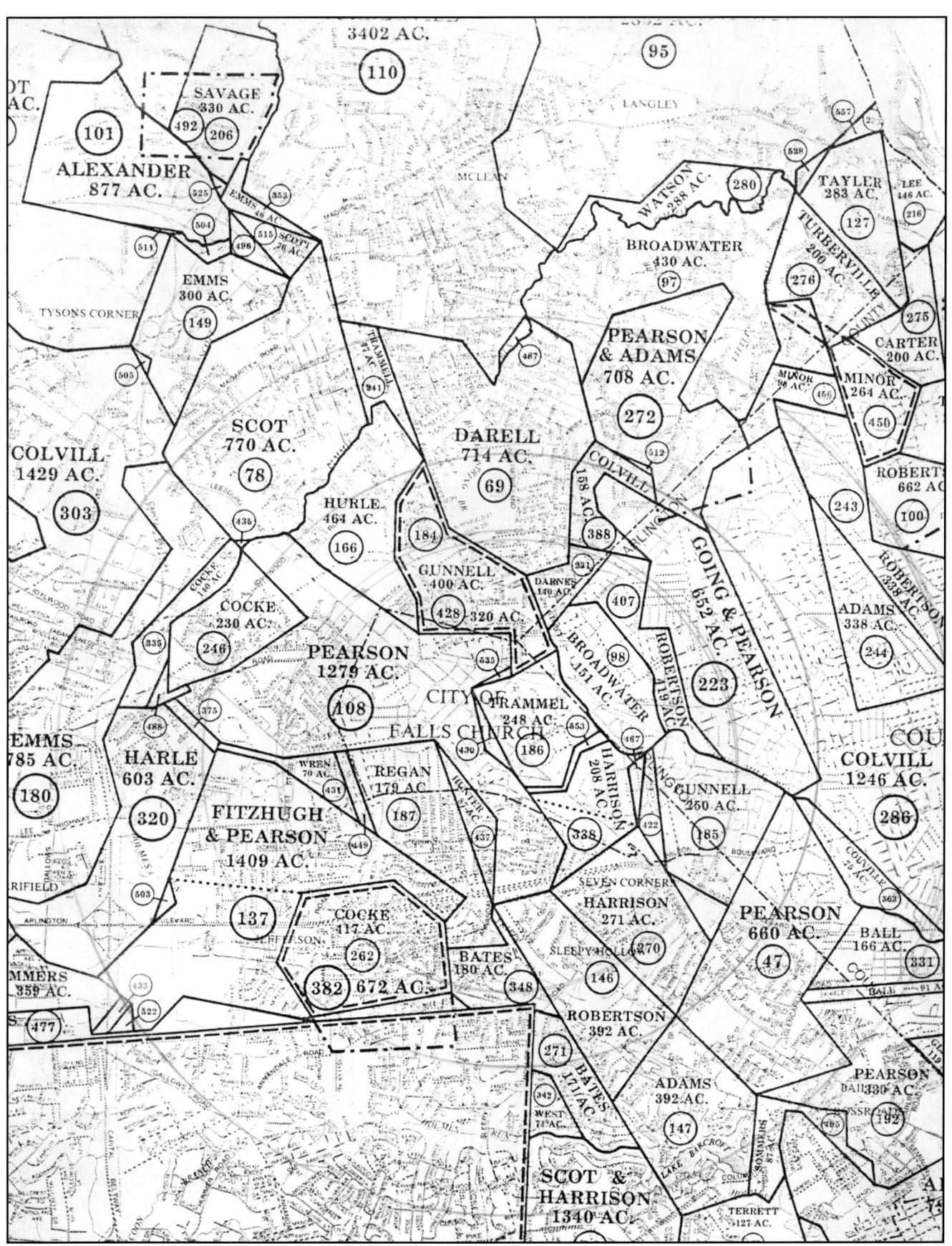

Map showing land patents granted to the Falls Church area's English settlers, 1715–1775, and subsequent land division or ownership, 1778–1837. This depiction, centered on The Falls Church (Episcopal), indicates the number of acres, abbreviated "ac.," comprising each patent and owners' names. Beth Mitchell, Beginning At a White Oak.

Big Chimneys, artist's sketch, showing a view circa 1900. This depiction, drawn with the aid of a photograph and with guidance of the home's last owners, shows the chimneystone bearing the date 1699 from which the community has accepted the date of settlement. F. Erle Prior, artist, 1948.

Opposite top:
"Virginians Defending Themselves Against Indians," from an engraving published in 1894. The native Americans occupying the Falls Church region departed quietly as the colonists began encroaching upon the lands which they hunted, fished, and farmed. The unfortunate state of relations between Indians and colonists depicted here was never the case in Falls Church. Lossing, Our Country.

Opposite bottom:
Big Chimneys, circa 1908. Early settlers built a large house of logs with large chimneys at either end which became known as "Big Chimneys." It is a cherished local tradition, based on an eyewitness account, that there was a large stone near the top of one chimney engraved with the year "1699." The dwelling was demolished between 1908 and 1914. Courtesy Marie Yochim.

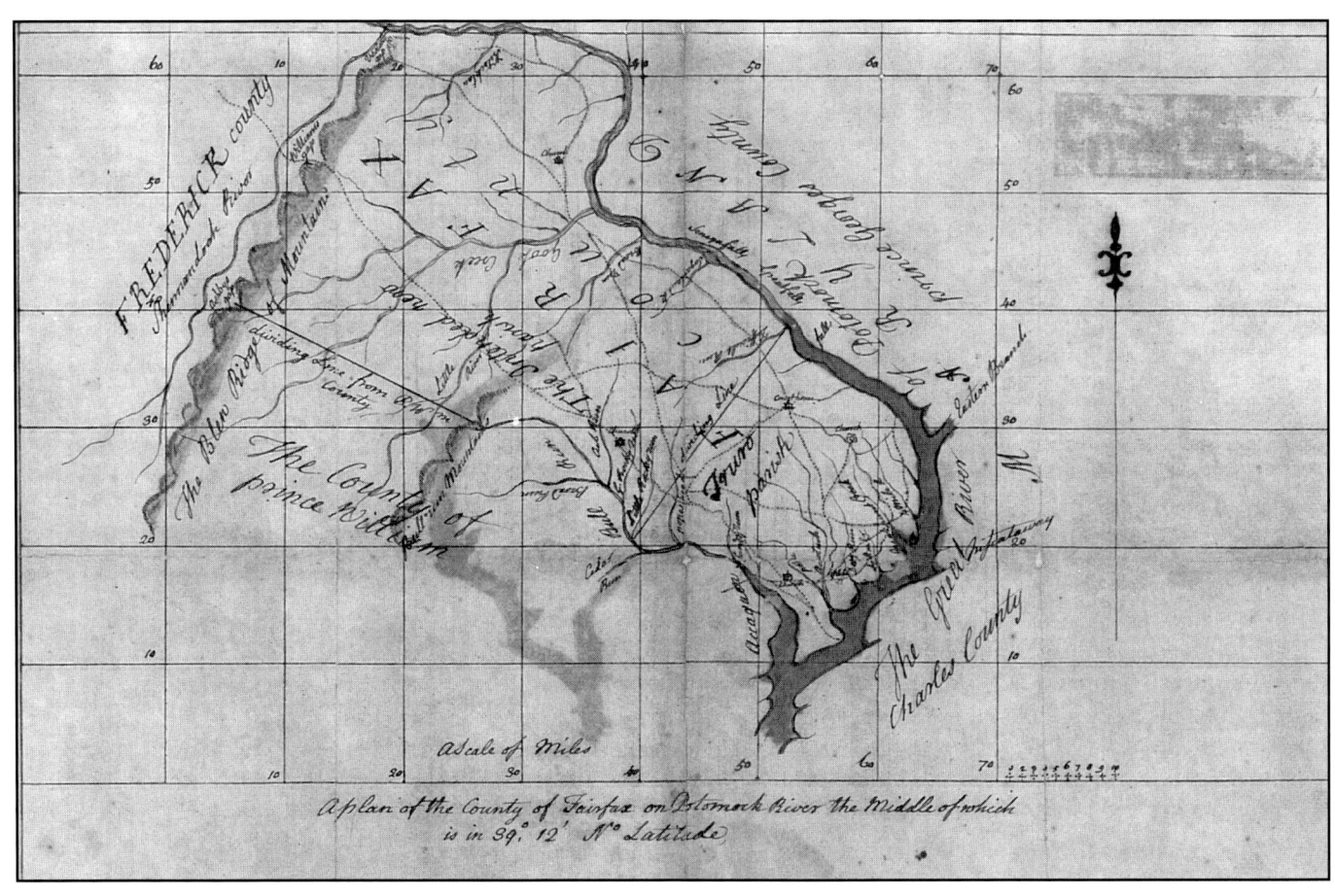

Truro Parish vestry map, circa 1747. This is the first map on which Falls Church appears, here rendered as "Church," for Upper Church. Courtesy Library of Congress, Geography and Map Division.

CHAPTER II

A Church "At the Cross Roads Near Michael Reagan's"

In colonial times, the Church of England was the official state church in Virginia and its parish governing bodies, called church vestries, had numerous religious and civic responsibilities. The vestrymen were men of property with social standing in their county and were by law responsible for the administration of religion and the moral health of all people in the parish. They had to provide a minister, build and maintain churches, provide for the poor, the sick and orphans, make presentment to the County Court in adultery cases, appoint processioners to establish boundaries of patented lands, and levy a poll tax annually on all tithables to pay for the costs. When a parish was organized, the first vestry was elected and from then on the group was self-perpetuating for they filled vacancies with their own appointees.[1]

The definition of tithables (taxable individuals) included all white males over 15, and all males and females over 15. All negroes under 15 were exempt. So, too, were all white women and white girls, no matter what their age.[2]

The General Assembly passed an Act in 1732 directing that Hamilton Parish in Prince William County be divided and a new Anglican parish called "Truro" be organized to include all of Prince William north of the Occoquan River and Bull Run and west to the Blue Ridge. Soon after Truro Parish was established, a meeting was held at the home of William Gunnell on upper Four Mile Run. In March 1733, the vestry decided to construct "a church at the cross roads near Michael Reagans." A purchase of two acres was made later with 50 shillings to landowner John Trammell. This is where The Falls Church has always stood; first as a wooden weather-boarded building designed and built in 1734 by Richard Blackburn and then in 1769, as a brick church designed and built by James Wren. The site was in Stafford County until 1730, from 1730 to 1742 in Prince William County, from 1742 to 1948 in Fairfax County, and from 1948 to the present, within the City of Falls Church.[3]

Truro Parish vestrymen played major roles in the early history of The Falls Church. Among them were Denis McCarty, Richard Blackburn, William Gunnell, John West, Charles Broadwater, William Fairfax, George William Fairfax, Augustine Washington, George Mason, George Washington, and James Wren.[4]

The first levy laid for Truro Parish took place in 1733 and furnished a fine example of life in a society where tobacco served as a medium of exchange. To take care of financial needs for the coming year in the parish, the vestry required 45,399 pounds of tobacco to be raised by collecting 67 pounds from each of 681 tithables.[5]

When Thomas, Sixth Lord Fairfax came to the Virginia colony in 1735 to discover for himself the potential of his Northern Neck Proprietary, he was favorably impressed. In order to determine the exact boundaries of the more than 5,200,000 acres involved he engaged John Warner in 1737 to survey the boundary lines and prepare a map for consideration by the King's Council in London. The Virginia colonial officials engaged surveyor William Mayo to

"Passing over the Alleghany Mountains," from an engraving published in 1894. George Washington of Mount Vernon, a Falls Church vestryman, touched off world conflict in 1754 when he fired the first shots of the French and Indian War, soon to widen into the global conflict called the Seven Years' War. Washington, with 150 Virginia militiamen, was sent into the wilds of the Ohio valley to challenge the growing French power there. The danger posed by the French and their Indian allies frightened colonists up and down the eastern seaboard. Small hamlets such as the one around The Falls Church were particularly vulnerable to the enemy's ire. Benson Lossing, Our Country, *1894.*

prepare a map as well. Ultimately, the Warner map was chosen as the official document.[6]

One of the landowners who lived near and attended The Falls Church was John Ball, a yeoman farmer, who received a proprietary grant in 1742 from Thomas, Sixth Lord Fairfax. His house was built on a 166-acre piece of land beside Four Mile Run, downstream from his local Anglican church which had been built in 1734. According to architectural historians, it was typical of an ordinary yeoman farmer's dwelling in the vicinity of The Falls Church at the time. Made of simple log construction, it has a clapboard roof. The dwelling exists today in Glencarlyn having survived for more than 250 years.[7]

John Ball, his wife Elizabeth and their five daughters all lived in this little house. County court records made after John Ball's death in 1766 indicate that he and his family had everything they needed to live a full life: axes to cut down the trees and clear the land; tools with which to build his house; and tools with which to make furniture. He had cows for milk, cream, and beef; pigs for pork and bacon; sheep for food and wool for clothes; geese for feathers for his beds; and bees for honey for his bread. He owned a mill to grind his wheat and corn; he had a distillery for strong drink; and a mare for transportation and plowing. He had guns for hunting and protection; tools to tend and cultivate his land; linen and wooden wheels for spinning; bed hides for warmth; earthen and wooden ware for dining; cooking utensils; knives and forks. An iron and a looking glass were listed. And after a day's work, he had his books, spectacles and even a fiddle for entertainment.[8] He was a well-documented example of a successful farmer who lived near The Falls Church in the mid-1700s.

During the French and Indian War (1755–1763), a force under the command of British Major General Edward Braddock was sent against the French in America at the forks of the Ohio River. Landing at the port of Alexandria, troops, artillery and heavy baggage were gradually moved overland up the Virginia and Maryland sides of the Potomac River to Fort Cumberland and then west toward Fort Duquesne and what was to be a major defeat.[9]

British Deputy Quarter Master General Sir John St. Clair had been assigned the task of clearing or building the necessary roads to Fort Duquesne and constructing boats that would be needed by the troops to cross streams and rivers along the way. After a thorough inspection of the routes beginning in January of 1755, St. Clair wrote describing the local roads at the time as: Williamsburg to Fredericksburg, very good; Fredericksburg to Winchester, very bad; and Winchester to Wills Creek, "85 miles of the worst road I ever travelled."[10]

Troops both British and American assembled at Alexandria for the arduous journey, most of them on foot. On April 7, 1755, three companies of Virginia Rangers left Alexandria for Wills Creek via Winchester. Sir Peter Halkett's Regiment of Foot (about 500 men) left camp at Alexandria on their way to Winchester and Fort Cumberland using the road past the country lane to John Ball's house and past The Falls Church. With the soldiers were marching drummers, horsemen, cannons on wheels, wagons carrying tents, baggage, regimental provisions, arms and ammunition. The sounds of many tramping feet and loud voices; horses with their squeaking leather harnesses; creaking loaded covered wagons; rumbling cannon gun carriages and colorful flags snapping in the breezes were virtually unknown noises for the sparsely-settled farm families who lived along the way.[11]

On this military expedition was one Madame Charlotte Browne, a widowed Englishwoman who was serving as a matron of nurses. She left Alexandria with a convoy on its way to Winchester on June 1, 1755. Twelve wagons and forty guards were in the group. They traveled past The Falls Church and stayed overnight at the Old Court House (near Tysons Corner). She commented in her diary entry the next morning, after bumping along in a wagon all the previous day: "The Roads were so Bad that I am almost disjointed."[12]

One result of this major colonial event was that the thoroughfare the military used (now Route 7, Broad Street) was called "Braddock's Road" in the community surrounding The Falls Church until the time of the Civil War—more than 100 years.[13]

In February 1765, the House of Burgesses established a new parish—Fairfax—out of part of the old parish—Truro. The very next year, a levy was laid for the building of two brick churches, one "where the old Falls Church stands and the other at Alexandria [now Christ Church], the undertakers to meet at The Falls Church and bring in their plans."[14] James Wren produced a plan which was chosen for both The Falls Church and the church at Alexandria. He had just been appointed a vestryman "in place of Edward Blackburn resigned."[15] James Wren (c. 1728–1815) proved to be an important man of the crossroads community which he served well. Not only was he an architect, builder, and a vestryman, but a planter and farmer, a court justice, sheriff, county official, and finally, an innkeeper.[16]

Population was steadily growing in Fairfax County, especially around Alexandria, and there was local demand for a separate parish. After some disagreements, the House of Burgesses reached a consensus and in May 1765, a boundary was defined between Truro Parish and the new Fairfax Parish in whose territory The Falls Church was now located. Being in bad repair, the old Truro Parish had already directed in 1765 that the wooden building be replaced with a new brick edifice. While the new brick church was under construction between 1767 and 1769, the decaying wooden building was

Drawing of John Ball homestead of 1767, undated. Ball's home, on Four Mile Run in what is now Arlington County, resembled the first European settlers homes in what is now Falls Church. Ball probably built his home between 1742 and 1750 and here enjoyed a surprisingly rich cultural life on his 166-acre farm, now evidenced by the detailed inventory of his property after his death. His home, now 250 years old, survives and is on the National Register of Historic Places. Sketch of the earliest portion of the Ball-Sellers house courtesy the artist, Rudolph Wendelin.

the scene of antisocial behavior by one John Hirst, Jr., who was later presented by the grand jury "for behaving in an indecent manner on Sunday the 17th instant at The Falls Church by bringing a mare to his stallion in presence of part of the Congregation in time of service." He was fined for this misdeed.[17]

Finally the beautiful brick church was finished. The Fairfax Parish vestry agreed that James Wren had completed his work at the new Falls Church at their vestry meeting held on December 20, 1769. Three months later, George

The Falls Church Episcopal, 1974. Established on this site, 1734; present structure erected 1767–69. George Washington, a vestryman of this church, rented a pew here with his family. Eighteenth and nineteenth century tombstones, one bearing the mark of a Civil War musket ball, dot the churchyard. The church, then Church of England, hosted colonial troops during the French and Indian War; served as a recruiting station during the Revolution; and as a hospital and stable during the Civil War. The south entrance (center, right) was the principal entrance during colonial times, and the Declaration of Independence was read from its steps to assembled villagers during the summer of 1776. National Register of Historic Places. William E. Barrett photo.

Washington entered in his "Ledger A": "By Mr. Wm. Adam for my Subscription toward decorating The Falls Church £1."[18]

International events were soon to change life in the colonies and particularly affect Falls Church vestrymen George Washington and George Mason. After the British Parliament closed the Port of Boston on June 1, 1774, Mason, with the help of others, wrote the Fairfax Resolves which called for, among other points, the need "to concert a general and uniform Plan for the Defense and Preservation of our common Rights."[19]

As war with Great Britain became a reality and recruitment of soldiers was held at The Falls Church for service in that conflict, Milcah Trammell was laid to rest in 1776. Her father had sold two acres of land to Truro Parish on which the 1734 and 1769 church buildings had been erected. Milcah, youngest of John and Susanna Trammell's seven children, had married wealthy Simon Pearson, a union which had ended in divorce, a rare action in those times.[20]

The Falls Church Episcopal, 1973. This rustic tombstone memorializes Milcah Trammell, youngest daughter in one of Falls Church's founding families, who died in 1776, the year the Colony of Virginia committed itself to overthrowing English rule. Lee Briggs photo.

The Apollo Room of the Raleigh Tavern in Williamsburg, Virginia's royal capital, from an engraving published in 1852. Lord Dunsmore, royal governor of Virginia, dissolved the colony's House of Burgesses when its revolutionary and reformist fervor became apparent. The councilors, including several from Fairfax County and two from Falls Church, promptly defied royal edict and reconvened in the Apollo Room to decide the colony's fate in the revolutionary movement. Their decision that day, for proactive change, helped alter the course of history. Lossing, Pictorial Field Book of the Revolution.

CHAPTER III

A War for Independence

The American Revolution proved a political and philosophical threshold for the colonists. The republic it created, governed "by laws, not men," represented a bold and brash experiment in politics and government. No fighting occurred in Northern Virginia and the war's effects on Falls Church were incidental. But the village may be justifiably proud of the actions of the men representing it in the Colony's revolutionary councils.

After Bostonians threw tea into their harbor to preclude its taxation by English authorities in 1773, Parliament in London enacted legislation punishing the colonies and demanding their obedience to policy. Virginia led the resistance to this legislation when its House of Burgesses (now the House of Delegates), meeting in the royal capital, Williamsburg, declared a day of fasting, prayer, and "humiliation." The Governor, John Murray, Fourth Earl of Dunmore, dissolved the Burgesses, which promptly reconvened and issued a call for the colonies to send deputies to a coordinating conference in Philadelphia. Hostilities soon commenced in Massachusetts and then in Virginia. Governor Dunmore fled Williamsburg, and the philosophical debates began.[1]

Key to these proceedings were the communications, called "resolves," from thirty-one of Virginia's counties conveying the sense of their citizens to the Colony's first revolutionary convention in 1774. Of particular note are the *Fairfax Resolves*. These resolves, written by George Mason of Fairfax County, were the most proactive and far-ranging of any presented. There were twenty-four separate resolutions each beginning with the single word, "Resolved"; three called for a continental congress of deputies from each colony to decide general policy toward Britain; war, if the Crown failed to redress grievances and publication of the names of citizens not subscribing to patriot views against England. These ideas proved influential in Virginia's revolutionary conventions and in the Continental Congress. The *Fairfax Resolves* were presented by George Washington of Mount Vernon and Col. Charles Broadwater, of Falls Church.[2]

The Colony's last revolutionary council convened in Williamsburg from May 6 through July 5, 1776. On May 15 its members, including Col. Broadwater and John West, Jr., unanimously instructed Virginia's delegates to the Continental Congress to introduce a resolution calling for independence. Richard Henry Lee of Virginia did so on June 7. Congress passed the motion on July 2 and two days later issued the Declaration of Independence, written by Thomas Jefferson.[3]

George Mason, a Fairfax County delegate to the revolutionary convention, drafted the Virginia Declaration of Rights adopted by the convention on June 12. This document, unmatched in its scope, guaranteed fundamental rights later repeated in the U.S. Bill of Rights and French Declaration of the Rights of Man and of the Citizen. These included freedom of religion, freedom of the press, and the right to a jury trial by peers in both civil and criminal cases.[4]

Mason also drafted a constitution for Virginia, which was a novel "first" for Englishmen anywhere who were not accustomed to a document defining and limiting the powers of government. Virginia's constitution, which declared its independence from England, fashioned a republic and commonwealth— a government of citizens united in their ideas of what constituted the common *weal*, or good.[5]

George Washington remained a vestryman of his parish through the Revolution, not resigning until 1784, although he was unable to attend to his duties on the church vestry while leading American armies afield. Revolutionaries from Falls Church included Col. Broadwater, who recruited soldiers for the local militia in The Falls Church; Col. James Wren, Col. Charles Little, John Follin, and Charles Simms.[6]

The Declaration of Independence, a copy of which arrived over the post road from Philadelphia, was read from the steps of The Falls Church sometime during the summer of 1776, as it was at many churches during those fateful days.[7]

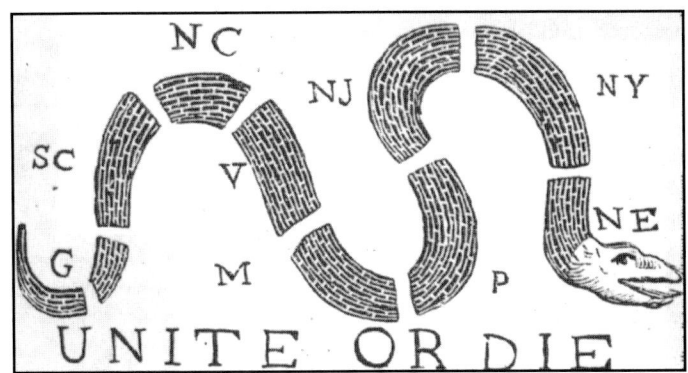

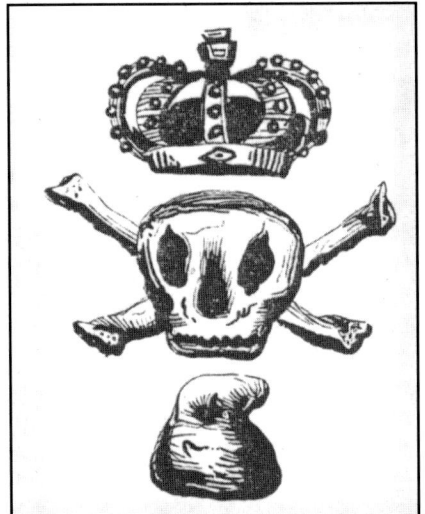

Facsimiles of engravings from the Revolution, circa 1775. Virginia's leading citizens, including several from Falls Church and Fairfax County, of which The Falls Church property was then a part, were important co-conspirators of the American Revolution. George Washington, vestryman of The Falls Church, led colonial armies. This sepulchral device, a skull and crossbones and crown hovering over the Cap of Liberty, suggested that "all was death and destruction between the Crown and liberty." So it seemed early-on to Virginians, who forced their royal governor to flee.

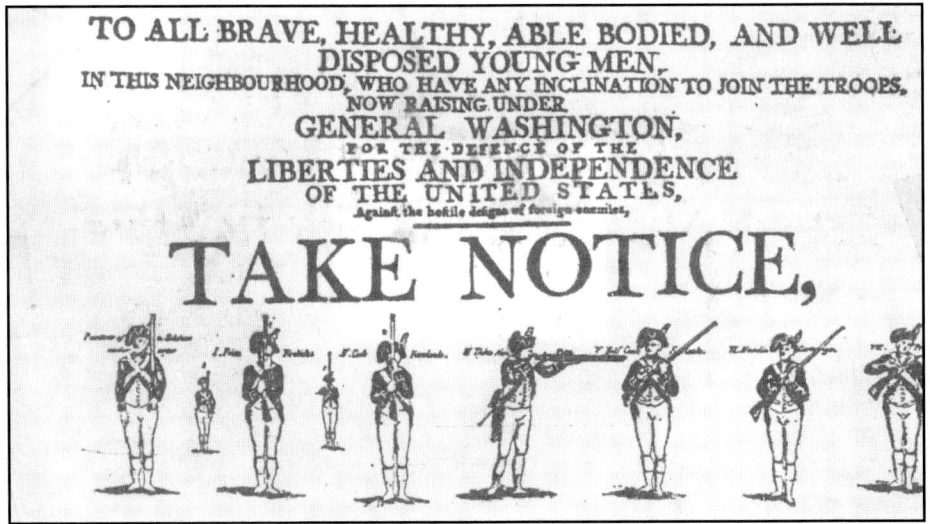

Colonial recruitment poster, circa 1776. Local tradition and a few written records indicate that recruiting of soldiers for Revolutionary War service was conducted at The Falls Church. This is a recruiting poster showing the manual of arms designed to encourage young men to rally to the cause. The pay was "$60 a year in gold and silver money." Courtesy George Washington's Office Museum, Winchester, Virginia.

George Washington of Mount Vernon, Falls Church vestryman before the Revolution. This bust by sculptor Jean Antoine Houdon, for which Washington posed, was the family's favorite likeness of its patriarch. Courtesy Mount Vernon Ladies' Association.

George Mason of Gunston Hall. Mason, a Falls Church vestryman and a guiding light of the Revolution, wrote the influential Fairfax Resolves *and Virginia's* Declaration of Rights, *from which Thomas Jefferson drew much of what became the United States Constitution. Etching by Albert Rosenthal, 1888. Courtesy Board of Regents, Gunston Hall Plantation.*

Fairfax Chapel was built for a new Methodist congregation after 1779 on the site now used for Oakwood Cemetery on Roosevelt Street. This view depicts the first recorded sermon of Harry Hoosier, the first African-American Methodist preacher, in 1781. "This circumstance was new, and the white people looked on with attention," wrote one observer. Artist's rendering, 1955.

CHAPTER IV

A Federal Seat of Government

A drastic change involving freedom of religion occurred almost simultaneously with the political and governmental revolution in Virginia and North America. During the Revolutionary War, in 1779, Thomas Jefferson wrote an Ordinance of Religious Freedom which was presented to the Virginia legislature and failed to be adopted. In December of 1785, however, a similar law was proposed by James Madison and was adopted as the Virginia Statute for Religious Freedom in January 1786. It was generally applicable but specifically abolished the Anglican Church which had been the official state church in the Virginia colony. Later serving as a model for the First Amendment of the U.S. Constitution, the statute declared that no man could be compelled to attend or support any church nor suffer any discrimination because of his religious beliefs. The Fairfax Parish vestry was represented at the First Convention of the new Protestant Episcopal Church in Virginia held at Richmond in May 1785.[1]

Methodism in Northern Virginia had begun to win converts before 1776, the year when the Fairfax Circuit was officially established at a Methodist conference held in Baltimore. At first local church meetings were held at "Church Hill," the home (now gone) of Col. and Mrs. William Adams at present-day Seven Corners. Fairfax Chapel was built and probably dedicated in 1779, located on the present-day site of Oakwood Cemetery. Itinerant Methodist Bishop Francis Asbury recorded in his journal that he preached at Fairfax Chapel in 1780. A year later Asbury recorded that he had preached at the chapel again, followed by a black preacher, Harry Hoosier, speaking to an interested white audience.

About 1798, the original wooden chapel building was replaced by a larger brick building on one acre of land later given to the Methodist Society by the descendants of Col. George Minor of "Minor's Hill." There was a gallery above the entrance where the African-American people sat. This second building was in use until the Civil War when Union troops destroyed it and used the bricks to build chimneys for their winter quarters.[2]

The Methodist Historical Society of Northern Virginia placed a plaque in Oakwood Cemetery in April 1969 commemorating the site of the first Methodist church in Northern Virginia, Fairfax Chapel.[3]

After much discussion about various locations, Congress authorized the establishment of the nation's ten-mile-square Federal District of Columbia on the Potomac River in 1790. Necessary land was ceded by Maryland and Virginia. Surveying of the territory took place in 1791 and 1792, forty boundary stones being set at approximately one-mile intervals. The work was done under the supervision of Major Andrew Ellicott, assisted by gifted astronomer Benjamin Banneker, a free black man.[4]

In 1980, the Heritage Conservation and Recreation Service of the Department of the Interior approved the naming of Southwest Boundary Stone 9, near Van Buren Street in Falls Church, after Benjamin Banneker to honor

District of Columbia boundary stone, Van Buren Street, 1961. This is the Southwest 9 boundary stone, or "Banneker Stone." In 1790, after much debate, Congress chose a Potomac River site for the new national capital. In 1791–92 Major Andrew Ellicott and his astronomer assistant, Benjamin Banneker, erected forty one-foot square sandstone markers in the wilderness to mark the boundary of the ten-mile square prospective city. In 1846 Congress returned the portion of the district that was south and west of the Potomac River to the Commonwealth of Virginia. Two of the original markers are on the Falls Church boundary line. Quentin Porter photo, courtesy Mary Riley Styles Public Library.

his life and contributions. It was also given the significant major designation as a National Historic Landmark.

The west cornerstone was surrounded with a protective iron fence by the Falls Church Chapter of the Daughters of the American Revolution in 1952. Arlington County, Fairfax County, and the City of Falls Church established the surrounding park in 1956. The stone was placed on the National Register of Historic Places in 1991. The Fairfax County Board of Supervisors approved the naming of the park after Andrew Ellicott in 1998. The naming of the boundary stones after Ellicott and Banneker was approved by the Arlington County Board and the Falls Church City Council in 1996. The Banneker Park was publicly dedicated on July 17, 1999.[5]

With the official establishment of the ten-mile square, the part of the new Federal District which encompassed Virginia land included the Town of Alexandria, Fairfax County's seat of government. The County had therefore to relocate their courthouse within the county boundaries. In 1798, the *Alexandria Gazette* announced that the Fairfax County Courthouse commissioners had selected the plan of architect James Wren for the new public buildings. Wren owned and operated an ordinary (inn) at the time near the brick Falls Church.[6]

The farm-to-market journey from the Shenandoah Valley, and Loudoun and Fairfax counties was greatly improved by the first bridge built over the Potomac River from the Virginia shore, at Little Falls. The covered wooden bridge, called the Falls Bridge, was constructed by the Georgetown Bridge Company in 1797. After this structure was washed away by high water, it was replaced in 1810 with a higher stone chain suspension bridge—"Chain Bridge."[7]

After Thomas Jefferson was chosen president of the United States by the House of Representatives in 1801, he experienced some difficulty in assembling his small official family.[8] Finally anticipating his arrival, Jefferson wrote his Secretary of State, James Madison, on April 30 about the wretched road conditions in Northern Virginia at the time. On the advice of Col. James Wren, Jefferson engaged two farmers to supply two horses to draw Madison's carriage "up the Bull run hill . . . really the worst I ever saw in a public road." The sitting president advised his colleague and friend, Madison: "You had better start as soon as you can see to drive, breakfast at Col. Wren's, and come here to dinner. We shall wait for you till 4 o'clock."[9]

The inn or tavern belonging to the gifted architect of Pohick Church, Christ Church and The Falls Church and the new Fairfax County Courthouse was a landmark in its time. On the map drawn in 1801 by Jonathon Lovett of his survey of the roads between Winchester and Alexandria, he designated as "Col. James Wren's" the location now known as Falls Church.[10]

Federal district West Cornerstone, 400 block of Meridian Street, 1994. This cornerstone, the "Ellicott Stone," marks the western tip of the original ten-mile square federal district. Each of the two boundary markers in Falls Church, placed in 1791, reads, "Jurisdiction of the United States" on one side and "Virginia" on the other. Each stone gives the year set, magnetic variation at that place and time, and distance from the previous stone. This stone remains the meeting point for Arlington and Fairfax counties and the City of Falls Church. Maurice J. Terman photo, courtesy Mary Riley Styles Public Library.

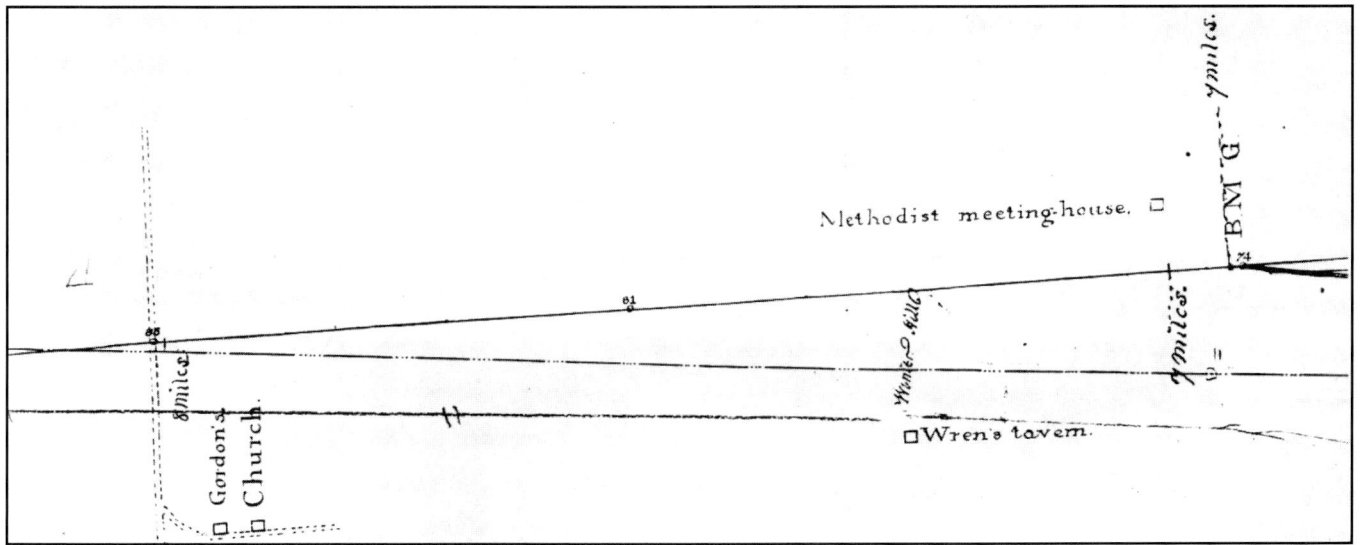

Map by Jonathon Lovett showing route of the Alexandria-Leesburg turnpike in present-day Falls Church, 1801. James Wren's tavern was for many years the best-known establishment near The Falls Church, and travelers—and sometimes mapmakers—referred to the area as "Wren's." Courtesy Mary Riley Styles Public Library.

Thomas Jefferson, from an engraving by Dequevauvillier after the painting by Desnoyers. This likeness is of Jefferson while serving as ambassador to France, 1784–89. Jefferson, upon returning to this country, was appalled by the state of Falls Church area roads. Foley, Jeffersonian Cyclopedia.

Engraving showing the burning of Washington by the British, 1814. This stylized rendering, which sites buildings and neighborhoods improperly, is correct in showing the destruction of the Washington Navy Yard, U.S. Capitol, and the city's churches, homes, and businesses. This conflagration was clearly seen from the Falls Church area, to which the Navy Yard's gunpowder was evacuated, and in which frightened refugees and residents gathered for safety. Courtesy Library of Congress, Prints and Photographs Division.

CHAPTER V

The War of 1812 Gunpowder and Refugees

As war with Britain approached in 1812, Fairfax County shipping companies found themselves victimized by an undeclared war upon the high seas. Between 1792 and 1801 French ships captured at least twenty Alexandria vessels. Until that point Virginians generally sided with the British in their quarrels with other Europeans. After Britain began impressing American seamen onto its ships at sea, local opinion shifted.

Until 1814 most of the fighting occurred far to the north of the mid-Atlantic region and when the British threatened Washington, the federal government could not comprehend the scope of the danger.[1] Most at fault was the secretary of war, John Armstrong, who refused to believe the British would target Washington. Pandemonium ensued in the government and among citizens as the British troops and fleet neared.[2]

Government offices evacuated their records across the river to Virginia on or about August 23, 1814. Wagons for this effort were in short supply, however, as all able-bodied citizens were fleeing the city in wagons piled high with their own personal goods. The scene was near bedlam in the city and on the bridges leading to Virginia.[3]

Col. George Minor and his 700-man Virginia Militia 60th Regiment were summoned on August 23 from Falls Church, where they had mustered at Wren's Tavern, to help protect Washington, but few came armed because an attack was so unexpected. And due to bureaucratic bungling among war department officials they were not sent to help defend the approaches to Washington at Bladensburg.[4]

As conflicting reports reached Washington concerning the whereabouts of the British troops, Commodore Thomas Tingey, commanding the Washington Navy Yard, ordered his senior clerk, Mordecai Booth, to move the gunpowder from the Yard's magazine to the interior of Virginia. Booth, detailed to take the powder to the farm of Sarah and Daniel Dulany, the commodore's daughter and son-in-law at Falls Church, experienced great difficulty in finding wagons enough to accomplish this task. After crossing the Potomac bridge he encountered Col. Minor, who assigned a six-man guard to accompany him and his cargo of explosives to Falls Church. Col. Minor and the rest of his regiment hurried on to Washington, where they camped for the night in the Capitol. Booth and his guard arrived at Wren's Tavern in Falls Church late on the night of August 23, still one mile from the Dulany farm, and there spent the night.[5]

Before dawn news reached the tavern that American forces were abandoning Washington to the British. Booth left for the Dulanys' farm at dawn, where he found that 75 of 124 barrels and two quarter-casks of powder had been unloaded and stored. The Dulanys' barn was woefully insecure, and Booth went to the house of another local man, Dozier Bennett, with whom he arranged to have a civilian guard posted at the barn until a Marine force could arrive. Booth then returned to the city.[6]

Dolley Madison, wife of President James Madison, from an artist's rendering published in 1868. Mrs. Madison fled the British destruction of Washington, attempting to find her husband and his cabinet, but was delayed in the roads around The Falls Church, which were jammed with frightened, fleeing citizens. Compounding her fears that night was rumor of a slave insurrection; the friends with whom she stayed the first night left their home the next morning for the safety of numbers in Falls Church.

President James Madison, from a drawing published in 1868. President Madison's military advisers seriously underestimated the threat represented by British forces during the War of 1812. Enemy troops occupied and destroyed Washington. The president took refuge in Falls Church, as did many refugees from Washington and Alexandria.

At the President's House (later the White House) the president's wife, Dolley Madison, waited in vain for her husband's return. By mid-afternoon Mrs. Madison wrote her sister, "Mr. Madison comes not. May God protect him! Two messengers, covered with dust, come to bid me fly. . . ." She refused to leave until the large portrait of George Washington was unscrewed from the wall, cut from its frame and dispatched for safekeeping. She then fled into Virginia, hoping to join her husband, who, with most of his cabinet officials, dispersed to various points.[7]

The roads between Falls Church and Washington were chaotic, disorderly, and full of stragglers from Washington. Booth returned to the Navy Yard from Falls Church to confer with officials and then rode out to determine the location of the British troops. He soon collided with British redcoats, who had just reached the District, and was fired upon. He fled back into the city, where he found the Capitol deserted. Riding quickly to the President's House he discovered it was dark, empty, and silent. A companion yanked violently on the front door bell-pull, but no one was there to answer. Only then did Booth realize the gravity of the situation: "the Metropolis of our Country was abandoned to its horrid fate."[8]

Booth returned to the Capitol, where he was fired on again by the arriving British, and then rode to the Navy Yard. Commodore Tingey, learning that the enemy was in the city and unopposed, bade Booth farewell and torched the Yard. It was twenty minutes past eight o'clock. In the Capitol the British Admiral Martin Cockburn and his troops piled high the books and draperies and set them afire. Booth, just reaching the Potomac bridge, looked back and saw the first flames from the Navy Yard and the fort on Greenleaf's Point leaping into the sky. By the time he ascended the hill on the Arlington end of the bridge the Capitol was in flames.[9]

Booth stood on the hill with many other people, transfixed with horror by the disaster unfolding before them. He reached Wren's Tavern in Falls Church at midnight, where he found his family, escaped from Washington, waiting for him. Everyone in the tavern was in a great state of excitement, and people and wagons were passing constantly on the road outside (East Broad Street).[10] President Madison, the attorney general, and his entourage struggled through the crowded roads toward Falls Church. Mrs. Madison, unable to make it that far in a heavy rainstorm, stopped for the night at Rokeby, near Chain Bridge, the home of her friend Mrs. Richard Love, northeast of Falls Church.[11] From there Mrs. Madison watched the flaring night sky. Her husband and his traveling companions stopped frequently to turn back and look at the burning city. The conflagration which was Washington—its burning ships, stores, homes, and public buildings—could be seen as far away as Leesburg and Baltimore, where worried residents still had no news of events. At daylight David Winchester of Baltimore wrote that no one knew what had happened in Washington; "We only know from the light during the night that the city was on fire."[12] In the Falls Church area, from which the burning city was clearly and distinctly visible, Miss Matilda Roberts, a seven-year-old refugee from Alexandria who never forgot that night, was awakened and taken outside to see Washington burn. "At first I thought the world was on fire," she recounted later. "Such a flame I have never seen since."[13]

Rumors bred in the chaos of that evening that slaves were revolting frightened Mrs. Love into fleeing Rokeby at daylight for the interior of Virginia. The rumors grew in strength the further she went and so she turned and raced for home. When her driver, a slave, remarked that he did not think the horses would make it by nightfall, she feared he was part of the rebellion and decided to shoot him if he stopped the wagon. He did not and they arrived to find that everyone at Rokeby had fled to Falls Church, "where there was safety in numbers." Mrs. Madison went to the home of Mrs. Minor, outside Falls Church, where she stayed the next two nights out of fear of the supposed rebellion.14

The next morning, August 25, Booth arose early at Wren's Tavern in Falls Church and, taking the tavernkeeper's son with him as guide, departed for Mrs. Minor's. There he was told President Madison had stopped briefly the night before but was no longer there. Booth returned to Wren's, where he was met by Sergeant-Major Forrest with a guard of about twenty-five men and boys, there to guard the Navy's gunpowder, and a troop of the Fairfax Dragoons. The presence of the explosive caused Falls Church residents and the refugees they hosted great consternation, and they petitioned Booth to remove the powder. This Booth agreed to do, and sent scouts to locate a better storage spot four to six miles further inland. The scouts failed to find any better location, and the powder remained stored in the Dulanys' barn.15

Returning to Wren's from the Dulany farm Booth discovered he had just missed President Madison, who had stopped at the inn in search of his wife. The president, whose movements were hampered first by reports that the British were en route to seize him and then by reports of the slave insurrection, eventually reunited with Mrs. Madison at Wiley's Tavern near Great Falls.16

On August 29 the British fleet arrived off Alexandria, where panicked citizens, the destruction of Washington fresh on their minds, quickly surrendered their city. Booth rode to Alexandria from Falls Church, where he felt sickened by the sight of the Union Jack flying above the District and the British fleet plundering Alexandria. After sacking the port town's warehouses, the enemy fleet moved downriver. The desperate Americans, in an ultimately vain attempt to stop the fleet, set up large guns at the destroyed President's House (which then had a seven-mile view downriver). Booth, galloping all the way to Dulany's farm, dispatched two wagon-loads of powder to the President's House. The powder was returned to Falls Church September 6 where it remained until the 10th.17

Falls Church's proximity to Washington bound it inexplicably to the defense of the capital. Future wars would follow in which this was also the case.

Signature of Thomas W. Tingey, commanding the Washington Navy yard during the War of 1812. Tingey, after dispatching the Navy's gunpowder to safety in Falls Church, torched the Yard to prevent its capture by the British. The powder was stored in a barn owned by Daniel Dulany, Tingey's son-in-law near the hamlet around The Falls Church.

Wren's Tavern signpost, artist's rendering, 1994. James Wren, architect of The Falls Church, established this tavern on East Broad Street (then known as the Alexandria-Leesburg road) sometime before the War of 1812. President James Madison stopped here briefly as he fled the British advance on Washington. The tavern and the road outside were the scene of frenzied activity during August 1814 in which the British burned Washington. Robin Bray, 1994, courtesy Mary Riley Styles Public Library.

Mount Hope, 203 South Oak Street, 1920. Mount Hope, built as early as 1790 but most probably in about 1815, and extensively enlarged in Victorian style in 1870, sits on the crest of a hill which it alone occupied until this century. Mount Hope faces Broad Street, to which it was connected via two tree-lined lanes; a side elevation of the home, not the front, faces Oak Street. Early meetings of the Presbyterian church occurred here, and it was the earliest known stop on the Falls Church mail route. Historic Falls Church, Inc., holds a preservation easement on this property. National Register of Historic Places. Courtesy Joseph Allison and Mary Riley Styles Public Library.

CHAPTER VI

Internal Improvements

Ever-increasing transportation opportunities, and the economic and other windfalls they created, were evident in Falls Church during most of the nineteenth century.

Virginia law, following English precedent, required the citizens living along its roadways to contribute work annually for their upkeep. This method became less popular in Falls Church and elsewhere as growing commerce increased wear and tear on the roads. The merchants of Leesburg, the gateway to the Shenandoah Valley, anxious to have a reliable connection with a market port, established the Leesburg Turnpike Company in 1808. The company built a road from Leesburg to Sugarland Run near Dranesville (at Route 7), where it met a connector road financed by Georgetown—present route 193, Georgetown Pike—connecting with Georgetown via the Chain Bridge. These were completed about 1820.[1]

Georgetown and Alexandria were locked in competition for business from the interior and from Baltimore and, when Georgetown's merchants fell on hard times in the late 1820s, Alexandria's commercial leaders arranged for a new, more direct link between their seaport town and Leesburg. These arrangements culminated in 1829 in the Middle Turnpike Company, which built a road from the eastern end of King Street along the colonial-era ridge road through Falls Church, and on to connect with the Leesburg Turnpike at Dranesville. Tolls were collected along this route beginning in about 1839. The new road and the commerce it brought allowed Falls Church, long a sleepy village, to begin robust growth.[2]

Another new road which impacted Falls Church was one completed in 1852, linking the new Aqueduct Bridge across the Potomac with Fairfax Court House. Its route between the bridge and Falls Church was, generally, that of modern Wilson Boulevard.[3]

Falls Church's strength during these times was its location—a short day's ride from Alexandria and Georgetown. Geography did not bless it with fast-flowing water sufficient to power a milling industry, and area farmers did not produce enough crops to export outside the local market, but Falls Church was well positioned to provide services for travelers. As the roads improved and commerce quickened the need for taverns and inns increased correspondingly. By 1827 there were four in the area: Gordon's near The Falls Church; Wren's, between the church and modern Seven Corners; Minor's, at Seven Corners, and Lindsay's (later McTear's), west of the village on Pimmit Run. Wren's, in business since at least 1785, was well-regarded and recommended by Thomas Jefferson. It, as well as the other taverns, were social centers in which public notices were posted, and official meetings and public sales of land and slaves occurred. One historian called taverns such as these the "dominant public spaces" of the era. By present-day standards these inns offered crude lodging. Travelers often shared beds and amenities were few. This changed as travelers became more prosperous and willing to pay for better services. The venerable

Leesburg and Alexandria Turnpike tollgate, 321 East Broad Street. In this 1874 sketch Nancy Williams is shown collecting toll from Mr. and Mrs. Henry J. Morgan. Roads were vital to the area's agricultural economy. The turnpike, chartered in 1813 and completed in 1839, carried most of the freight between Alexandria's port and inland markets until superceded by railroads in the 1850s. Henry J. Morgan, 1874. Courtesy Elizabeth Tabb Stewart and Mary Riley Styles Public Library.

Birch House, 312 East Board Street, 1981. Built about 1840 and owned by the Birch family from 1852 until 1976, this house bears little resemblance to its original appearance, although its appearance has not changed in over 120 years. Historic Falls Church, Inc., organized in 1975 to save this property from destruction, did so and holds preservation easements on it and other historic properties in which its intervention was instrumental. National Register of Historic Places. William E. Barrett photo, courtesy Mary Riley Styles Public Library.

and long-lived Star Tavern, also located near The Falls Church, joined local roadside hostelries by mid-century.[4]

Better roads also offered greater convenience to practice religious faith, and several churches were added to the village by mid-century. Falls Church was home to a vigorous Methodism as early as 1774—the second such place in Virginia, and one of the earliest in America. By 1780 the Falls Church Methodist meeting place was called Fairfax Chapel. The first chapel, of log and clapboard, was built in the late 1770s. In Falls Church and throughout the former colonies Methodism soon replaced Anglicanism as the most popular faith, and the small chapel was replaced in 1798 by a larger structure which was, in turn, replaced by the last chapel, in what is now Oakwood Cemetery, in early 1819. Fairfax Chapel was the second church in the area, after The Falls Church. Circuit riders staffed the pulpit. The last Chapel, a substantial building constructed of thick brick walls, was forty-by-sixty feet in width and length, and included a large gallery used for the "colored people." This Chapel was dismantled by soldiers during the Civil War who used its brick to build chimney flues in their encampments on the hills nearby.[5]

Presbyterianism was represented informally in the area beginning in 1812, when a minister of that denomination began preaching occasionally in Falls Church until his death in 1828. Presbyterian services were much more infrequent from 1828 until 1848, when regular preaching resumed in Falls Church in the homes of various members. Services were interrupted by the Civil War and did not resume until afterward.[6]

The Columbia Baptist Church congregation was established in 1856 and built a wood-frame home with a steeple in 1857 next to The Falls Church.

Cherry Hill, 312 Park Avenue, 1880. Cherry Hill's patent, granted in 1729, consisted of 248 acres, of which about ten acres remain. A lane of cherry trees extended from the house to Broad Street, giving the farm its name. The farmhouse, built about 1845, is an excellent example of the solid and masterful carpentry which is Falls Church's architectural heritage. National Register of Historic Places. Airbrushed photo courtesy Bier Barrett and Mary Riley Styles Public Library.

Services in this church were also interrupted by the advent of civil strife. The church may be seen in a Mathew Brady photograph taken during the war and in lithographs published in *Harper's Weekly*.

The Falls Church, progenitor of them all, fell upon hard times in the decades following the Revolution. After the close of hostilities Virginia formally eschewed the official state Church of England and its followers moved to the newly-established Protestant Episcopal Church. Stripped of its guarantee of parish revenue and humbled by its prior association with English colonial authorities, The Falls Church lost much of its congregation and closed its doors sometime between 1799 and 1806. It soon fell into disrepair and, missing doors and windows, was open to the elements. One passer-by noted that animals lived within. This state of affairs lasted until 1823, when several area residents attempted to reestablish it. While this attempt to reopen The Falls Church was aborted it produced much-needed repairs, including, apparently, a new roof.[7]

After 1823, and for the next fourteen years, the church again stood deserted amidst unkempt surroundings, even as the village prospered. It was used for meetings of the new Falls Church Temperance Society in 1831, which met the first Saturday of every month to promote among its members a liquor-free existence. In about 1835 students from the new Fairfax Seminary in Alexandria became interested in The Falls Church and their labors led to reorganization of its congregation in 1836. The church was again led by a rector from 1837 to

Lawton House/Home Hill, 203 Lawton Street, circa 1890. Built in 1854–56. During the Civil War, Confederate General James Longstreet used this house as his military headquarters while Southern forces controlled Falls Church. From here Longstreet and his officers directed the Army of Northern Virginia. Over one hundred years later a piece of rafter was found in the attic bearing the identification of soldiers. In 1889 the home was purchased by Henry Ware Lawton, an army general later killed during the Philippine Insurrection after the Spanish-American War. Historic Falls Church, Inc., holds a preservation easement on this property. Courtesy Mary Riley Styles Public Library.

William Henry Greenburg Lynch, circa 1855. Lynch was a local merchant whose family remained in Falls Church for over one hundred years. Lynch was well-known as a Confederate sympathizer during the Civil War. This daguerreotype image is the earliest known image of a Falls Church citizen of importance. Courtesy Willard Piggott and Mary Riley Styles Public Library.

1861, and in 1838, with Captain Henry Fairfax's help, the new rector raised funds enough to repair the church. (Fairfax, killed at Saltillo, Mexico, in the war with that country in 1848, is buried in the churchyard). Records from this period, however, were destroyed or lost during the Civil War when Federal soldiers occupied the building and looted the rector's home.[8]

Catholicism in Falls Church received a late start. In 1871 St. Mary's Catholic Church, Alexandria, began serving Falls Church Catholics in the home of Sabilla Sewall on South West Street, later called Walnut Hill. A parish church was built on West Street in 1873–74, beside the present St. James cemetery.[9]

Turnpikes launched Falls Church's success as a village, but were themselves succeeded by a later invention, the railroad. By the time of the Civil War era, turnpikes were seriously threatened, and advances in railroading during the war completed their destruction. The General Assembly chartered the Alexandria and Harper's Ferry Railroad Company to establish this line in 1847, providing service between those two points through Falls Church. In 1854 the Assembly changed the company's name to Alexandria, Loudoun, and Hampshire Railroad Company. Work began on the line in 1855. Originally intended to be an extension of the Baltimore & Ohio's lines into Virginia, it opened late enough that it was, in effect, a northerly extension of Virginia's railroad network centered on Petersburg. Its first sections opened for business in 1858, and the first train ran the full line in the spring of 1861, just in time to provide a valuable and highly contested service for both the Confederacy and Union in the Civil War which was just then erupting. By 1860 the new railroad had offered service from Alexandria to Falls Church for a fare of fifty cents. The thirty-five minute ride was considerably shorter than the half-day's ride offered by the turnpike, and traffic and passengers increasingly shifted to the railroad.[10]

Falls Church got a new neighbor in 1846, or, rather, an old neighbor returning to the Commonwealth of Virginia with a new name. The District of Columbia was created in 1791 and 1792 from part of Fairfax County, Virginia, and portions of Montgomery and Prince George's counties in Maryland. The inclusion of Alexandria, D.C. (now Arlington) County, on the Virginia side of the Potomac River, proved disadvantageous to Virginia's commerce and especially to its merchants, who instigated a retrocession of the county to the Commonwealth in 1846. Falls Church was no longer adjacent to the national capital territory, but to a newly created Virginia county.[11]

Fairfax County's population decreased between 1810 and 1830, after which it began to increase. This population growth created the need for a post office at Falls Church, which it received in 1849. During this time legal tender circulated in Falls Church and Fairfax County included notes of the chartered banks of Virginia—the Bank of Virginia, the Farmer's Bank of Virginia, and all of the chartered banks in the District of Columbia (which included Alexandria until 1847).[12] Part of the increase in population was fed by Yankees, mostly from New York and New England, attracted by the cheaper farmland, a longer growing season, and a better climate. They brought with them a wish to recreate what they had left: an orderly, tidy, tree-shaded community of respectable residences and well-kept farms. Falls Church's architectural legacy of solid, pleasant, unpretentious homes was established during this period by the addition of a number of homes, many of which remain.[13]

By the end of the 1850s, Falls Church was an established crossroads village. Its fertile farms and fields provided a good standard of living for area residents. Many Victorian homes built in the last half of the century still exist today. It was, according to some, "A comparative Eden." But October 17, 1859 changed all that. On that quiet Monday morning the wires of the "magnetic telegraph" carried a disquieting dispatch from Frederick, Maryland, via Baltimore: "There is an insurrection at Harper's Ferry. A band of armed Abolitionists have full possession of United States Arsenal . . . The band is composed of a gang of about 250 whites, followed by a band of negroes, who are now fighting." Rumors quickly began circulating, many of which were not founded in fact. News of the outbreak at Harper's Ferry "has come upon us as suddenly and unexpectedly as would a peal of thunder fall upon the ear on a cloudless day," declared the *Alexandria Gazette* soberly. News of insurrection and subsequent fighting between abolitionists and townspeople in Harper's Ferry spread quickly throughout Fairfax County, where it became the "principal theme of conversation." After the Commonwealth executed John Brown, leader of the abolitionists at Harper's Ferry, and Virginians and fellow Southerners realized that Brown was becoming a Northern hero, "the horror they felt can scarcely be exaggerated." John Brown's raid, as it came to be called, frightened Southerners with the spectre of racial uprisings and, more than any other single thing, estranged the north and the south.[14]

Talk of the Commonwealth's secession was in the air. Northern Virginia's "comparative Eden" was drawing to a close.

Route schedule of the newly opened Alexandria, Loudoun and Hampshire Railroad Company 1860. The road, built to link Virginia's piedmont and mountain counties of Loudoun and Hampshire (now West Virginia) with the port of Alexandria, rendered the turnpikes obsolete. Within twenty years the turnpike companies were assumed by county government. H. H. Harwood, Rails to the Blue Ridge.

TIME TABLE--NO. 1,
Alexandria, Loudoun, and Hampshire Railroad Company,
To take effect on and after MONDAY, January 16, 1860.

TRAIN GOING WEST.	Fares.	NAMES OF STATIONS.	Distances.	TRAIN GOING EAST.
Leave at 10 A.M.		..ALEXANDRIA..		Arrive at 2.30 p.m.
		3		
" " 10.9 "	15	.... Old Factory	3	" " 2.21 "
		2¼		
" " 10.15 "	25	... Arlington Mills	5½	" " 2.15 "
		1¼		
" " 10.25 "	30	.... Carlinville	6¾	" " 2.10 "
		3¾		
" " 10.35 "	50	.... Falls Church	10½	" " 1.55 "
		4½		
" " 10.55 "	75	.... Vienna	15	" " 1.35 "
		3		
" " 11.08 "	90	.... Hunter's Mill	18	" " 1.20 "
		3		
" " 11.20 "	1.00	..... Thornton	21	" " 1.10 "
		2½		
" " 11.30 "	1.10	..... Herndon.....	23½	" " 1.00 "
		3¾		
" " 11.45 "	1.25	..... Guilford.....	27	" " 12.45 "
		4		
Arrive at 12.00 M.	1.40	..FARMWELL..	31	Leave at 12.30 P.M.

"Map of the Seat of War" showing the locations of the First Battle of Manassas and Balls' Bluff. The events at Manassas had great impact on Falls Church, the modern limits of which extend, roughly, from Barrett's Hill to Upton's Hill, shown here with the location of "Rebel" camps. V. P. Corbett, 1861. Courtesy New York State Library.

CHAPTER VII

Balloons and Minié Balls
The Civil War

Although the situation appeared grim after John Brown's raid at Harper's Ferry, many in Virginia hoped to preserve the Union. But moderation was overtaken by events.

In April 1861 South Carolina began hostilities by firing on Fort Sumter and on May 23, 1861 Virginians voted to remove the Commonwealth from the Union. In Fairfax County the vote was pro-secession. In Falls Church the vote, while pro-secessionist, was badly split 44 to 26. Armed secessionist bands in and around the Falls Church and nearby voting stations frightened the area's northern sympathizers, a number of whom voted for secession, or stayed at home, in fear of their lives. "Vote this ticket," said one secessionist to Philip H. Minor of Minor's Hill. "If not, you are gone for. . ."[1]

Federal troops immediately occupied Alexandria and moved quickly from the initial bridgeheads toward Falls Church and Ball's Cross Roads (modern Ballston). On June 1 the troops skirmished with secessionists—as Southerners were called—near Bailey's Crossroads and at Fairfax Court House, the first local events of the war.[2]

General Daniel Tyler and troops comprising several Connecticut militias established a headquarters in Taylor's Tavern at Falls Church (on the hill above modern-day East Broad Street at its intersection with Roosevelt Street). Falls Church at this time was a compact village clustered around The Falls Church. Between Taylor's Tavern and the village were tidy farmhouses, orchards, farm land, and woods. In addition to its principal taverns, Taylor's and the Star, across from The Falls Church, the prosperous little village and its environs included four churches and about twenty-five houses. According to one contemporary observer the homes were ". . . of a superior character, proving the owners to be persons of more than ordinary wealth and taste. Rows of cedar trees adorn each side of the street, and the yards around different residences give it a most beautiful appearance."[3]

But Falls Church's beautiful appearance belied the disharmony which overtook the area. Fairfax Chapel closed its doors in the early spring of 1861, its members divided by sectional loyalties and fearful of oncoming events. Columbia Baptist Church fared little better. The stressful days of 1860 took their toll as talk of possible secession by Virginia roiled the congregation. In that year the secretary of the Potomac Association of Baptist churches recorded in his minutes, "Columbia—Laboring under discouragements and opposition. No cheering news to write. They are embarrassed for their house."[4]

This schism was reflected at the state level by the disintegration of the General Assembly. In June 1861 delegates loyal to the Union met at Wheeling, in Virginia's panhandle, and, declaring Virginia's governmental offices "vacant," established the "Restored" state government. Francis Harrison Pierpont was elected governor. Fairfax County, Falls Church, and Alexandria were represented, and Falls Church resident Daniel F. Dulany served as Pierpont's aide. In 1863 Virginia's western counties seceded to form West Virginia, and the capital

Taylor's Tavern, located on the hill at what is now the intersection of East Broad Street and North Roosevelt Street, Mathew Brady photo, circa 1862. During the opening days of the Civil War Union General Daniel Tyler established his Union army headquarters here. Courtesy Library of Congress, Prints and Photographs Division.

of the Restored government moved to Alexandria.[5]

Meanwhile, full-scale operations by both sides began in the Falls Church area. The Union controlled the territory from Taylor's Tavern east to Alexandria, and the village center much more tenuously, but the country immediately beyond Falls Church was in Confederate hands. On June 20, 1861, General Daniel Tyler telegraphed to the defensive forts in Arlington from Falls Church that he believed an attack was imminent and asked for reinforcement. Two days later General Tyler telegraphed the forts another alarm from Falls Church but, again, no action occurred.[6]

One innovation of this war was aerial reconnaissance—in this case from hot air balloons. On June 22, 1861, Professor Thaddeus S. C. Lowe with his balloon, the *Enterprise*, skirting Rebel scouting parties at Bailey's Cross Roads, traveled to Taylor's Tavern at Falls Church, where it was used constantly during the next two days. These ascensions appear to be the first aerial military reconnaissance in the Western Hemisphere, and probably anywhere in the world.[7]

On June 26 *The Charleston* [S.C.] *Mercury* incorrectly reported that Union forces had taken Falls Church with a force of 5,000 men, confirming the confused state of affairs in and around the village. Vice President Hannibal Hamlin visited the picket line at Falls Church at around this time, "being anxious to see how a Rebel looked at short range."[8]

Union and Confederate armies began massing for the first great battle of the war, on the banks of Bull Run near Manassas, on July 21. Three massive columns of Union soldiers marched west, with one column, numbering about 15,000 men, passing through the Falls Church area. The affair at Bull Run was expected by all in Washington to be a short one, in which Federal troops would put a quick end to the rebellion. The Confederates, however, had a different agenda and superior leadership. The fighting, the cannonading of which was clearly heard in Falls Church, turned against the Federals. Their advance halted and they began an orderly retreat, which quickly degenerated into a panic-stricken rout. Union soldiers "ran blindly, like beasts from a fire."[9]

In Falls Church the ragged Federals began streaming through the village in twilight. Pro-Unionist local citizens, who had believed they would be protected by Union forces, found the seemingly endless retreating Union soldiers unnerving. Many quickly packed and left.[10]

Frightened soldiers passed through Falls Church all night long, and morning dawned over a village and countryside which, one Falls Church observer said "seemed filled with disheveled soldiers." During the night of July 22, the day after the battle, advancing Confederate scouts, coming on the heels of the last of the Union forces, penetrated the village.[11]

After the Union disaster at Manassas, Confederates advanced east through the village to Munson's and Upton's hills, which they then occupied. General James Longstreet established his headquarters in what is now the Lawton House at Falls Church, to which he extended the Confederate Military Telegraph, and from which he conducted councils of war directing the Army of Northern Virginia. J.E.B. Stuart and his 1st Virginia Cavalry established themselves on Munson's Hill, in full view of the U.S. Capitol. Stuart took great delight in directing his artillery to take "practice" shots at Professor Lowe's balloon, which now ascended from the forts in Alexandria County (now Arlington County) to observe their movements, and in causing the "Long Roll" (battle and mobilization signal, sounded by drums) to sound all along the Union front by feigning attacks. This was probably the first incidence of anti-aircraft fire anywhere.[12]

For the Confederates their time in Falls Church was a holding action, intended to divert Federal attention from the build-up of their forces under way at Centreville. They constructed fake earthworks on Upton's and Munson's hills and "fortified" them with fake cannons.[13]

An early and major battle of the local front of the war occurred in and around Lewinsville on September 10, 1861. Numerous companies of Union and Confederate soldiers, the latter from Falls Church, engaged in sharp clashes in the darkness of the roads and woods between Falls Church and Lewinsville. It was a terrible night for the Union soldiers, who were outmaneuvered and outgunned by their opponents. On the evening of September 13 Professor Lowe, ascending in his balloon from Chain Bridge, saw what appeared to be two burning buildings just east of Falls Church and another on an adjacent hill, surrounded by large crowds of cheering and boisterous rebel soldiers: the Confederates were celebrating their victory at Lewinsville.[14]

On September 24 Professor Lowe made military history when he ascended from the Arlington Heights and targeted fire from Fort Ethan Allen (near Chain Bridge) on Confederate forces at Falls Church. This was the first aerially directed artillery fire in American history. Using a telegraph machine in the balloon basket Lowe signaled the fort, three miles away, to correct its fire when firing fell short. Confederates at Falls Church

Lithograph showing the arrival of Connecticut infantry regiments at Falls Church on June 19, 1861. The troops encamped at Taylor's Tavern, although that is not the building depicted here. They were sent to reinforce General Daniel Tyler, whose headquarters were at the Tavern and whose pickets were harassed by the Rebels. Frank Leslie's Pictorial History of the American Civil War.

Arrival of a U.S. Cavalry force at the Star Tavern in Falls Church on June 19, 1861. Columbia Baptist Church (with steeple) and the Presbyterians' Groot Hall (to its right) shown in background. The cavalry was in a "state of wild excitement" caused by the Rebels' capture of their captain, with the aid of sisters Artemisia and America Virginia Scott. Mounted cavalry are shown branching off down the Leesburg Pike and the road to Fairfax Court House (South Washington Street) in pursuit. This view faces east along Leesburg Pike (Broad Street). Frank Leslie's New York Illustrated Magazine, *June 29, 1861.*

Harper's Weekly *account of the capture of the Misses Scott—Artemisia and America Virginia Scott—of Falls Church. Both young ladies assisted in taking a Union captain captive, for which they were arrested but later released.*

soon linked the appearance of Lowe's balloon with increasingly threatening fire. And thus Falls Church earned the dubious distinction of becoming the first community in history to be bombarded by aerially-directed fire—to become common in future wars.[15]

A smaller engagement occurred on September 25 as the 600-man Seventeenth Virginia Infantry, encamped at and around The Falls Church, was joined by the Second South Carolina Infantry and the Washington Artillery for an attack on federal troops at Lewinsville and Langley. ". . . While loitering around the church," William A. Andrews of the First Georgia Infantry later wrote, "everything apparently at peace with the world, the long roll was beat to arms. The regiment was quickly formed in the road. Couriers were dashing at breakneck speed in every direction. Gen. Longstreet, whose headquarters was not far from the church, was soon in the saddle. It was not long before the Ninth Georgia, the Second South Carolina, Thirteenth Virginia, Col. Stuart's regiment of Black Horse Cavalry, and Capt. Rosser's battery of artillery was on the grounds, and away we went in the direction of Lewinsville." Another Confederate victory ensued, after which the southern forces returned after nightfall to Falls Church, where their hearts were "gladdened by the camp fires of about 20,000 Confederate soldiers."[16]

One consequence of Lowe's frequent ascensions to view rebel forces at Falls Church was his discovery that the ominous "fortifications" on the hills outside the village were not backed by corresponding levels of troops and equipment. But the ruse had served its purpose: Confederate forces were nearly finished fortifying Centreville.[17]

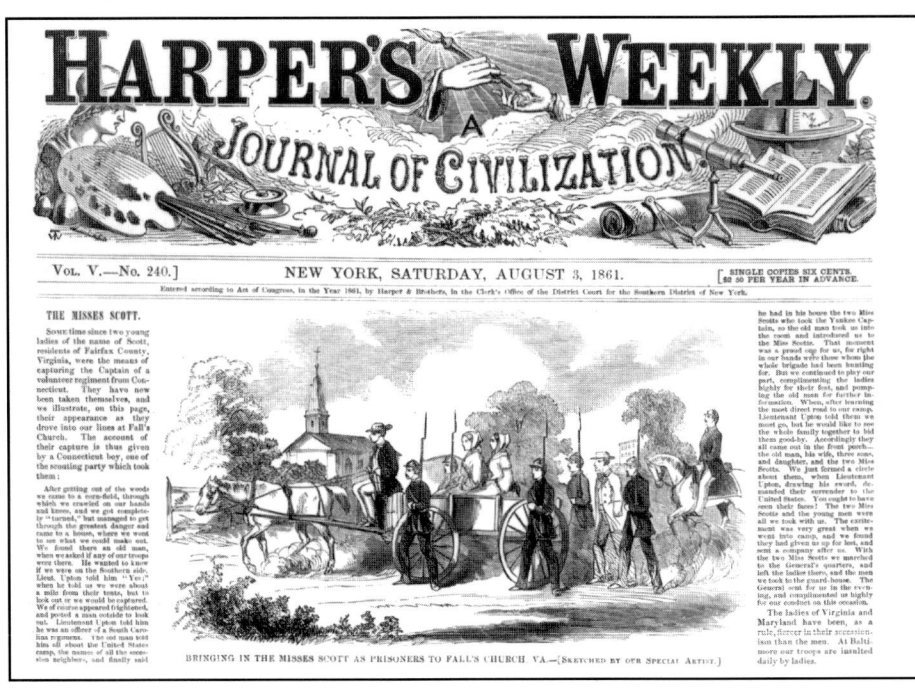

On September 29 the Confederates quietly evacuated Falls Church and its hills for their "impregnable" position on the Centreville heights and a forward post at Fairfax Court House. Surprised Federal troops quickly reoccupied Falls Church and its hills. The next day, reflecting on the day's events, a pleased but surprised General Heintzelman, not yet comprehending the successful two-month long Confederate feint which had just concluded, wrote, "We have possession of Fall's Church and Munson's Hill . . . There was no resistance."[18]

Almost as soon as Union forces reoccupied the area some of them wreaked vengeance or damage on unfortunate southerners. Members of the Twenty-second New York Infantry dismantled Fairfax Chapel in the winter of 1862 and used its brick for chimneys at their winter headquarters nearby. Members of the Twentieth New York Infantry Regiment defaced the interior of The Falls Church with graffiti (their names and regimental identification) in the winter of 1861; their commanding officer made them return the church to its former state. But other units soon followed suit. This damage paled in comparison with what would happen to the church later in the war. Union forces first used it as a hospital and later as a stable, tearing out the furnishings, floor, and walls below the windows to afford their horses better ingress and egress. Columbia Baptist Church was damaged by secessionist forces during their occupation of the town. And it is difficult if not impossible to tally the losses suffered by villagers whose homes, crops, and fields were harmed.[19]

The Falls Church figures prominently in the accounts of soldiers of both sides of the conflict. One soldier of the Twenty-third New York Infantry, attended services held there by his regimental chaplain on November 9, 1861: "Nearly all the men went, more, I guess, out of curiosity and novelty than from a desire to attend church. We carried our arms which were stacked in front of the building . . ." The church, "which has obtained such a notoriety in the present struggle," he writes, is not grand; "It is its age and association connected with it that gives it its sacredness which, in fact, has almost entirely shielded it from devastation."[20]

Several nurses, volunteers dispatched by the U.S. Sanitary Commission, ministered to the sick in Union hospitals in Falls Church. Two of them, wealthy socialites from New York City, arrived in the winter of 1861–62 and found men from a nearby New York regimental unit, most suffering from typhoid in a field hospital in The Falls Church. The patients, they recounted,

Lithograph, 1861, showing the clapboard Columbia Baptist Church, with its distinctive New England-style steeple, on the Leesburg Pike, with The Falls Church in the background. The village is identified as "Fall's Church," reflecting the tendency of soldiers of both sides to think the village was named for a resident named Fall. By the time this lithograph was published federal troops had abandoned the area a few days earlier and the village was occupied by Confederate forces. Harper's Weekly, August 3, 1861.

were emaciated and pale. "Come and take care of me, and I shall get well," said one soldier when the ladies first entered. "If you do not come, I shall die." When they began service in the hospital it held thirty-nine patients, with six former patients lying dead but unburied in the "dead-house."[21]

Falls Church was then the only village between Alexandria and Vienna, and many soldiers identified themselves in letters home as being posted "near Falls Church." In truth, most were posted on the hills west and northwest of the village center—Minor's, Munson's, Perkins' and Upton's hills, for which Falls Church was the only identifiable point of reference. Soldier camps dotted the slopes of Minor's and Upton's hills, in particular, causing nearby farms great damage as soldiers removed fence rails to use as firewood; fruits and vegetables for eating; hay and other crops for feeding horses; and cattle, hogs, and pigs for slaughtering. Valuable timber was felled, and left lying on the ground, in order to clear gunnery ranges from the forts on Upton's and Perkins' hills: much of what is now the eastern areas of the City of Falls Church were entirely denuded of trees. It is difficult to say how many soldiers were encamped in and around Falls Church at any one time, as companies came and went frequently, but it appears safe to say that at certain times during the war several thousand soldiers were posted within two miles of the village center.

The Manassas region was again the center of a major battle in August and September 1862. The second Battle of Manassas, or Bull Run, disrupted life in Falls Church as Union officials, preparing to burn the village to prevent its use by the Confederacy, ordered the village evacuated. Local residents fled with as much livestock and personal belongings as they could carry, and again Falls Church was deserted. Rebel armies moved in opposite directions, however, sparing the village from a fiery fate.[22]

Within days of the second battle at Bull Run a human tidal wave of misery and suffering descended on the village as 1,600 sick and wounded soldiers were brought to Falls Church. The Presbyterians' Groot Hall, Columbia Baptist Church, The Falls Church, and many homes were pressed into service as hospitals. Five days after the battle ambulances continued to arrive hourly in Falls Church.[23]

Aerially-directed artillery fire, later a staple in armed conflicts around the globe, got its ignoble start in Falls Church during the Civil War. Thaddeus Lowe, shown here with his hot-air balloon near Fairfax Court House, ascended from the Arlington Heights on September 24, 1861 and directed Union artillery fire onto Confederate positions in Falls Church. Lowe also ascended from Falls Church before it passed from Union control to make among the first-ever aerial reconnaissance of enemy troops. New York Illustrated News, *July 12, 1861.*

Armed skirmishes and incursions were a continuing and often daily facet of life in and around Falls Church throughout the war. Some were larger than others: one, involving the 84th New York Infantry and the 300-man First Virginia Cavalry, occurred one mile west of the village in November 1861 as the Virginians were intercepted while attempting to gather "valuable information" from the vicinity.[24]

In May 1864 the Thirteenth New York Cavalry headquartered itself in Falls Church. Its commander soon complained that Col. John S. Mosby's highly successful raiders were "continually around us" and observed that "the small force of cavalry here can hardly damage the enemy. We number hundreds, and they thousands." The erstwhile commander must certainly have been dismayed by the September 14, 1864 lightning raid by Mosby against his headquarters, in which Mosby captured the brigade butcher and then returned to capture a quartermaster's establishment which was only three hundred yards from a cavalry brigade.[25]

The Thirteenth New York Cavalry scored a victory against Col. Mosby on October 2, 1864 when it captured his arsenal and personal saber and brought them to Falls Church. Revenge, pure and sweet, may have been on the minds of Mosby and 75 of his raiders as they attacked Falls Church at 2 a.m. October 18, killing two members of the village's home guard and capturing pickets of the Sixteenth New York Infantry. Their raid was disturbed by J. B. Read, pastor of Columbia Baptist Church, who blew a horn to alert the rest of the village guard and the 16th. Mosby's men captured Pastor Read and later executed him. "That Baptist preacher Read got what was coming to him," said one. His wife and daughter were granted safe passage to drive a wagon to Tyson's Corner to retrieve his body. He is buried in The Falls Church yard.[26]

The Falls Church was witness to many more wartime funerals than just Read's. Many Union soldiers were interred there, some in unmarked (and presently unknown) graves. Their funerals, commemorating deaths of unusual and cruel variety ("rapid consumption"; purpura haemorrhagica, "a very rare disease"; typhoid; death by freezing; and, of course, death in battle) were sad affairs conducted with regal, but simple, military pageantry.[27]

Mathew Brady, circa 1860. Brady and his photography wagon visited Falls Church twice during the early portion of the Civil War, taking images of Columbia Baptist Church and The Falls Church. Courtesy National Archives.

As the war closed in 1865 Falls Church again observed massive troop movements—these all passing through the village, many camping in or near it, destined for the final review of troops by the president in Washington. The village and its inhabitants suffered many privations in the course of the conflict—churches shuttered, congregations divided; families split on basis of sectional loyalties; the prosperous and fertile fields alternately trampled and neglected; the village deserted during the most dangerous points during the war; a local pastor killed; and the local economy in ruins. Falls Church, just outside the capital's defensive fortifications, and never in the complete and uncontested control of either side, had been a particularly busy area during the Civil War. Over eighty-five regiments are known to have camped in or passed through the area. The hopes and fears of the Confederate nation were met in bloody battlefields on the "sacred soil" of Virginia, and Falls Church played a role. Reconstruction, of a most personal and wrenching kind, would occupy the villagers of Falls Church for a long time.

The Falls Church, 1862. Union soldiers stand in the west doorway and sit with sabres on horses outside. This photo was taken before the church's use as a stable, during which the brick below the windows along the south wall—shown here intact— was removed to allow horses easier ingress and egress. After the war the federal government paid to have the damage repaired. Courtesy National Archives.

Interior of The Falls Church during wartime, showing soldiers posing before graffiti covering much of the east wall. Pewboxes, pews, and railings have been removed. The church was used by Union soldiers as a hospital, stable, and then again as a hospital. The flooring, removed during use as a stable, is shown here largely intact, probably dating this photo during the early part of the war. One soldier, attending services conducted by the Twenty-second New York Infantry Regiment in November 1861, remarked "In every direction the walls . . . are literally covered with names." Courtesy U.S. Army Military History Institute.

Interior of The Falls Church. This photo, taken by Mathew Brady, probably in 1862, shows the north wall. The tablet on the left, which appears damaged, contains the Episcopal Creed. The center tablet lists the Ten Commandments from the Book of Exodus, chapter 20, and the tablet on the right the Lord's Prayer. These tablets, and almost all other furnishings, were spirited away during war by Union soldiers. Graffiti is visible above the tablets. Two of the names belong to members of the 141st New York Infantry Regiment. Courtesy National Archives.

Close-up of a larger photograph of Union soldiers at The Falls Church. Most images of soldiers at the church show them as distant, inscrutable figures, too far away to allow the viewer to discern emotion or see facial expressions. Courtesy National Archives.

53

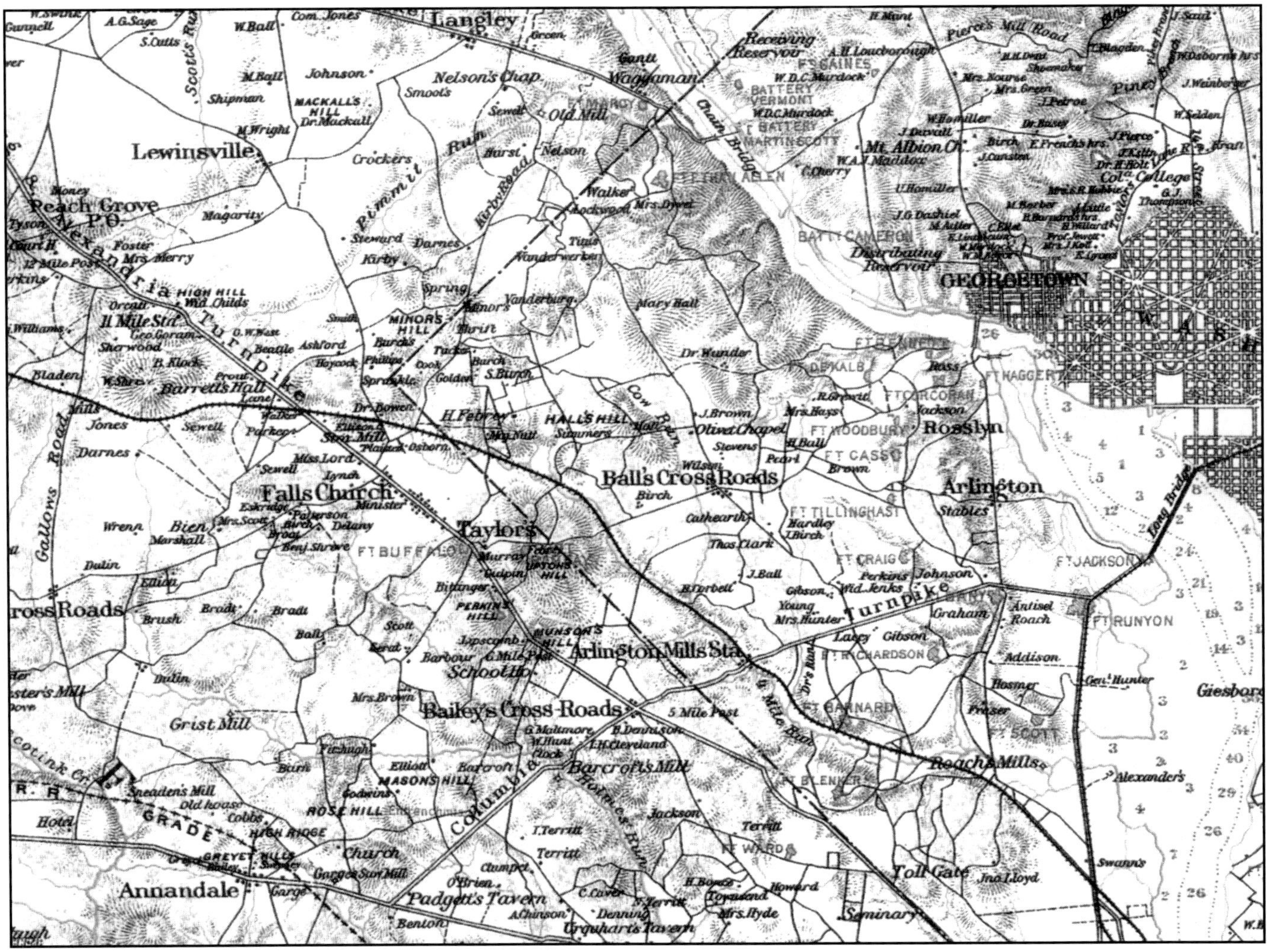

U.S. Government map showing some of the hills, fortifications, roads, and villages significant during the Civil War. Geographic features, especially hills, were very important during the Civil War, and fortifications were built on the "Falls Church hills" (Upton's, Munson's, Perkins' and Minor's hills) and at Taylor's Tavern. Engagements of note occurred at Mills Cross Roads (Merrifield), Balls Cross Roads (Ballston), Annandale, Lewinsville, and at the farms of Major Nutt and William Dulin. Falls Church itself was the site of numerous raids and skirmishes throughout the war. Courtesy Mary Riley Styles Public Library.

"Secession scouts seen at Falls Church with the aid of an opera glass." It is unknown which Confederate regiment these men represented, as many, including Mosby's Rangers, operated in and around the village throughout the war. Trees were cleared for great distances surrounding every fortification to allow unobstructed cannon fire, insuring vistas unknown today. Each side frequently spied the other through looking glasses. Pictorial War Record.

This depiction of the vagaries and extremes of area weather was drawn by an artist who happened to be present to witness it. Although no other accounts of this Feb. 24, 1862 storm are known, it appears to match two others in severity. "It was terrific," a soldier wrote of an October 6, 1861 storm. A Nov. 2, 1861 storm caused another to write, "The winds hurled the tents from the pinnings as though they were toys." Two of the soldiers depicted here appear to be experiencing the very same occurrence. Pictorial War Record.

"Treeing a Rebel." This lithograph shows troops from the Thirty-seventh New York Infantry trapping a Rebel soldier in a tree near Falls Church. Occasionally Rebel soldiers trapped federals in trees too. In September 1861 an Alabama soldier shot a Yankee soldier out of a tree near Falls Church, probably killing him. Frank Leslie's Pictorial History of the American Civil War.

Union General George McClellan (to right of stump, leaning on it) and his staff on Upton's Hill. Falls Church and its environs were the headquarters of some of the great minds of the Confederate and Union militaries during the war. Courtesy Library of Congress, Prints and Photographs Division.

Lithograph of Union fortifications at Fort Buffalo adjacent to Munson's Hill. The soldier with the looking glass (telescope) is probably peering westward, toward the village of Falls Church. Pictorial War Record.

Union cannon emplacements at Fort Ramsay on Upton's Hill. The tower seen atop the home in the background was a signal station with line-of-sight communications with the half-finished Washington Monument in the capital. The cannon and the man with the looking glass are facing east, although most of the cannons were probably mounted facing west, toward the village of Falls Church, the direction from which the enemy most likely would come. Courtesy Library of Congress, Prints and Photographs Division.

Fort Ramsay on Upton's Hill. Officers' tents are shown in front of the house, which served as headquarters. The full height of the signal corps tower constructed atop the house may be seen. This view is from the east; the road passing between the fort and house is now Wilson Boulevard. The horses and wagon have just ascended the steep incline from Four Mile Run which is still evident today. It was from here that Julia Ward Howe observed campfires and returned to her quarters in Washington's Willard Hotel to write the poem, "Battle Hymn of the Republic." Charles A. Vanderhoof. American Century, Century Collection of Civil War Art, *1974.*

John Singleton Mosby, Confederate army officer, during the war. This photo was taken in the Confederate capital, Richmond. Several of Mosby's accoutrements, such as his saber and looking glasses (binoculars) were probably stage props provided by the photographer. Colonel Mosby commanded a small group of partisan rangers in Northern Virginia in 1863–64; the "Gray Ghost" became a folk hero and the subject of legend and myth. Commercially available postcard image.

Top right: John D. Read, undated photo. Read, pastor of Columbia Baptist Church, or a portion of its congregation, and a Union sympathizer, was a member of Falls Church's village home guard. In the early morning of October 18, 1864, John Mosby and seventy-five of his Rangers attacked Falls Church. Read blew a horn to alert the nearby Sixteenth New York Infantry Regiment, encamped in the village. He was captured by Mosby's men and executed. Courtesy Mary Riley Styles Public Library.

Frederick Forrest Foote and George W. Thomas, 1864. Both were associated with two freedmen's communities in south Falls Church. Foote settled in the Fort Buffalo area and owned property there which his descendents sold to developers in the 1950s. The area is now known as Seven Corners after the mall which was built on the former farm. Scrapbook of Barbara Williams.

The DePutron family of Falls Church. Top row: Corinne Louise and Edith Sophia; bottom row: Beatrix and Maurice Bentley. Note the child's doll in foreground. This studio portrait was probably taken in Washington as Falls Church had no photographic studios. Courtesy Kay Speakman.

CHAPTER VIII

A Sense of Community

A deep sense of community developed in the little village of Falls Church following the Civil War. It increased among the people who were native to the place and was augmented by the arrival of substantial numbers of newcomers from New England, the mid-Atlantic states, and the mid-West. Attracted to the area by good farmland available at bargain prices, a relatively mild climate and prospects of economic growth, these Northerners brought new energy, new capital and new ideas about how to get things done.

The incorporation of the village into the Town of Falls Church in 1875 gave it new legal status with control of part of its taxes, roads, schools, and other public facilities. For the next quarter of a century, the town grew in population and prosperity as it increased its agricultural output for sale to Georgetown, Washington, and Alexandria merchants.

Churches were organized to serve as both religious and community centers. The Falls Church, Fairfax Methodist Chapel, and Columbia Baptist had been built prior to the Civil War. Shortly after hostilities ceased, the "colored settlement" built both the Galloway Methodist and Second Baptist churches. The white community then built, in a period of fewer than twenty years, Dulin Methodist, Crossman Methodist, St. James Catholic Chapel, First Congregational, and Falls Church Presbyterian churches.[1]

Virginia's 1869 Underwood Constitution made many changes including new laws regulating both the county forms of government and universal public education in the Commonwealth. Where appointed justices had formerly been responsible for administration of county affairs, the new rules called for eventual division of each county into magisterial districts within which voters would select a representative to serve on a Board of County Supervisors. Court justices were to be responsible for judicial affairs only. Universal education was promised, although separate schools were to be provided for white and black children.[2]

A Board of School Trustees for each magisterial district was responsible initially for adopting rules for government of schools within their district. On March 6, 1871, a public notice was printed and distributed for the Falls Church school district announcing seventeen rules. The many daily procedures to be followed included opening exercises requiring reading of sacred scriptures. Pupils were to appear in school with proper neatness; a pupil possessing a pistol or other dangerous weapon was to be suspended; and no teacher or pupil was permitted to use tobacco in any form during school hours.[3]

Efforts were made to put together broken pieces of things everywhere, especially where railroads were concerned. The Alexandria, Loudoun and Hampshire Railroad bridges had to be rebuilt. Tracks were replaced and nature herself had to be pushed back in the places where she was reclaiming the right-of-way with rapidly growing saplings, shrubs, and vines. When the railroad was again functioning and renamed the Washington and Ohio Railroad, President U. S. Grant and members of his cabinet rode it through Falls Church in 1873

These Falls Church ladies enjoyed shady summer comfort in this leafy bower, about 1900. Courtesy University of Virginia - Alderman Library.

on a day-long junket to visit Leesburg and the exhibition of the Agricultural Society at the Fair Grounds. They listened to the town band and had dinner with Col. John W. Fairfax.[4]

By a Virginia Act of Assembly approved in 1875, portions of Fairfax and Alexandria (now Arlington) counties were "made a town corporate" named Falls Church. Besides being incorporated, the town's charter was adopted. A long-standing tradition holds that Joseph Riley of "Cherry Hill" lobbied the act through the legislature to successful passage. Town councilmen appointed were J. J. Moran, T. T. Fowler, J. E. Birch, Isaac Crossman, L. E. Gott, G. B. Ives, and Joel Carter. Henry J. England was appointed Town Clerk and E. Frank Crocker, Town Sergeant.[5]

At the first organizational meeting of the mayor, J. J. Moran and the first councilmen, J. S. Riley was asked to deliver in person the official notice to the Hon. James Love, Fairfax County's Commonwealth's Attorney, that the Council had been organized following the incorporation by the Virginia Assembly of the Town of Falls Church.[6] Ordinances of the Towns of Keyser and Hamilton were to be used as models for drafting suitable ordinances for the Town of Falls Church.[7]

The first ordinance adopted regulated fireworks, guns and pistols "and things pertaining to the same." Subsequent ordinances were adopted for pre-

Dulin United Methodist Church, as it has looked since 1926, in a 1972 photo. The Civil War divided Falls Church's original Methodist congregation into northern and southern factions, each of which established separate churches which continue to exist. The southern faction constructed Dulin in 1869. Stained glass windows, a tower, and the present entrance were added in 1892. Courtesy Mary Riley Styles Public Library.

vention of: intoxication and vagrancy; public lewdness or indecency, graffiti, indecent painting, engraving, prints or sculpture. Illustrative of the rural nature of the town at the time was the passage of an ordinance making it unlawful to hitch or turn at large any cow, horse, or hog to graze on any of the sidewalks or highways of the town.[8]

Frederick Forrest Foote, Jr., a respected black businessman in the community, served the Town of Falls Church for ten or more years, first as town sergeant from 1876 to 1880, and then as a town councilman from 1880 to 1889. No Town Council minutes have survived for the years 1885 to 1897.[9]

One subject which appeared on the Council's agenda at almost every meeting was the need of repairs for roads, bridges, and sidewalks. Loads of stone were bought at 25, 50, or 75 cents per ton, hauled and broken up by hand using large stone hammers or a mechanical stone crusher, and placed in the gaping holes in the non-hard-surfaced roadways.[10] Bridges were usually built of wooden planks and they quickly rotted from use and weather and had to be replaced.[11]

Sometimes standing water was a problem. Councilman G. M. Thompson complained at one Council meeting that he needed sidewalks for his house as he "could scarcely get in or out after a heavy rain and his dooryard was at times navigable for small boats."[12]

Public school education was a major concern of the Town. G.A.C. Merrifield presented a petition signed by taxpayers to the Council in 1876 to levy a tax for the purpose of sustaining public free schools in the Corporation.[13] More than two years later, the Town Council called a public school meeting to devise means of continuing the graded school and to form a committee to determine the advisability of being relieved from the County tax for schools.[14]

The following year, 1879, the Town Council recorded in the minutes a high degree of frustration over the school situation: "Whereas, the State of Virginia having failed to provide for the maintenance of County and District public schools in accordance with the provisions of the constitution of the state of Virginia and the necessity of a public school in the Town of Falls Church" a resolution was passed by the Council calling for a school-age population census and making a determination of the amount of assistance available for conducting a corporation public school from the State, County, District or other funding sources. "The said school shall be under the control and direction of the Council of Falls Church and their delegated appointments."[15] J. S. Riley, who had been elected to the Town Council in October 1876, stated for the record that "this matter of public schools is of vast importance and something should be done by the Council in order that an effort may be made to have a public school in the Corporation." Mayor Ives appointed to the Committee on Schools: J. S. Riley, G. M. Thompson and J.C.H. Brown.[16] Action begun immediately resulted in the opening of the

"Highland View," built about 1870 as the country home of a Washington banker, in a 1949 view. Edmund Flagg, U.S. Consul to Venice, moved here in 1871 and wrote several books here. The Flagg family owned the house, which stands on the hill overlooking Leesburg Pike opposite George Mason High School, until 1991. The home has a side tower, long veranda and mansard roof with widow's walk. Courtesy Mrs. George Galleher.

Second Baptist Church, an African-American congregation off Annandale Road, 1921. This building, constructed in 1870, was abandoned in favor of the building in use today, built in 1926. The church was founded in the area of the Town of Falls Church gerrymandered to Fairfax County in 1887. Scrapbook of Barbara Williams.

Jefferson Institute Elementary School on Cherry Street, off Broad Street, in October 1882.[17]

An issue which had long been under discussion in the town was finally resolved when the Council voted to purchase three acres of land adjoining the old Methodist Chapel grounds for a cemetery. A large committee of prominent citizens was appointed to view the proposed site.[18]

Another problem was fire fighting. The Council discussed various measures in 1879 and early in 1880 ordered fire buckets and wood with which to build six fire ladders of different lengths.[19] Petitions signed by more than a two-thirds majority of voters favored purchase of fire apparatus in 1899, with a levy for purchase of fifteen cents tax per $100 carried. The Council approved the bid of the C. T. Halloway Fire Engine Co. of Baltimore for the purchase of a fire engine.[20]

One of the present businesses in Falls Church was established in 1883. James W. Brown came to Falls Church from Loudoun County where he had grown up and been a school teacher. He purchased for his store and home a structure built by Edward Birch in 1866. Between 1872 and 1881 it was also used as the post office.[21]

The Village Improvement Society of Falls Church was organized in the fall of 1885. It was modeled after the famous Laurel Hill Society of Stockbridge, Massachusetts and its objectives were to aid in improving the condition of the village. In 1892, the Society inaugurated the first observance of Arbor Day in the Commonwealth of Virginia. It was held at the Jefferson Institute.[22]

A section of the town south of the thoroughfare then known as the Falls Church and Fairfax Courthouse Road was by a Virginia Act of Assembly returned to the jurisdiction of Fairfax County. This amendment, passed in 1887, directed the transfer of the boundary of the section of land then called "the colored settlement" to outside the corporate limits of the town.[23] Since 26 percent of the black males voted Republican the boundary change gerrymandered the territory in favor of the remaining Town voters who were mainly Democrats.[24]

Communications were markedly improved when the Falls Church Telephone Company was incorporated by an Act of the General Assembly in 1888. Its incorporators were forward-looking citizens of the Town and included Robert Morrison, W. H. Doolittle, Schuyler Duryee, E. J. Northrup, Dr. T.

M. Talbott, D. D. Munson and Dr. Merton E. Church.²⁵

A clear indication of the rapidly-increasing popularity of Falls Church as a residential village was given in the *Fairfax Herald* in 1891. A special train was run from Washington on a Tuesday in June bringing about 400 people to a sale of lots in the new Sherwood subdivision. "The bidding was active from the start, and ninety-two lots were sold at an aggregate price of $23,000." Developer Church must have been pleased.²⁶

Merton Elbridge Church was born in Orleans County, Vermont in 1858, son of Joshua and Mary Elizabeth (Cobb) Church. After his father died while serving in the Union Army, in 1862, his mother married George S. Spofford and eventually moved to Virginia.

Merton E. Church was a talented entrepreneur. He was trained as a pharmacist in Fitchburg, Massachusetts and owned pharmacies in Herndon and Falls Church. He went into the real estate and insurance business and developed a telephone system throughout Northern Virginia which he eventually sold to the Chesapeake & Potomac Telephone Company in 1916. The Falls Church Improvement Company, of which he was general manager and a large stockholder, successfully developed "Sherwood" in Falls Church, west of the present-day Lincoln Avenue, and one of the first subdivisions put on the market in Fairfax County. He was a founder and director of the Falls Church Bank and served on the boards of several others, and was an ardent supporter of railway service to Northern Virginia. Ironically, Church was also a strong advocate for another improvement—road building.²⁷ Gradually roads replaced rails for preferred transportation.

The Reverend George W. Powell, pastor of Second Baptist Church, circa 1890. Second Baptist, an African-American congregation, was begun in south Falls Church in 1870, before that area transferred from the town to the county. Second Baptist has enjoyed a remarkable stability in its leadership and has been served by very few pastors each serving many years. Scrapbook of Barbara Williams.

Isaac Crossman House, 421 North Washington Street, circa 1890. This home, actually two separate houses joined together in a T-shape, was built in 1870 on a site thought to have been an Indian camp. Two rows of maples led from the house to the street. Crossman purchased the farm from Seth Osborne in 1864, at the close of the Civil War; the Osbornes lived in a log cabin which dated from the 1760s. The farm attached to this house included most of what became East Falls Church; its last portion was not sold until the 1950s. This home looks substantially the same today, although the former Crossman lot is now occupied by offices. The house itself was moved two blocks to the west. Courtesy Mary Riley Styles Public Library.

First Congregational Church, 222 North Washington Street, circa 1900. This Gothic structure was built in 1879. The church disbanded in 1910 and the building has since served as library, town hall, city hall, school, polling place, police station, drug store, and recreation center. Now known as Washington House and minus its steepled bell tower, the building has been home to the Falls Church Woman's Club since 1961. Courtesy Eleanor Fenwick and Mary Riley Styles Public Library.

Shadow Lawn, 335 Little Falls Street, circa 1955. Intermittently known as Whitehall Sanitarium, this home, constructed sometime between 1862 and 1878, has been expanded significantly, in phases, and bears little resemblance to the original house. As presently configured Shadow Lawn contains fifty-two rooms and numerous baths and half-baths. Mattie Gundry, proprietor of the Virginia Training School on West Broad Street, and Willie May Darby jointly operated a sanitarium here from 1931 until Gundry's death in 1947. Shadow Lawn is currently a private residence. Courtesy Tony Chaves.

Crossman Methodist Episcopal Church (North), 1904. Crossman was founded by the northern faction of Falls Church's original Methodist congregation after the Civil War. The structure shown here was built in 1875 and demolished in 1963. The current building was built in 1957. Courtesy Mary Riley Styles Public Library.

Dr. John J. Moran, first mayor of the newly-established Town of Falls Church in 1875, in a photo taken sometime between 1868 and 1875. Egbert Guy Fowx photo, courtesy Mary Riley Styles Public Library.

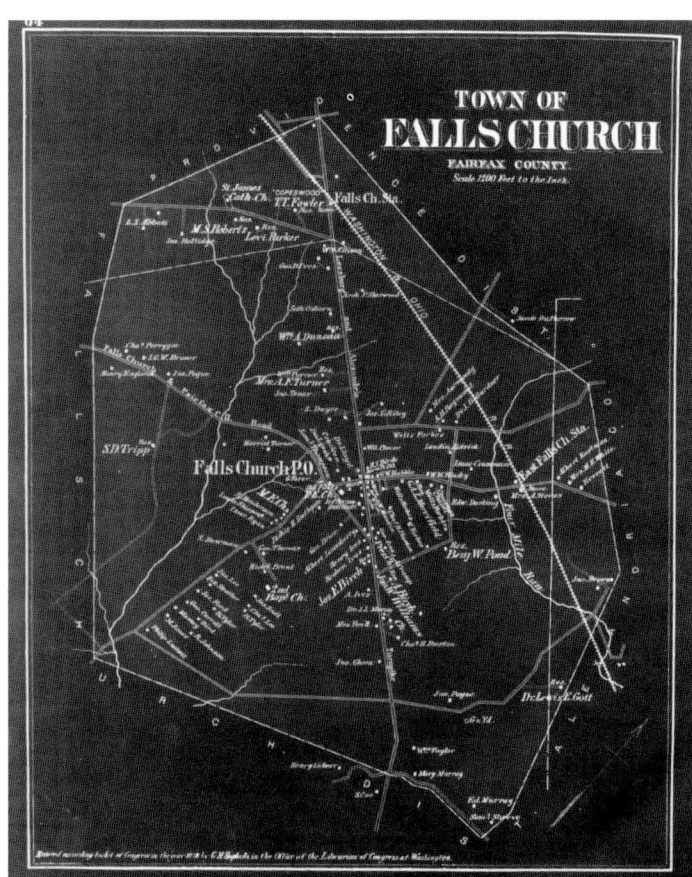

Eighteen seventy-eight Hopkins Atlas Map of the new Town of Falls Church, incorporated in 1875. The southern boundary changed in 1887 when a portion was gerrymandered out of the town limit, and the eastern boundary changed in 1936 when the Arlington County portion of the town, East Falls Church, was removed by court order. Courtesy Mary Riley Styles Public Library.

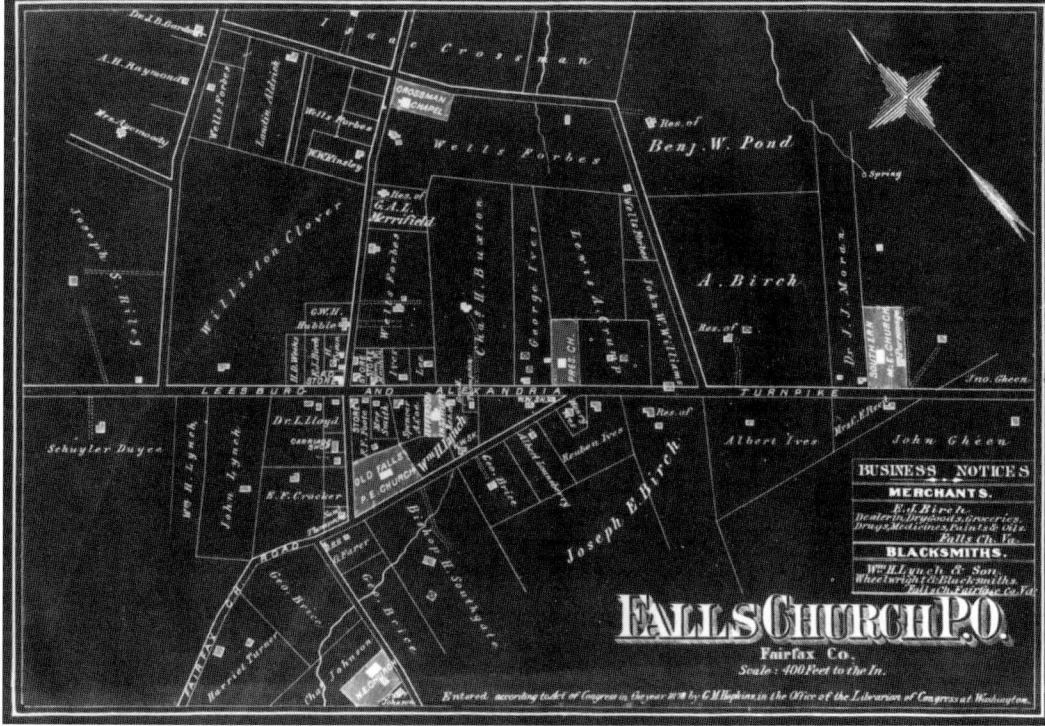

Hopkins Atlas map (1878) of area served by the Falls Church post office. "The three Falls Churches"—East, West, and the village center—were eventually served by a like number of post offices until reorganized as one post office in the 1930s. Courtesy Mary Riley Styles Public Library.

Jefferson Institute, East Broad Street at Cherry Street, 1891. The Institute was Falls Church's first public school and met in the Columbia Baptist Church from 1875 until 1882, when this building was opened for students. The brick two-story building with its prominent belfry was used until 1956. It was demolished as a fire hazard in 1959 and is now the site of the Childhood Development Center. The town's first Arbor Day ceremony was held here in 1892. Courtesy Mary Riley Styles Public Library.

St. James Roman Catholic Church, South West Street at Fowler Street, 1880. Falls Church's small Catholic community worshipped in this church, originally a mission church, until 1902 when it moved to larger quarters in the present church on Park Avenue. The parish cemetery remains at this site; the former rectory was next door. Courtesy Tony Chaves.

Falls Church Presbyterian Church, East Broad Street and Fairfax Street, circa 1900. This Gothic-style church, the first stone building in Falls Church, and built of stone quarried on South Washington Street at Tripps Run, was erected in 1884. Later additions have remained sympathetic to the original style. Courtesy Mary Riley Styles Public Library.

The Ladies Aid Society of Falls Church Presbyterian Church, circa 1890. These philanthropic and community-oriented women formed one of Falls Church's first fraternal and charitable organizations. Courtesy Mary Riley Styles Public Library.

Frederick Forrest Foote, Jr., circa 1885. Foote, a prosperous merchant, served on the town council, 1880–89. Foote's election to the council came after the time of Reconstruction imposed on the former Confederate states and illustrated the high regard in which he was held by the Falls Church community at large. G. W. Davis Studio, courtesy Mary Riley Styles Public Library.

Rollins House, 109 East Columbia Street, 1890. The large front tower is octagonal on the first floor and circular on the second floor. This house, built in 1888, contains twenty rooms, four baths, and five fireplaces. Courtesy Mary Riley Styles Public Library.

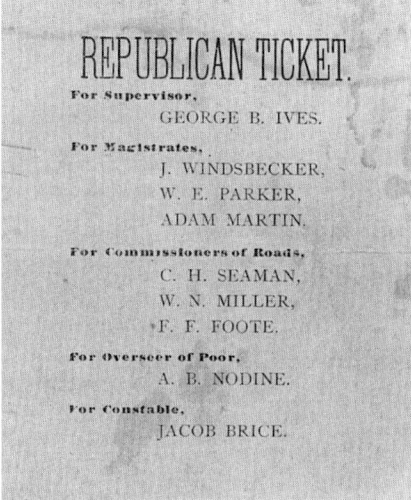

Republican office-seekers appearing on Falls Church election ticket, undated. Frederick F. Foote, a prominent area African-American, is listed as a candidate. George Ives was a candidate for overseer. Scrapbook of Barbara Williams.

Woodbrook, 1011 Fowler Street, circa 1972. Woodbrook, with the only remaining windmill in Falls Church, was built in 1890 and contains many architectural niceties including sliding doors and front and back stairs leading to the upper hallway. The attic contains a large tank into which water was pumped by the windmill for gravity flow throughout the house. Courtesy Mary Riley Styles Public Library.

Spofford and Church Drug Store, 113–115 West Broad Street, circa 1890. Pharmacist Merton E. Church, co-owner and soon the town's leading businessman, is seated at right. Falls Church's first telephone and telephone exchange were here (see sign, left foreground). Courtesy Mary Riley Styles Public Library.

Guy Northrop Church, 1890. Young Church's pram is parked outside the drug store co-owned by his father, Merton E. Church. The son, who joined the military, later witnessed—and survived—one of the seminal moments in American history, the Japanese attack on Pearl Harbor, Hawaii, in 1941. Courtesy Mary Riley Styles Public Library.

Schuyler Duryee House, 309 West Broad Street, circa 1890. Mattie Gundry expanded the home after purchasing it in about 1899 for her renowned Virginia Training School. The Duryee House was demolished in 1948, one year after Miss Gundry's death closed her school, to make way for a massive development of apartments. Most are gone now; the surviving ones are condominiums. Courtesy Mary Riley Styles Public Library.

Brown's Hardware and Grocery Store, West Broad Street at Washington Street, circa 1890. The Brown family opened the store in 1883 and it remains in business today as the city's oldest family-owned business. Courtesy Mary Riley Styles Public Library.

I.O.O.F. Hall, 248 West Broad Street, 1966. Falls Church's chapter of the International Order of Odd Fellows, once a preeminent fraternal organization, built this hall, the town's only public meeting place for many years, in 1891. The building was demolished in 1970 and made way for an undistinguished structure which shares none of its predecessor's solid architectural presence. Quentin Porter photo, courtesy Mary Riley Styles Public Library.

Dulin Methodist Episcopal Church (South), 1909. After the Civil War, during which Falls Church's original Methodist congregation split into regional factions, the southern group erected this church in 1869 at 513 East Broad Street. In 1892 two chandeliers with six kerosene lamps, shown here, were installed in the sanctuary. They hung from pulleys in the ceiling with weights in the attic and were pulled down with a pole for lighting, cleaning, and filling. The chandeliers were replaced in 1926. Courtesy Mrs. Joe Copley and Mary Riley Styles Public Library.

Erwin House, 300 Great Falls Street, 1972. This home, built in 1893, is the most opulent of those constructed during the late Victorian era in Falls Church. The house employs varied materials and textures—shingles, clapboards, and panels—and includes two projecting balconies. William E. Barrett photo, courtesy Mary Riley Styles Public Library.

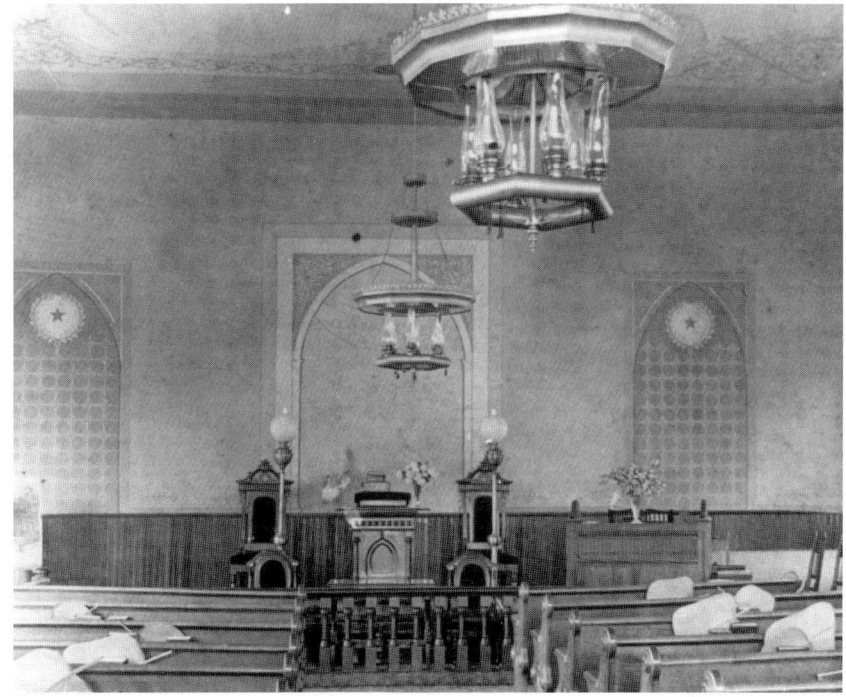

DePutron House, 508 Lincoln Avenue, circa 1912. Jacob DePutron built this two-story gabled brick Victorian-style house in 1893. The western point of the original ten mile square District of Columbia is on what was the DePutron farm. The bricks for the home were made on the property, except for the facing bricks on the front; the interior walls are made of solid brick. One of the towers encloses a water storage tank. This house is believed to have installed the first modern bathroom in Falls Church. This was later the home of Falls Church's longest-serving mayor, L. P. Daniel. Courtesy Kay Speakman.

Albert P. Eastman family, circa 1893. Left to right: William R., Albert P., Sarah N., and Frank. The photogenic Eastmans, of East Falls Church, were longtime residents of the town when its eastern portion seceded in 1936 to Arlington County. Their home, at Washington Boulevard and Lee Highway, was spared by the construction of Interstate 66 and retains its white picket fence. Courtesy Eleanor Fenwick and Mary Riley Styles Public Library.

Bonnie Brier, 502 Walden Court, undated photo. The Casilears built this large two-story, gable-roofed house around 1895. A summer house, sheep house, concrete icehouse (a luxury in the days before electric or gas-powered refrigerators), and barn were also located on the site. In the front was an orchard extending to Lincoln Avenue, now occupied by the houses of Walden Court. Courtesy Mary Riley Styles Public Library.

Maurice Bentley DePutron at the West Falls Church railroad station, located near where the tracks (now the regional park trail) crossed West Broad Street. This station was for freight; passengers generally used the East Falls Church station. Courtesy Kay Speakman.

Ship's company of the battleship USS Maine. *Falls Church resident Charles Parker Galpin, who survived the explosion which marked the ship's end, may be the sailor shown in the second row from top, second from right. The crew, photographed in happier times before the ship's ill-fated visit to Havana, was known for its high morale and collegiality. Library of Congress, Prints and Photographs Division.*

CHAPTER IX

The Summer Soldiers of 1898 Falls Church and Camp Alger

The sinking of the warship *Maine* on February 15, 1898 signaled one of the most momentous events in Falls Church history. Shortly after the war began state militias were mobilized and citizen soldiers from New York, Pennsylvania, Ohio, Indiana, Illinois, Connecticut, and other states found themselves telegraphing home the news, "Ordered to Falls Church, Va."[1] The various state militias were in need of training before deployment. The War Department in Washington secured a two-square mile tract of land west of Falls Church which it named Camp Russell A. Alger after the secretary of war. Camp Alger occupied the area roughly bounded by the present Lee Highway, Hollywood Road, Gallows Road, Arlington Boulevard and Graham Road.[2] Over twenty regiments forming the U.S. Second Corps took residence there, totaling almost 30,000 soldiers.

Typhoid broke out in mid-July 1898. Most soldiers and officers blamed the "water famine," caused by lack of drinkable water for the fever and for the cases of diarrhea which plagued the camp. The incidence of typhoid, which sickened many and accounted for most of the seventy-three deaths reported there, figured prominently in soldiers' diary entries and letters home, prompting recriminations felt in the state capitals and in Washington.[3]

But all was not hardship. Troops made excursions into Washington, where they usually visited the Capitol, Navy Yard, Library of Congress, and Smithsonian. These trips to and from Falls Church overwhelmed the train stations and streets, causing disarray and chaos in the town. Provost guards from Camp Alger encamped permanently at East Falls Church to assist in maintaining order and directing traffic. One soldier wrote, "The pandemonium [at East Falls Church's trolley station] here is something frightful. Tickets are purchased in the store across the track, while lemonade, soda water and candy vendors combine with colored bootblack and clothes brush boys, not to mention the hackmen, to raise a rumpus which is absolutely unforgettable."[4]

Falls Church residents sometimes bore the brunt of soldier roughhousing and war games. On the evening of July 2, men of the Sixth Pennsylvania Infantry, erroneously believing themselves released for the Independence Day weekend, left on foot. Troop "A" of the New York Cavalry was called to arms: "We galloped over the main road [Lee Highway] to Falls Church, a cloud of dust enveloping all but the first two sets of fours." The troops must have made an impressive appearance, as the leaders, followed by the moving cloud, thundered down the steep hills with their weapons clashing, and the drawn sabres gleaming in the moonlight at intervals through the dust. Falls Church, however, was "quiet as the grave." Troop "A" then "commenced a wild chase, scouring the surrounding country on every side in the direction of Washington." One by one the missing Pennsylvanians were rounded up, sometimes thirty men at a time.[5]

The colorful Troop "A" visited Falls Church again en masse, this time to make a "grand attack" on the village. They were careful to leave blank car-

Falls Church resident Charles Parker Galpin, sailor aboard the USS Maine. *Galpin survived the explosion which sank his ship in the harbor of Havana, Cuba, igniting the Spanish-American War. Courtesy Clarence R. Hartman and Mary Riley Styles Public Library.*

Stereopticon image of the First Rhode Island Volunteers, Camp Alger, 1898. "The new recruits . . . promised to 'Remember the Maine,*' and we fully believe they will." The Spanish-American War was among the shortest in American history, and many soldiers at Camp Alger were never called upon to prove themselves in battle. These men appear sharply attired but not all soldiers were as lucky. Uniforms and equipment were late in arriving for many at Camp Alger. Library of Congress, Prints and Photographs Division.*

tridges behind at camp so that "the villagers might not suppose that the civil war had recommenced." They were then surprised by Troop "C," which did not leave behind blank cartridges, and a "lively" (and surely noisy) engagement followed.[6]

Falls Church residents found Camp Alger a very noisy neighbor indeed. Much of the village was within earshot of the gunfire emanating from the practice skirmishes there. Each day began and closed with regimental buglers sounding reveille and taps, the notes echoing over the fields and woods. "The neighing of horses, the rattle of empty wagons, tramp of the troops, while above all sounded the ceaseless roll of drums or practice of bands . . . made a life of activity comparable to nothing outside the army," wrote one soldier, adding, "Singing, as in all camps, was a favorite pastime with the men . . . Each company had its glee club, and after supper, as night fell, you were sure to hear from every [company] street the familiar choruses by the men, varied by occasional solos by the best singers. 'Break the News to Mother,' 'Say Au Revoir,' 'Nearer, My God, to Thee,' 'Marching Through Georgia,' 'The Old Oaken Bucket,' etc., were favorites of an endless repertoire."[7]

Coexistence of the massive camp with the adjacent town of Falls Church was always tenuous. Temperance leaders in the village were incensed by the "boom-town" called the Midway Plaisance, named for the carnival strip made famous by the Chicago World's Columbian Exposition of 1893, which grew along the Warrenton Pike (present-day Lee Highway) in the vicinity of Merrifield. The tents, shacks, stalls and vendors' stands of the Plaisance supplied the soldiers with alcohol which, many in the village felt, was cause of much of the carousing by soldiers which took place there. Coexistence of the two—village and camp—was also sorely tested by Falls Church residents' dislike of being stopped by army road patrols while going about their own business.

The visit of President William McKinley provided Camp Alger its biggest day on May 22 as he brought several cabinet officers and foreign dignitaries to review the troops. Fifteen thousand soldiers prepared to parade before the president and his entourage, and the troops assigned to escort him from the train station busily polished brass and brushed off uniforms, but to no avail: ". . . the yellow Virginia dust commenced to rise, and with the pounding of almost two hundred horses' hoofs on a heavy trot, the suffocating *ochreous* cloud was so thick that only the troopers directly in front could be distin-

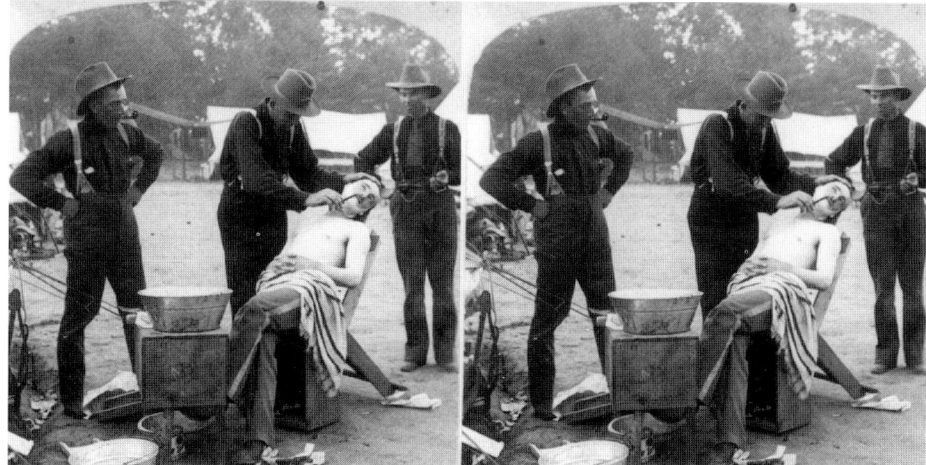

Stereoscope image of a barber's establishment at Camp Alger, 1898. "The neighing of horses, the rattle of empty wagons, tramp of the troops, while above all sounded the ceaseless roll of drums or practice of bands, with all the necessary accompaniments of a great camp, made a life of activity comparable to nothing outside the army. Entire streets, bordered with restaurants, jewelers, photographers, seemed to spring up in a night . . ." according to one report. The upended crate on which the wash basin rests is marked "Marvel Slipper Co., Ladies Slippers." Library of Congress, Prints and Photographs Division.

guished, and then only as faint silhouettes, the sides of the road being lost to view." After a bit the order came to part, allowing the presidential party, which had been choking in the dust, to the forefront.[8]

The president was by no means the only dignitary to visit Camp Alger. Clara Barton, Dr. Walter Reed, representatives of the German Embassy and Chinese Legation and of the Norwegian and revolutionary Cuban armies all paid calls, as did members of Congress. And Carl Sandburg, a soldier at the time, wrote that "near Falls Church, Virginia, only a few miles from the Capitol dome, I lived in a tent, answered roll call six and eight times a days, cut saplings and built myself a bunk, more than once made a practice march in hot weather . . ."[9]

The timely and welcome news that the Navy had destroyed the Spanish fleet at Santiago de Cuba, Cuba, enlivened Independence Day celebrations at Camp Alger. Soldiers played baseball, held foot races, wheelbarrow races, hurdle races, wrestling and boxing matches, visited Washington, attended the camp theater, enjoyed sarsaparilla and ice cream, and viewed what must have been Falls Church's greatest fireworks display until recent years.[10]

But the war was among the shortest in American history. Most at Camp Alger never saw combat. Even after the Kingdom of Spain signed peace protocols, insurrection continued in the Philippine Islands, requiring garrison troops, but Camp Alger's role was ended. The last of the regiments departed September 8. The troops had wreaked such havoc on the land that it was "a bleak sand waste" and unproductive for many years to come.[11]

Lessons learned in 1898—the necessity and ability to coexist with welcome and unwelcome circumstances, developments, and conditions—were to prove instrumental to Falls Church's success in the century soon to dawn. The villagers' new-found flexibility and adaptability would soon assert itself in positioning the town for growth and prosperity during what many would come to call "the American century." The Spanish-American War proved a valuable litmus test for Falls Church for the changes soon to come.

Smartly-attired New York Cavalrymen parade in their "cool and comfortable" new white helmets, a gift from an organization of friends and family in New York. Uniforms and equipment were provided the troops by their respective states in varying degrees of effectiveness. One poorly-supplied Missouri troop marched before President William McKinley in a review on May 28 wearing "ragged civilian clothes and without arms." A moved crowd cheered wildly, offering thunderous applause, and an embarrassed state government quickly forwarded the needed uniforms and arms. Library of Congress, Prints and Photographs Division.

East Falls Church and its rail station, 1898. "The pandemonium here is something frightful. Tickets are purchased in the store across the track, while lemonade, soda water and candy venders combine with colored bootblack and clothes brush boys, not to mention the hackmen, to raise a rumpus which is absolutely unforgettable," wrote one soldier. An electric trolley is seen unloading or taking on passengers. Buggies queue to take paying passengers from the station to Camp Alger, a training facility during the Spanish-American War. The fare was "invariably 25 cents one way, no difference whether one rides in a farm wagon or a surrey." Courtesy Mary Riley Styles Public Library.

Military guards stationed on street corners in Falls Church and its rail stations maintained order. This scene shows the East Falls Church provost encampment by day; at night "The [East] Falls Church station . . . surpasses itself for noise and confusion. . . ." Thayer, History of Company K . . .

Private Paul L. Wheelock, Private William C. Johnson, and Corporal Frederick L. Appleton, Camp Alger, 1898. Wheelock, who hated the Virginia sun, Johnson, a perpetual inventory clerk for a manufacturing company, and Appleton, who was "full of unrest and ready to travel," demonstrated the cross-section of society represented at Camp Alger. Thayer, History of Company K . . .

Encampment of the Twenty-second Kansas Infantry Regiment at Camp Alger, 1898. "The long, hazy days of summer are dragging slowly along for us. Every day, every week and every month is alike to us . . . The inactivity of this great army is tiresome in the extreme. . . ." Courtesy Kansas State Historical Society.

Unidentified soldiers in the woods surrounding Camp Alger. They appear to be accompanied by civilians. The soldiers each sport the regulation camping and marching gear, including metal drinking cans, suitable for campfires; rolled tenting; and rifles. Courtesy National Archives.

Doctor Henry DeHaven Cameron of Co. C, New York Cavalry. Dr. Cameron, who "never seemed to think of his own comfort and was ready, day or night, for service" enjoyed the "perfect confidence" of the men in his care but was ill-prepared by the medical science of the day to attend to the many sicknesses, including dysentery and typhoid fever, which ran unchecked through Camp Alger. Cammann, History of Troop A . . .

Band of the Twenty-second Kansas Infantry Regiment at Camp Alger, 1898. Courtesy Kansas State Historical Society.

Brown's Hardware Store, undated photo. Left to right: Mr. Rinker, a store clerk; Mr. Brown, proprietor; the identity of the young man is unknown. Courtesy Hugh Brown and Mary Riley Styles Public Library.

CHAPTER X

Domestic Tranquility

After Camp Alger closed down and Spanish-American War soldiers' activities had ceased to have an impact on Falls Church, the Town Council turned its attention to local problems. Fire equipment was purchased and the Fire Company was invited to participate in the Fourth of July parade.[1] Many community affinity groups had been organized in Falls Church by 1899. They included a wide variety of interests: the Potomac Fruit Growers Association, a farmers' cooperative; the Independent Order of Good Templars; the Village Improvement Society; the International Order of Odd Fellows; the Kemper Masonic Lodge, the Volunteer Fire Department; and the R. E. Lee Chapter, Daughters of the Confederacy.[2]

The future for the new twentieth century looked especially bright with the establishment of a highly-respected training school under an energetic and well-trained principal, Mattie Gundry, and a Falls Church library which was in the next hundred years to become a vital cultural and educational center for residents of town and city.[3]

Educator Miss Mattie Gundry purchased residential property on West Broad Street near Little Falls Street from Schuyler Duryee in 1899. She enlarged the building and developed a campus for the Virginia Training School which she operated successfully for almost fifty years. She taught her mentally disadvantaged students useful knowledge and skills to enrich their lives.[4]

Nonfunctioning oil street lamps or problems with the lamplighter seemed to appear almost every month in the council's 1899 minutes. Complaints about the poor maintenance of the electric trolley crossings on the public streets were almost as frequent. One petition asked that someone fix the culvert at a crossing "to at least make the water run downhill."[5] Living with the railroads was not easy. One resident requested that the mayor effect abatement of the noise made by the Southern Railway's locomotive whistles.[6]

Vandalism had become a problem and by 1901, the council adopted a resolution authorizing the mayor to put the town sergeant on active duty to control disorderly conduct or to appoint special policemen for the purpose.[7] Litter was another ever-present source of irritation. The Village Improvement Society requested at a council meeting that same year that the litter ordinance be strictly enforced.[8]

Future author James Thurber and his family, including two brothers, lived in a rented house on Maple Street in the summers of 1901 and 1902, when he was six years old. In letters to Mrs. Frank Acosta in 1958 and 1959, Thurber recalled some of his vivid memories of Falls Church. Fascinated by one of the town's employees, he wrote: "Our garbage was collected by an ancient white-haired negro, no more that five feet tall, whose two-wheeled oxcart was pulled by a brace of oxen. His appearance never failed to enchant us boys, for he was not only out of the South, but out of the past, even out of fiction, as remarkable as old Uncle Tom himself." It was in Falls Church that Thurber lost one of his eyes as the result of a childhood accident.[9]

George Erwin's bakery, undated photo. The bakery probably used manually-stoked ovens fueled by wood or coal and kerosene lamps for lighting, as Falls Church did not get electricity until 1912. It proved so popular that by 1912 the town found it necessary to grant permission for the new electric utility to string lines "Provided that all poles shall be neat and symmetrical." Courtesy Mary Riley Styles Public Library.

The Thurbers were followed by many renters for both summer and winter. By 1903, real estate agents, subdivision developers and potential residents of Falls Church were using the trolley services. In addition to land purchases, renters were eager to live in Falls Church in all seasons. The *Fairfax Herald's* Falls Church correspondent published the information that "more people have recently rented houses in our town for the winter than was ever known before. A house is scarcely vacated by the summer residents before a new tenant moves in."[10]

Cultural enrichment was beginning to be a part of village life. The Falls Church Library had only been in existence for four years when the Library Association and its Board of Control published a *Catalogue of Books* listing all of the 650 items in their collection. The civic-minded officers for 1903 were Pickering Dodge, president; Dr. George B. Fadeley, vice president; William A. Ball, secretary; and George W. Hawxhurst, librarian. Advertisers whose ads helped pay for the publication were business people from Falls Church, Leesburg, and Washington, D.C.[11]

A strong interest in protecting native birds was formalized in 1903 when the Virginia State Audubon Society was established in Falls Church. John B. Henderson was the first president. One of the principal goals of the organization was to promote a popular interest in bird study. Children under sixteen paid no dues but signed pledge cards agreeing not to harm birds or their eggs.[12] It was around this time that Joseph Harvey Riley of Cherry Hill in Falls Church embarked upon his life career as a renowned professional ornithologist at the Smithsonian.[13] A successor branch organization, the Fairfax Audubon Society, now meets monthly at the National Wildlife Federation in Vienna.[14]

In his book *Falls Church: A Virginia Village* published in 1904, Charles A. Stewart noted that there were then few old houses in the village. One comment he wrote is of interest: "The old big chimney house situated in the field opposite the Odd Fellows' Hall was built in Revolutionary times and is probably the oldest dwelling in this vicinity."[15]

Stewart also wrote of the "colored settlement" a short distance south of the town limits, consisting of about a hundred cottages with a population between four and five hundred. "They have a school building and three churches and many of the little cottages and surroundings indicate industry and thrift in the occupants."[16]

Stewart described Falls Church as the place where

> . . . the tired city man can afford all of the enjoyment of retirement and tranquility. With an abundance of green lawns, well shaded walks and drives, pure water, good schools and the necessary stores, what more could the seeker desire to complete his ideal of a country home. Falls Church welcomes the jaded fathers and mothers from the city to the place where chil-

dren may enjoy life with nature, where the climate, conducive to refreshing sleep, soothes tired nerves and makes life to such again buoyant with youthful hopes and joys.[17]

A new church building and a parochial school were built in the town between 1902 and 1906. The stone building of St. James Roman Catholic Church was erected in 1902 and the St. James Catholic Elementary School was built facing Broad Street in 1906. They are still located across from one another on Spring Street.[18]

If any evidence was needed in 1910 that Falls Church was in at least one regard still a sleepy little country town, it was provided by an earlier council ordinance passed again that year. In part, it read: ". . . It shall not be lawful for any person to fasten, turn at large or permit any cow, ox, horse, mule or hogs or other animals to graze on any of the sidewalks or highways of the town . . ."[19]

Major changes were made the very next year. The Rosslyn Gas Company was extending its lines to Falls Church.[20] And after years of council discussions the decision was made to electrify the town. Requests for bids were released but the only response was made by Merton E. Church, General Manager of the Arlington Electric Company. The council accepted his offer to buy the franchise for $10.00. The formal letter of notification and acceptance was dated January 11, 1912.[21] After all of the years of problems with kerosene street lamps, the council was surely relieved to direct that lighting of kerosene street lamps be discontinued at the end of April 1912.[22]

After lengthy discussions had been held at many meetings before the Falls Church town council, it adopted on December 14, 1914, the Virginia state act approved March 12, 1912, providing for designation of segregated districts for residence of white and colored persons.[23]

Five men from the black community appeared at the following January 1915 council meeting protesting passage of the segregation ordinance. J. B. Tinner, Rev. Y. W. Powell, Rev. J. W. Colbert, E. B. Henderson, and G. W. Simmons spoke on the subject.[24] The ordinance was enacted and the council's segregation committee was instructed to prepare a map showing the boundaries of segregation districts Nos. 1 and 2.[25]

Early in 1915, however, E. B. Henderson had called a meeting with leading black citizens of Falls Church to oppose the proposed segregation ordinance for the town of Falls Church. The group organized the Colored Citizens Protective League (CCPL) and Henderson urged them to elect Joseph Tinner president. Later that year, the organization became the Falls Church and

Falls Church Post Office, 1898. This building, erected in 1895, was the first dedicated post office in town. Courtesy Mrs. Myron Thompson and Mary Riley Styles Public Library.

Francis Holmes Styles, age 4, and Elizabeth Morgan Styles, age 6, Easter 1900. The Styles siblings lived at Cherry Hill Farm, the longtime family home. In the 1950s both gave the new city the land on which the public library sits, opposite their farm house. Their father, Samuel Styles, was a prominent council member in the new town of Falls Church, which he helped found. Photograph by Nolte, courtesy Mary Riley Styles Public Library.

Vicinity Branch of the National Association for the Advancement of Colored People (NAACP). This group engaged Washington, D.C. attorneys James E. Cobb and George E. C. Hayes who were active in NAACP affairs. The lawyers submitted a brief to the town council noting the unconstitutionality of the Falls Church segregation plan and the council abandoned efforts to enforce the ordinance.[26]

Decades passed during which federal legislation was passed to eliminate segregation and its many inequities. An important Supreme Court decision was made in 1954 calling for equal opportunity in public education. In 1964, the Civil Rights Act provided the first federal fair employment practices law, prohibiting discrimination on the basis of race, color, religion, national origin, or sex by employers, employment agencies, and union. Fair housing was mandated by additional statutes. The 1915 segregation ordinance was repealed by the Falls Church City Council in February 1999.[27]

Electric trolley station and steam railroad station, East Falls Church, circa 1900. A portion of East Falls Church's vibrant business district, destroyed during the 1960s to make way for Interstate 66, may be seen here. Note separate sets of tracks for the electric and steam railroads. Soldiers from nearby Camp Alger thronged these two stations in 1898, forcing the army to post a permanent provost guard to maintain order. Courtesy Dexter Tutbull and Mary Riley Styles Public Library.

Independence Day, 1900. Many in the crowd shield themselves with parasols from the hot summer sun. Courtesy Eleanor Fenwick and Mary Riley Styles Public Library.

Galloway Methodist Church, 306 East Annandale Road, 1979. Galloway, an African-American congregation, built this structure in 1901. Rapid growth caused the church to tear it down and build a handsome and imposing replacement on the same site in 1991. Lee Briggs photo, courtesy Mary Riley Styles Public Library.

St. James Roman Catholic Church, Park Avenue at Spring Street, 1968. This church, built in 1902, was expanded in 1952. Wings added during the expansion matched the original style and shaped the church in the form of a Roman cross. Setback buttresses surround the church, which is an example of English Gothic architecture. Gothic tracery beautifies the lead-glass windows. Courtesy Mary Riley Styles Public Library.

Lynch family at home, 304 East Broad Street, 1902. Left to right: Talbott, twins Cora and William Henry, father William Nathan, and mother Sarah Ellen. Talbott is holding a stereopticon, or "magic lantern," similar to the Viewmaster of more modern times. Courtesy Willard Piggott, courtesy Mary Riley Styles Public Library.

Broad Street at Washington Street, circa 1902. Horse-drawn buggies figure prominently in this pre-automobile era photo. Courtesy Tony Chaves.

Washington Street looking north from Broad Street, circa 1902. Telephone or telegraph poles may be seen; electric service did not arrive until 1912. Courtesy Tony Chaves.

Pete Gillam in front of Brown's Hardware Store, Broad and Washington Street, circa 1905. Gillam was the man described by author James Thurber, who lived in Falls Church and later recalled, "Our garbage was collected by an ancient white-haired negro, not more than five feet tall, whose two-wheeled oxcart was pulled by a brace of oxen. His appearance never failed to enchant us boys, for he was not only out of the South, but out of the past, even out of fiction, as remarkable as old Uncle Tom himself." Scrapbook of Barbara Williams.

Independence Day, Garner family home, East Columbia Street, 1906. The flag flies forty-four stars, although there were forty-five states in the Union: Utah, the forty-fifth, was admitted in 1896. Courtesy Wally Garner and Mary Riley Styles Public Library.

Arringdon Hall, 223 North Washington Street, Christmas 1906. Major W. S. Hopkins lived in this spacious home with its imposing Grecian columns and lovely grounds. Demolished late 1960s. Courtesy University of Virginia, Alderman Library.

Rust/Bonnell/Douglas House, 201 North West Street, 1972. The house dates from about 1907. Shown here are a three-story water tower and one-story combination acetylene gas and ice house. The water tower was used until 1936, when Falls Church inaugurated town water service. Acetylene gas was used for lighting until sometime after Falls Church received electric service in 1912. General Leonard Wood is said to have lived in this house during World War I. Courtesy Mary Riley Styles Public Library.

Picnic at Groot Hall, Falls Church Presbyterian Church yard, 1908. The meeting hall, constructed in 1856 during the antebellum period for Presbyterian meetings, was used as an army hospital during the aftermath of the Battle of Second Manassas during the Civil War. It was torn down in 1925. Courtesy Jane B. Shaw, courtesy Mary Riley Styles Public Library.

Rosslyn Mill, North Oak Street, 1910. Falls Church, though small, has always been home to light industry. Courtesy James E. Anderson and Mary Riley Styles Public Library.

Columbia Baptist Church, 1927, showing the 1926 addition (at left). Begun in 1909 and completed one year later, this building was constructed of native stone quarried on South Washington Street at Tripps Run. Building Columbia a new home was a community-wide, ecumenical event: every denomination in town except the Catholics furnished a representative to the building committee and rendered substantial assistance; the Catholics contributed a stained-glass window from their old church. The building was demolished in 1968 and its stone used to construct the addition to Falls Church Presbyterian. Courtesy Clarence Hartman and Mary Riley Styles Public Library.

The 100 block of East Broad Street, circa 1910. Brick sidewalks provided by the Village Improvement Society and trees planted after the Civil War provided a pleasing pedestrian experience. The trees have been felled and replanted at least twice and perhaps three times during the life of the street. Falls Church residents remain attached to their lush forest canopy. Courtesy Mary Riley Styles Public Library.

Signboard of J. G. Abbott, general merchandiser, whose store was located in the 100 block of West Broad Street. Courtesy Galkin family and Mary Riley Styles Public Library.

Summerfield Taylor's market and apothecary, East Broad and Washington Street, circa 1910. The streetlamp in the foreground was gas-powered; electric service did not come to Falls Church until 1912. Courtesy Mary Riley Styles Public Library.

Electric trolley station, William B. Thompson's grocery store, and the U.S. Post Office, East Falls Church, circa 1910. For many years the "three Falls Churches" each had a post office. Man seated at right may be a waiting trolley passenger. Courtesy Mary Riley Styles Public Library.

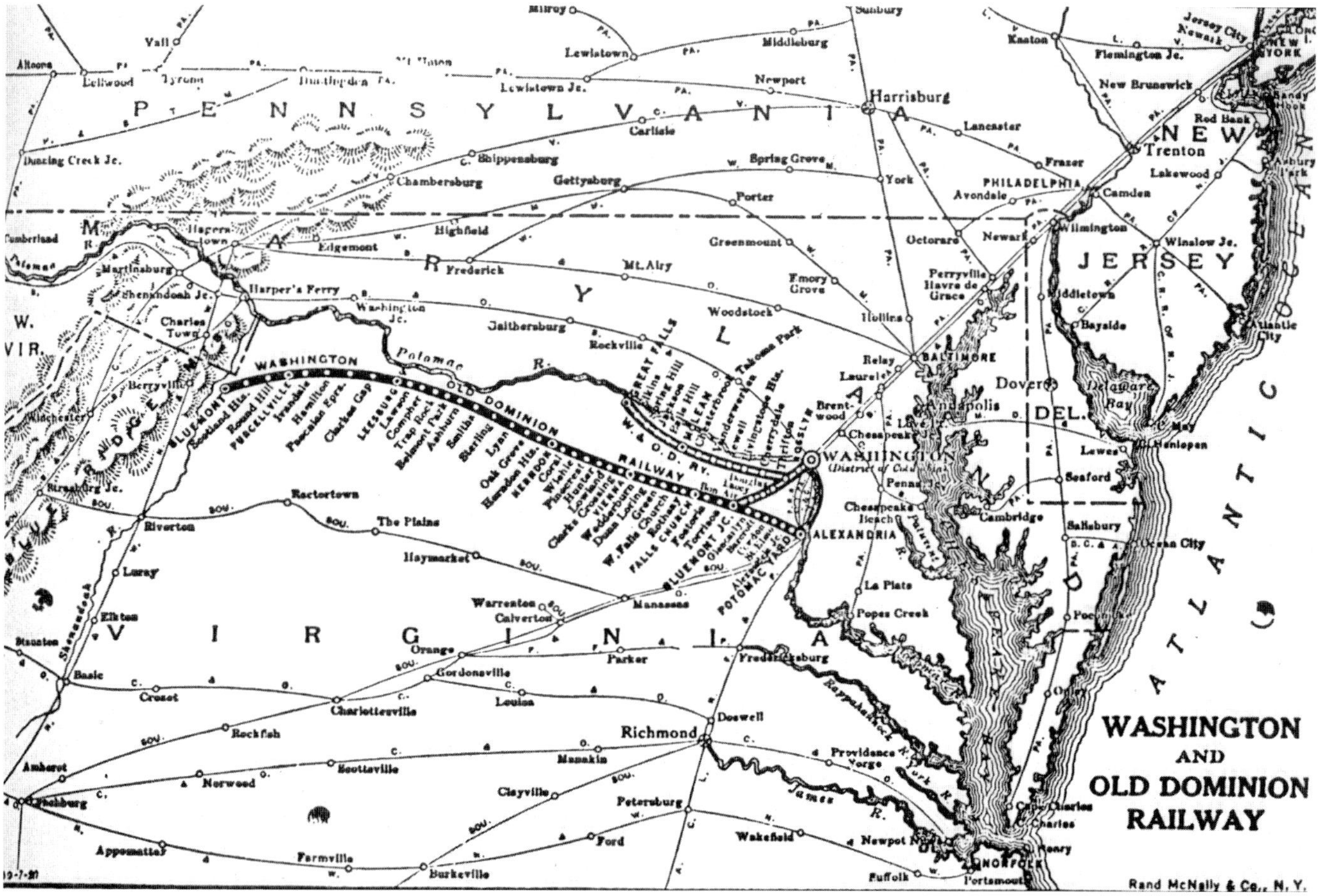

Washington and Old Dominion Railroad 1912 system map, showing the road's connections to the state and national networks. Three of its station stops, Fostoria in East Falls Church, Falls Church, Rothsay, and West Falls Church were within the town limit.

Quaker Oats Company product promotion, circa 1912. The truck features an enclosed glass-walled chamber in which puffed rice and wheat, advertised on the side of the truck, were popped. Courtesy Hugh Brown and Mary Riley Styles Public Library.

President William Howard Taft speaking at the residence of Dr. T. C. Quick in Falls Church, July 21, 1912. Taft stopped en route to Manassas to commemorate the fiftieth anniversary of the First Battle of Manassas there. Several American presidents have visited Falls Church, including George Washington, Thomas Jefferson, James Madison, and William McKinley. Courtesy Virginia Quick and Mary Riley Styles Public Library.

Ladies of Dulin Methodist Episcopal Church (South), 1913. The church is shown in its original brick appearance; it was stuccoed white in 1926. Courtesy Ruth Mankin Hildebrand and Mary Riley Styles Public Library.

Merton E. Church, 1914. Church, who co-owned a drug store in town, also provided its first telephone service in 1888 and electric service in 1912. In 1898 he lobbied the war department to situate a training camp for thirty thousand soldiers just outside town by promising to extend telephone and telegraph wires to the camp. In the early 1920s he headed a local good roads movement, lobbied successfully to have the new Lee Highway routed through Falls Church, and led the effort to privately fund its construction. He established Falls Church's first bank, and in the 1930s he rescued the electric trolley line from bankruptcy. Courtesy Mrs. H. Willis Jones and Mary Riley Styles Public Library.

Green Gables, 313 Lincoln Avenue as it appeared sometime before 1939. Dr. John Smallwood built this California-style bungalow in 1916 and later added a small physician's office and trolley stop for his patients. Courtesy M. L. Steadman and Mary Riley Styles Public Library.

Valentine's Day in the Birch family home, 312 East Broad Street, circa 1916. Note the heart-shaped decorations adorning the room. Courtesy Mary Riley Styles Public Library.

"It was Hell on earth." Falls Church doughboys Mac Fadely, Phil Hough, and Lawrence Hough, circa 1917. Most of the ninety-five identified Falls Church soldiers spent several months during World War I in training at Camp Lee, Virginia, and then fought in some of Europe's bloodiest battles. It was a far cry from the peaceful farms and quiet tree-shaded lanes they left behind. Courtesy Mary Riley Styles Public Library.

CHAPTER XI

The Great War

"The lamps are going out all over Europe, we shall not see them lit again in our lifetime," mused Edward Grey, the British foreign secretary in 1914, as diplomacy failed and war loomed.[1] On April 6, 1917, Congress declared war on the Central Powers.

Compulsory draft registration began in May. Falls Church registrar George T. Mankin soon found himself very busy, registering 114 men by early June, a larger number than any other area of the county save Vienna.[2]

The need for land around Washington on which to conduct war activities became acute as the war effort moved into high gear. "SELECT OLD CAMP ALGER," the *Fairfax Herald* boomed, editorializing, somewhat romantically, that "the country [near Falls Church] is gently rolling, well drained, and with no nearby marshes to breed malaria. The health of the recruits would be safeguarded by selecting this point." Several thousand Spanish-American War veterans of Camp Alger would probably have contested this point. And perhaps they did: the Army inspected the old camp site and rejected it in favor of land at what became Fort Belvoir. Had the Camp Alger site been chosen Falls Church would have embarked on a very different course, with a giant, permanent, military base just outside town limits.[3]

Consumer goods were redirected to the war front to feed soldiers and as war materiel. By winter 1917 Falls Church felt the brunt of mandatory rationing as coal, an important home heating fuel, became scarce. By early 1918 the fuel crunch was so severe that meetings were canceled so that citizens might conserve their fuel supplies.[4]

Food supplies were equally problematic. J. Parker Milburn, the Fairfax County food administrator, urged citizens to observe meatless Tuesdays and wheatless Wednesdays. Mondays later joined Wednesdays in wheatless fare, and at least one meal of every day was to be wheatless and another meatless. Lack of wheat became so dire it spawned the creation of "Victory Bread," an unappetizing wartime recipe which county bakers were required to prepare using alternative ingredients. Flour and sugar soon joined the list of rationed foods, and by April 1918 local citizens were urged to forego the use of wheat completely until at least September. "BLOOD OR BREAK," read one notice in an area newspaper. "Others are giving their blood. You will shorten the war and save life if you eat only what you need, and waste nothing."[5]

Falls Church leaders were particularly active in supporting the war effort. Town residents played an active role in the county War Camp Recreation Society, assisted by the Village Improvement Society, and carried out an ambitious fund-raising program. The Red Cross chapter in Falls Church raised almost $2,000 during one drive, nearly three times the goal. Local residents assisted the county Red Cross in purchasing a motorized ambulance and motorcycle for use at the front. The Young Men's Christian Association (Y.M.C.A.) directed locally by Merton E. Church, also raised funds successfully.[6]

A sad bedtime story. Germans, or "Fritzies," were humiliated and economically ravaged by the peace treaty which ended World War I—and Falls Church would only too soon find itself called upon to endure the privations and offer its young people to fight another apocryphal war.

Americans financed the war via a series of four Liberty Loans. Falls Church residents committed $7,700 through their local bank during the first loan drive and $22,000 in the second drive, with many, it was assumed, pledging in Washington, D.C. banks, for a much greater total. Each of the four local loan drives was oversubscribed.[7]

Falls Church men formed a home defense league, the Colonial Rifles, which was active throughout the war. The town council appropriated money for uniforms, but not guns, and the company never received rifles for all its men. Its membership peaked at approximately forty-five.[8]

Yet no one in Falls Church contributed more to the war than those men at the front. Newly-drafted soldiers spent the first few months of the war in training camps, and, fully seven months after Congress declared war, most of the twenty-four Falls Church men then serving in the armed forces were still at Camp Lee outside Petersburg, Virginia. Reports began returning of wounds and deaths as local men made it to the front. Twenty-nine year old Edward G. Fenwick, of the University of Virginia ambulance corps, shot through a cheek, appears to have been the first man wounded abroad. Stephen P. McGroarty, 23, became the first Falls Church and Fairfax County battle fatality. He was followed by Walter L. Taverner and Ralph Stambaugh. The terrible litany of reports of wounds and deaths at the front would be broken only by the war's end.[9]

Death struck more than the soldiers. The greatest pandemic in recorded history, the Spanish Influenza, or, "the Flu," bred in the trenches and mass population movements engendered by the war, attacked 40–50 percent of the world's population, killing 22,000,000. Unlike most viral episodes the Spanish Flu attacked young and active adults—those classes of population usually least susceptible. Virologists believe the elderly bore antibodies developed in the late nineteenth century when a similar, though lesser flu passed through the area—to which younger people bore no resistance. "Cover up each cough and sneeze; if you don't you'll spread disease," went the popular admonition, but disease visited Fairfax County despite public effort. Falls Church and the portions of the county nearest Alexandria and Washington were particularly hard hit. Schools and churches closed and all meetings of any kind were suspended for over a month in October-November 1918, until infection rates lessened.[10]

When the Armistice ended the conflict in November 1918 almost one hundred soldiers from Falls Church, a large percentage of its population of fourteen hundred, were then serving. Falls Church greeted the peace which followed the Armistice with relief and jubilation. Rationing was curtailed and then ended. The flu gradually played itself out, and the veterans began returning from the front. Falls Church had been a busy place during the war. Merton E. Church, the town banker, noted that with "the increased number of Government clerks and war activities in Washington the housing problem has become very acute . . . Every house in Falls Church is rented and we could rent many more if we had them."[11] But slowly the local economy and war-weary Falls Church returned to normal.

Falls Church garage, Lee Highway at Four Mile Run in East Falls Church, 1917. This garage, one of the first in the area established solely to service the new "machines," or personal automobiles, probably saw its business plummet during World War I. Wartime rationing of gasoline and rubber caused many local drivers to park their machines until the war, and consumer rationing, came to an end. Courtesy Mary Riley Styles Public Library.

Heightened patriotism during the war years probably accounts for this bunting-bedecked wagon on Independence Day in 1918. The gentlemen are Mr. Fox and Benjamin F. Elliott. Courtesy Village Preservation and Improvement Society and Mary Riley Styles Public Library.

A series of four Liberty Loan bond drives financed the government war effort. The Fourth Liberty Loan drive, advertised here, was interrupted in Falls Church by the advent of the world's worst pandemic ever: the Spanish Flu. Churches, schools, and many businesses closed for over a month in 1918 to lessen the disease's infection rate, but 531 people perished in Fairfax County. Falls Church residents overwhelmingly supported the Liberty Loans, oversubscribing to each. Library of Congress, Prints and Photographs Division.

Joseph B. Tinner, undated photo. Tinner and his family, of Tinner Hill, were known for their fine stonemasonry, examples of which still exist in Falls Church. At E. B. Henderson's request, Tinner served as president of Falls Church's branch of the NAACP, the National Association for the Advancement of Colored People, at the branch's formation in 1915. Henderson, History of the Fairfax County Branch of the NAACP.

CHAPTER XII

The Great Depression and Interwar Years

After the Great War, Falls Church turned its attention to other matters. One, in particular, caught the attention of local business leaders: the terrible state of area roads. The first privately owned automobile, or "machine," as they were called, made its appearance in Falls Church about 1907. It was owned by Ralph and Mabel Garland, and was top-of-the-line (it had headlamps). Other Falls Church inhabitants bought machines and soon they outnumbered horses and buggies.[1]

At the dawn of the automobile age roads in the Falls Church area were a detriment to travel. "The automobile was born into a roadless world," according to one contemporary Washington editorialist.[2] It was an era in which roads and highways developed by local usage and not through concerted government policy. They bore names, not numbers, and were usually short-haul. Falls Church business leaders recognized that linking the village via good roads with Washington would increase markets by expanding trade.

A group of visionary citizens known as the Lee Highway Association was attempting to build a coast-to-coast highway across the southern United States to be named in honor of Robert E. Lee, as companion to one being built across the northern tier of states in honor of Abraham Lincoln.[3] The genius of the Lee Highway effort was that it promised travelers a highway bearing the same designation—then a novelty—and passable in all seasons along its entire length.[4]

Sensing an historic opportunity, Falls Church's preeminent citizens convinced the Lee Highway Association to reroute the proposed road through the town.[5] They organized a local branch of the association to rally efforts,[6] paid substantial subscription fees, and arranged large-scale private financing to get the road built.[7] The road they proffered—the present Lee Highway, U.S. Highway 29—consisted of worn-out pavement for a mile east of the village center, while west of town between Falls Church and Fairfax Court House it was a narrow dirt track reliable only in dry weather.[8]

Falls Church's gamble paid off. Real estate agents reported "one thousand per cent increase in sales and one hundred per cent increase in value" of property along the new highway. Yes, Falls Church citizens paid a lot of money to garner the highway, but, according to the mollified town banker, Merton E. Church, "WE NEVER MADE A BETTER INVESTMENT."[9]

Pleased by the commercial success of the new Lee Highway and boasting immodestly, "we will not rest until the United States is paved,"[10] the Lee Highway Association and Falls Church citizens almost immediately began planning the route now known as Arlington Boulevard (U.S. Highway 50), intending for it to pass through Falls Church. The route, also honoring Robert E. Lee and called Lee Boulevard (until renamed in honor of Arlington House, Lee's home, to allay the confusion) was never national in scope. It was to link Washington with the new Shenandoah National Park.[11] Falls Church residents hosted the road's groundbreaking ceremony at Fort Buffalo (as Seven Corners

Charles Tinner residence, 107 Tinner Hill, circa 1920. Lee Briggs photo.

Edna Evans and Frank Tinner on Tinner Hill, circa 1920. The Evanses and Tinners were prominent families in the area for decades, and Tinner Hill was named for the Tinners, who own a portion of it. Scrapbook of Barbara Williams.

was called until the 1950s) and were among its greatest financial backers, but the economics of increasing road frontage prevailed, and the new road passed outside of the town limit.[12]

Another consequence of the advent of the personal automobile was the decline of railroad ridership. The electric trolley, the Washington-Virginia Railway, long linking East and West Falls church to downtown Washington, entered a period of steep decline and was liquidated in 1927. Merton E. Church organized the Arlington and Fairfax Railway Company, or A&F, out of its remnants and led it energetically until his death four years later. Soon afterward, however, the A&F lost its right-of-way to Washington and, in the face of ever-increasing automobile ownership, closed for good in 1939.[13]

The 1920s were a time of great prosperity, both in the country at large and in Falls Church. Among the era's most important achievements was the right of women to vote, granted by a federal constitutional amendment in 1920. In Falls Church Miss Mattie Gundry, proprietor of a home and school for the mentally handicapped, and Mrs. P. H. Smyth were elected to the town council in 1921. Miss Gundry, a firebrand, became well-known for her leadership and research in national matters concerning mental handicaps.[14]

The town council was advised of a new problem in 1920 when the electric company wrote them that it was going to bill the town for all light bulbs broken by vandals. There were other similar annoyances as reported by a Village Improvement Society committee in November pointing out many depredations made by boys of the town recently. Falls Church's electric street lamps, in place only eight years, made an inviting new target for youthful mayhem.[15]

Perhaps the most momentous event occurring during the interwar years was the separation of East Falls Church from the town. Until separation Falls Church and West Falls Church were within Fairfax County and East Falls

Church was within Arlington County. Separation sentiment was first voiced in 1921 but little activity occurred on the question until 1932, when East Falls Church citizens, citing "intolerable confusion of overlapping governmental agencies," successfully petitioned the circuit court for permission to leave the town. By court order, Arlington County was required to pay 29.6 percent of the principal and interest due on outstanding school bonds and 18 percent of the water bonds. The eastern area of the town, containing 25 percent of its population and area, 30 percent of its taxable value and 60 percent of its stores and businesses, was not, as now, geographically isolated from the rest of Falls Church by interstate highway 66. Falls Church promptly appealed the decision but lost, and East Falls Church withdrew from the town on April 30, 1936.[16] The East Falls Church business district was largely eradicated by the advent of interstate highway 66 in the 1970s.

The Great Depression, which defined the life and character of the times in most other places, had but limited impact on Falls Church, where most residents held secure government jobs. Their guaranteed salaries, in turn, meant continued prosperity, or at least solvency, for the merchants and services in town which supported them. The few area residents falling into harm's way economically were helped by local citizens and organizations, which saw to it they obtained health care and were provided food, shelter, and clothing, and by the new federal programs designed for this purpose. Falls Church's energetic town government availed itself of the new federal largesse whenever possible, to the permanent benefit of its citizens.[17]

Residents of Falls Church and its immediate environs benefitted markedly between 1930 and 1940 from Mayor L. P. Daniel's leadership and the support of the town councils and citizens. Municipal services expanded greatly. Full-fledged municipal sewer service was assured in 1936, thanks to the hard-working Mayor Daniel, his town council and two of Franklin Roosevelt's New

Family portrait of Edwin Bancroft (E. B.) Henderson, his wife, Mary Ellen Meriwether Henderson, and their sons in 1922. Henderson was critical to the early and continued success of Falls Church's African-American community in fighting for educational opportunities and civil rights and was nationally known for his book, The Negro in Sports. *Mrs. Henderson was principal of the Falls Church Negro School and later the James Lee Elementary School, which provided quality education to Falls Church area minority students until local schools were desegregated. Courtesy James Henderson.*

Falls Church Negro School, circa 1920s. The school, on Annandale Road in south Falls Church, was later replaced by the James Lee Elementary School, a Fairfax County facility. Black high school students were bused to a regional black high school in Manassas until 1954. Scrapbook of Barbara Williams.

Falls Church Negro School, circa 1920s. The school served younger pupils; older pupils were bused to school in Manassas. Scrapbook of Barbara Williams.

Deal "alphabet soup" agencies, the Works Project Administration and Public Works Administration. Periodic drought conditions and a more than doubling of the town's population—from 1,007 in 1900 to 2,109 in 1930—had an adverse effect on the level of the underground water table by which shallow domestic dug wells and the somewhat deeper drilled wells were supplied. By 1930, failure of the water supply in the town had been felt by 40 percent of the 316 households. The town council contracted to deliver water to householders by truck and in September and October, over 33,000 gallons were supplied at cost.[18]

After careful investigation, the council found that the cost of purchasing water from Arlington County would be excessive. On advice from a consultant in the United States Geological Survey, the mayor and council decided to provide the needed water from town-drilled wells into a new central piping system. The first of four wells was drilled on a lot behind the old First Congregational Church, where the town's first water storage tank was built.[19]

By the mid-1940s, a more dependable water source was needed because of increased demands. A connection was made with Arlington County near Chain Bridge from which water was piped to Falls Church and the Fort Buffalo (now Seven Corners) area. By the 1950s, now a city, Falls Church completed its own Potomac River crossing and a direct connection to the Dalecarlia Treatment Plant in Maryland. Currently, the City of Falls Church provides water to approximately 120,000 people in and around Falls Church. It operates six pumping stations and nine storage tanks strategically located within the service area.[20]

Prior to 1937, when the U.S. government gave a Public Works Administration grant to the town, each Falls Church residence had a privy or a septic tank. In that year, the first public sewer system was constructed after the successful passage of a sewer bond issue by the town's voters. As early as 1901, the local Board of Health had received numerous complaints of unsanitary privies in town and the complaints continued for decades.[21]

With periodic improvements to the system, the service area now includes 3,300 homes within the city and approximately 650 homes adjacent to the city. The City's waste water is treated under contract either with Arlington County's Four Mile Run system or Fairfax County's Tripps Run system.[22]

House to house garbage collection began in 1937, the fruit of a campaign by the Falls Church Woman's Club.[23] An equally important municipal improvement was the incorporation of the volunteer fire department in 1925.

Education took great leaps in 1924 when the Commonwealth granted Falls Church its own school district. In 1926 Madison Elementary School opened, with grades 1–7, and the venerable Jefferson Institute became a four-year high school.

The relative affluence of Falls Church was highlighted in January 1936 when the State Theater opened. Local pundits called it "the finest theater in Arlington and Fairfax counties." It seated over eight hundred, featured a large stage to be used for plays and public events and a lounge which could be used for teas, bridge parties, and meetings. Its parking lot accommodated 250 cars and its interior was air-conditioned—an innovation not yet available in typical homes. ("Manufacturing its own weather throughout the year," boasted the firm which installed the air-conditioning system.) The State's strong but subdued Art-Deco (a phrase not yet coined) architectural motifs would bolster preservationists' successful attempts to save it from the wrecking ball sixty years later.[24]

Increasing traffic on area roads during the interwar years caused Lee Highway to be widened to three lanes. Trees, long a major concern in Falls Church, became a contentious issue when the state highway department announced plans to cut all the shade trees lining Broad Street as part of its widening. As community opposition to the trees' removal grew, even the Parent-Teacher Association became involved—on the side of the trees, of course. Henry G. Shirley, state commissioner of highways, issued Falls Church an ultimatum: it could have its shade trees, or it could have a new forty-foot road. The need to rebuild Broad Street took precedence over the trees, which were said to be reaching the end of their life spans. The state highway department replanted the rebuilt Broad Street with pin oaks and Chinese elms, so Falls Church and Henry Shirley both won.[25]

African-American Boy Scouts of America troop, Tinner Hill, undated. Scrapbook of Barbara Williams.

In September 1938 a family which was to become renowned moved to the home later known as Tallwood on East Broad Street: Milton S. Eisenhower and his wife, Helen. Dr. Eisenhower, the elder brother of Dwight D. Eisenhower, was a high-ranking official in President Roosevelt's administration and was known and envied for his access to the president, with whom he dined alone frequently.[26]

Coming world events were to influence Falls Church and the Eisenhowers in ways which no one could have imagined. The era of peaceful prosperity was drawing to a close.

Members of the fashionable Birch family pose for a wedding, circa 1920s. The Birches lived at 112 East Broad Street from the 1840s through 1968, and owned it until 1976. Carter-Bailey Studio, courtesy Mary Riley Styles Public Library.

Electric trolley station, 1101 West Broad Street, in 1922. The electric trolley line reached East Falls Church in 1897 and was extended along Lincoln Avenue to the West End by 1901. The Shepard House, shown here, doubled as both station and station master's residence. Trolley service ended in 1939. Courtesy Mrs. Clarence Fox, Sr., courtesy Mary Riley Styles Public Library.

Falls Church trolley station, 1922. The young man numbered "4" is Burns "Bunny" Gibson, longtime Falls Church resident and businessman. Gibson's colleagues, both outside and inside the car, are difficult to identify. The motorcycle (left) is the earliest photographed in the town. Courtesy J.L.B. Williams and Mary Riley Styles Public Library.

Lee Highway between Falls Church and Fairfax Court House, circa 1923. The dirt road, despaired by many as a seasonal mud wallow, was selected to carry the designation Lee Highway, a newly-established route crossing the country from coast to coast. It was very difficult to drive anywhere, and unified routes such as this one bearing but one name proved so popular they were later numbered. Courtesy Mary Riley Styles Public Library.

Paving South Washington Street, circa 1920s. This photo shows the feed store which stood at the southeast corner of the intersection with East Broad Street until about 1926. This view, showing Broad Street in the foreground, looks south. The road workers appear to be African-American. Courtesy Hugh Brown and courtesy Mary Riley Styles Public Library.

Traveling advertisement, 1924. Merton E. Church, the town's preeminent realtor, was quick to realize the utility of mobile advertising, then a novelty. The background of this image has been substantially retouched. Courtesy Mary Riley Styles Public Library.

The Sherman M. Wells family, 216 East Fairfax Street, circa 1925. Left to right: Sherman, Harry, Stanley, Shirley, Claude, Glenn, and Ruth, with their 1922 Buick machine (automobile). Harry and Claude grew up to serve the young City of Falls Church in a variety of ways, and City Hall is named for Harry E. Wells. Courtesy Harry E. Wells and Mary Riley Styles Public Library.

Lee Highway between Falls Church and Fairfax Court House, circa 1926. Falls Church businessman Merton E. Church, with foot on the automobile's running board, shows off the newly improved road, now eighteen feet wide and paved with concrete. The main trunk telephone line between Falls Church and Fairfax Court House, also built by Church, is seen at right. Courtesy Mary Riley Styles Public Library.

Falls Church Filling Station, circa 1928. Town banker Merton E. Church constructed this station on the southeast corner of Broad and Washington Streets in 1926. It was built of native granite quarried on Tripps Run and pointed by the Tinner family of Tinner Hill. The gasoline pumps were exactly that: customers hand-pumped gas up into the large glass jar on top of the pump, from which it drained into the customer's automobile. Demolished, 1963. Courtesy Marjorie McElroy Acevedo and Mary Riley Styles Public Library.

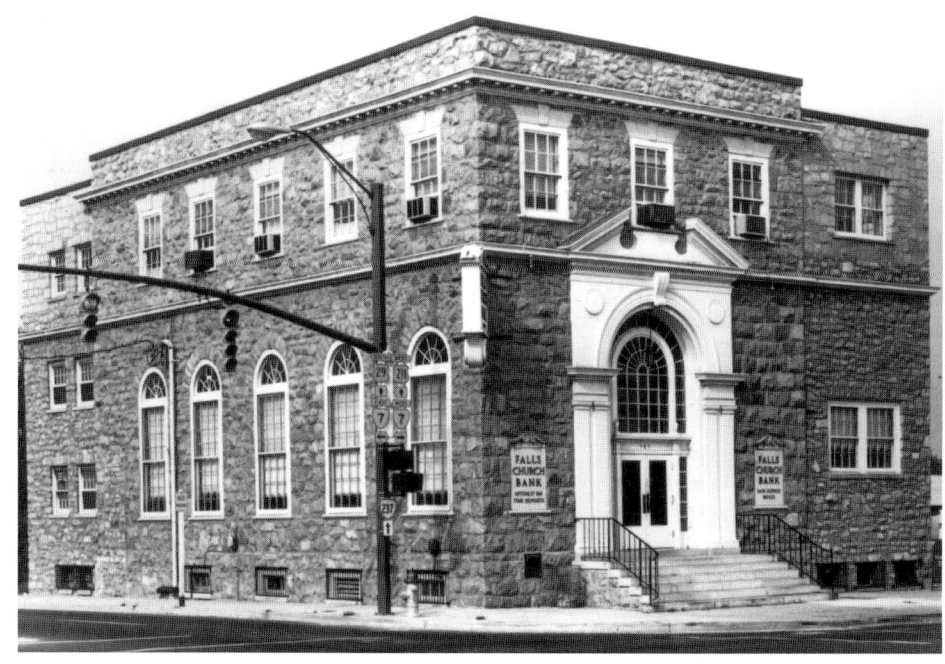

Falls Church Bank, circa 1960s. Merton E. Church constructed the bank of native granite quarried locally on Tripps Run in the 1920s. The bank, the town's first, was demolished in 1974 to make way for a corporate headquarters highrise which was never built. George Mason Square has occupied the site since 1984. William E. Barrett photo, courtesy Mary Riley Styles Public Library.

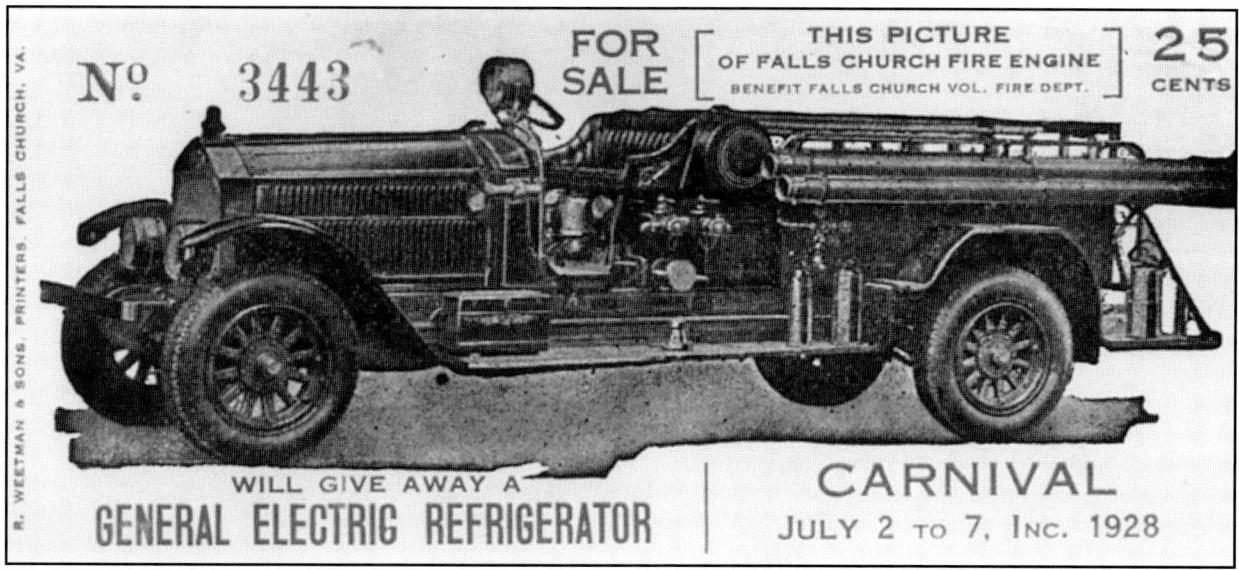

Raffle ticket sold by the Falls Church Volunteer Fire Department, 1928. The winner of the raffle received an electric refrigerator—a luxury item. Most people relied on iceboxes which were cooled by blocks of ice delivered regularly by the local ice plant. Courtesy Mary Riley Styles Public Library.

Wendelyn "Tin-Tin-John" Masarik, circa 1928. Masarik, probably a Hungarian emigre, roamed the Falls Church area repairing pots, pans, and umbrellas. He was among the last of a breed of drifters once common, especially during the Great Depression. Scrapbook of Barbara Williams.

Little Falls Street, looking north toward the intersection with Great Falls Street, 1928. The semi-rural life of Falls Church was already changing as this photo was taken. Courtesy Harold Parrott and Mary Riley Styles Public Library.

Better roads and increasing numbers of automobiles revolutionized outings such as this one at Chain Bridge, circa 1920s. Left to right are: Elizabeth Morgan Styles, Kathleen C. Mercer, and Jay H. Sypher. Undated photo, courtesy Mary Riley Styles Public Library.

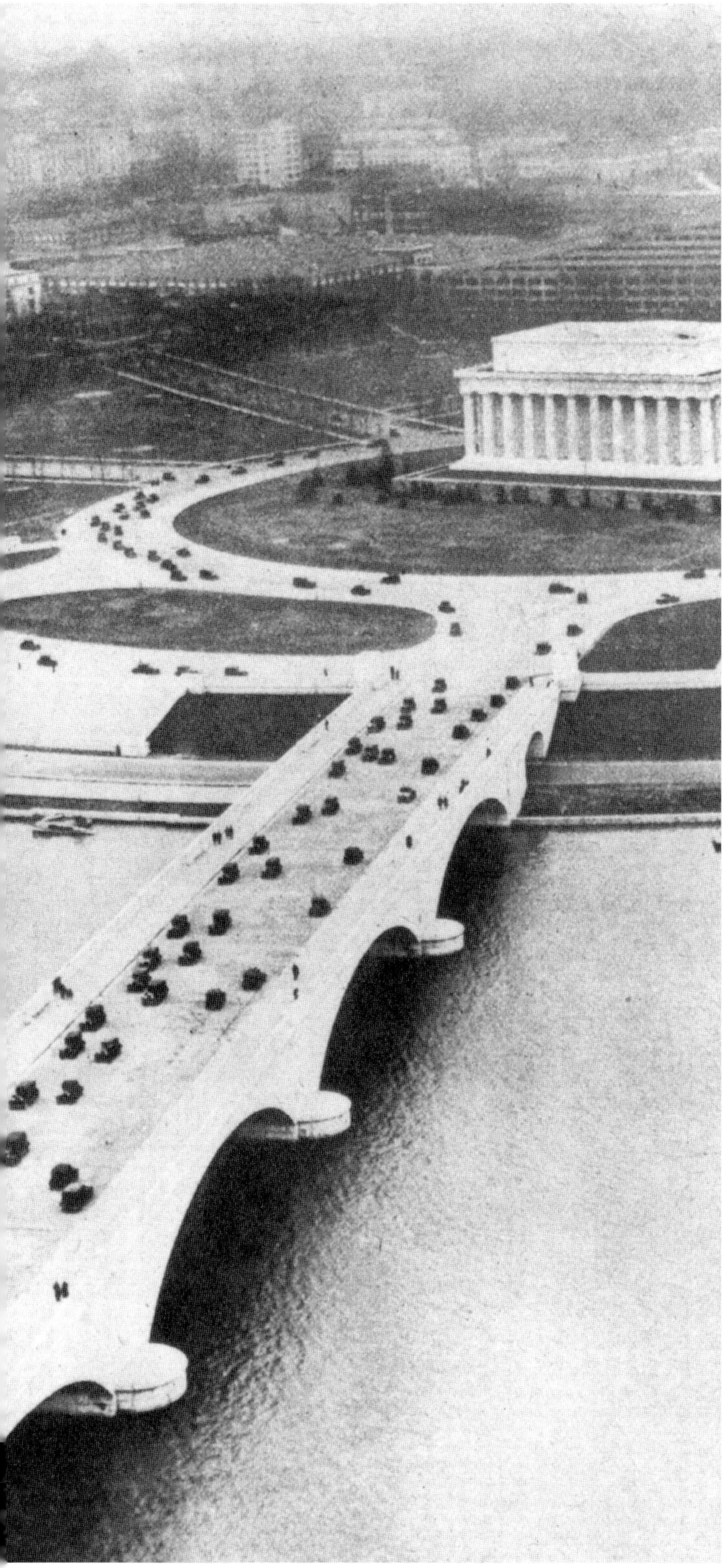

Arlington Memorial Bridge just after opening, 1932. The bridge carried the new Lee Boulevard (modern Arlington Boulevard) across the Potomac River. Business leaders in Falls Church, who caused the Lee Highway to be routed through the town, believed this new bridge and boulevard the key to their economic futures. Goods from Falls Church would now enjoy new markets in the capital. Lee Highway, in particular, proved a spectacular commercial success. Undated clipping. Courtesy Michael Spangler.

Newspaper photograph of L. P. Daniel, Falls Church's longest serving mayor, for whom Mount Daniel and the city elementary school at its summit is named. Also shown is Milton E. Roberts, for whom Roberts Park is named. The Evening Star, *June 11, 1930.*

Maryland and Virginia

1930

DANIEL ELECTED IN MAYOR CONTEST AT FALLS CHURCH

Spirited Race Brings Out the Heaviest Vote Ever Cast in Town.

TWO MEMBERS OF TICKET CARRIED WITH CHIEF

Chapman Wins at Fairfax and Fulmer Is Re-elected in Clifton Balloting.

Special Dispatch to The Star.

FALLS CHURCH, Va., June 11.—Maj. L. P. Daniel yesterday was elected mayor of Falls Church in a spirited contest which polled the largest number of votes ever cast in a Falls Church town election. Capt. John Bethune, the present mayor, received 188 votes, with 30 cast for the third candidate, W. S. Shacklette. A total of 439 ballots was cast, the highest previous record for a town election being 306. There were a large number of mismarked ballots for mayor, where the voter had scratched only one instead of two names.

Two members of Daniel's ticket also achieved victory, Frank L. Birch of the first ward defeating the incumbent, W. T. Westcott, 223 to 205, and J. V. Turner of the second ward defeating Philip Talbott, incumbent, 254 to 173. Milton E. Roberts, present councilman from the third ward, was re-elected, receiving 254 votes to 175 for Dr. Joseph Allison.

The council room was filled last night with interested citizens, who watched the count of the votes until the result was announced at 10 p.m. The term of the present council will not expire until September 1.

CHAPMAN WINS AT FAIRFAX.

NEARBY VIRGINIA ELECTION WINNERS

MAJ. L. P. DANIEL,
Elected mayor of Falls Church for the term starting September 1.

THOMAS P. CHAPMAN, SR.,
Yesterday re-elected mayor of Fairfax, Va.

FRANK L. BIRCH,
Elected to represent the first ward on the Falls Church town council.

MILTON E. ROBERTS,
Re-elected councilman from the third ward in Falls Church.

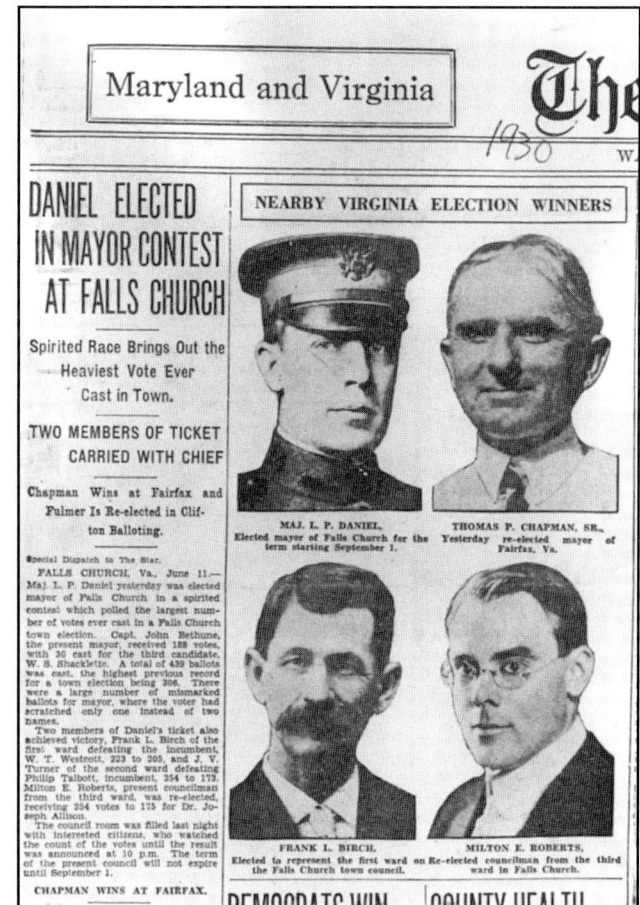

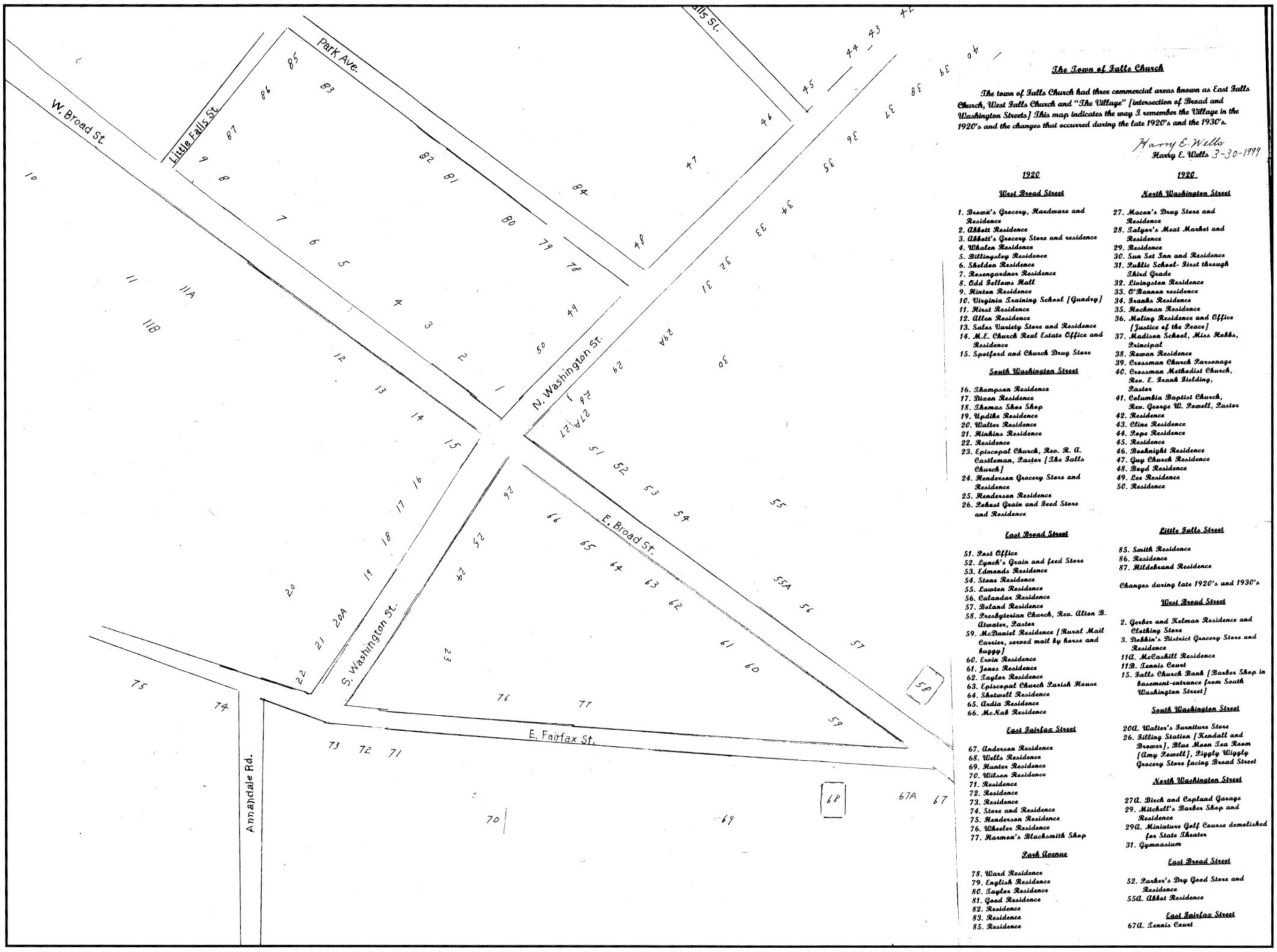

Hand-drawn map of downtown Falls Church by lifelong resident Harry E. Wells, 1999. This view indicates businesses and residences in the village center as they existed during the 1920s and 1930s prior to the region's rapid growth and change. Courtesy Harry E. Wells.

Postcard, Quarry Inn, South Washington Street at Tripps Run, circa 1930s. The Inn was a product of the Automobile Age. Increasing mobility meant larger numbers of travelers seeking lodging. The Inn still exists at the same location, though minus tourist cabins and Rock Creek root beer. Courtesy Tony Chaves.

West Broad Street, looking west, at the railroad crossing (now the regional park trail bridge), circa 1930s. Broad Street is gravel and two lanes. Courtesy Washington & Old Dominion Railroad Regional Park.

Joseph Harvey Riley, circa 1930s. Riley, an accomplished ornithologist, became associate curator of the Smithsonian Institution's Division of Birds in 1932. Riley lived at Cherry Hill Farm, where his interest in bird habitats led him to plant a variety of trees, many of which remain. The grove of pine trees across from Mary Riley Styles Public Library is perhaps the most visible. Courtesy Mary Riley Styles Public Library.

"Manufacturing its own weather year round. . . ." The State Theater, which opened in 1936 and operated continuously until 1989, was an example of what later came to be called Art Deco architecture, and featured air conditioning at a time when few homes had it. The State got a new lease on life recently when it was restored to its former grandeur and reopened. Quentin Porter photo, courtesy Mary Riley Styles Public Library.

The Great Falls Diversion Dam on the Potomac River and the gatehouse at the Georgetown Reservoir, both parts of the Washington Aqueduct system from which Falls Church takes its water. The Aqueduct, operated by the U.S. Army Corps of Engineers, ensured a steady source of water for Falls Church, making possible the rapid growth after World War II. Courtesy Baltimore District, U.S. Army Corps of Engineers.

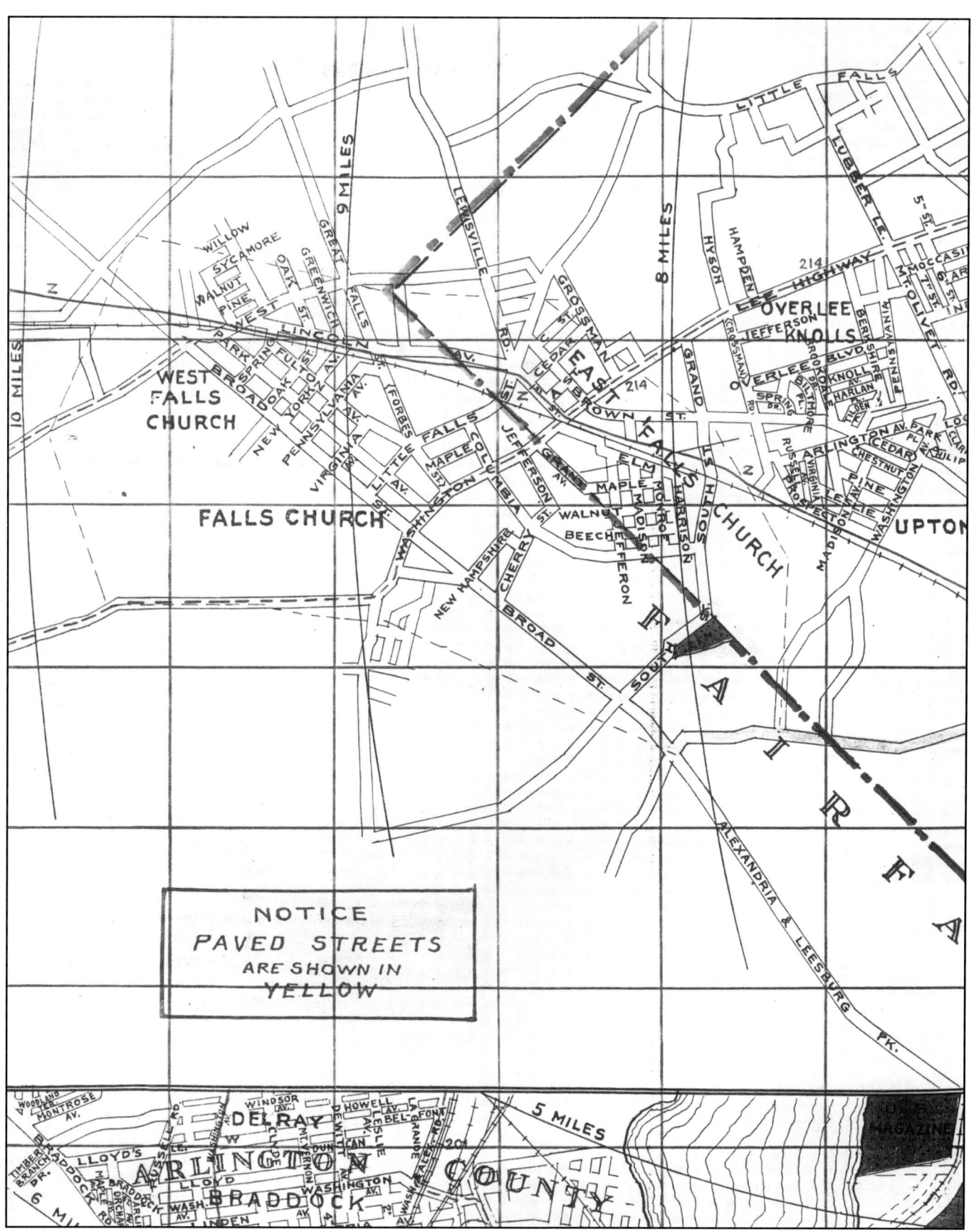

Nineteen twenty-eight map showing the "three Falls Churches"—East, West, and the village center, within the town limit which had remained inviolate since 1887. Eight years later the Arlington County portion of East Falls Church was removed from the town. Wagner's Complete Map of District of Columbia, Arlington County, Va., and Surrounding Territory.

Falls Church Police Station, 100 block South Washington Street, 1939. Originally built to house the municipal offices of the newly-established Town of Falls Church in 1875, this long-lived building served until torn down in 1954. Today's police force, headquartered in City Hall, numbers approximately thirty male and female officers and is more diverse than the all-male, all-Caucasian police force of 1939. Courtesy Malcolm Smith and Mary Riley Styles Public Library.

Macon Ware's drug store, 1939. The store opened in the former First Congregational Church, now the Falls Church Woman's Club, in 1937. The Woman's Club purchased the building in 1961. The bell tower has since been removed. The Bell Telephone symbol at the door, advertising telephone service within, was once an American icon. Courtesy Mary Riley Styles Public Library.

Mother's Day in the Birch family home on North Underwood Street, 1939. Clockwise from top: Milton, Isaac, Essie, and Mary Birch. Congress established Mother's Day as a nationally commemorated event in 1913. George Studio, courtesy Mrs. Julian Ninde, Jr. and Mary Riley Styles Public Library.

Pope-Leighey House, Falls Church, 1940. "Of course I am ready to give you a house," replied architect Frank Lloyd Wright in 1939 to an entreaty by Loren Pope. The home Wright built, nestled in rolling woodland at 1005 Locust Street just outside the town limit, was a Usonian house with concrete floors coated with red-colored wax, piano hinges on the doors, and radiant heating. Wright visited Falls Church numerous times during construction in 1940. Library of Congress, Prints and Photographs Division.

Interior of the Pope-Leighey House, Falls Church, 1940. "The Mongols astride their wild ponies never constituted the threat to Western culture that do these Mongoloids astride their slide rules and T-squares," fumed a livid Loren Pope in 1962 upon learning that his former home in Falls Church, designed by renowned architect Frank Lloyd Wright, was slated for destruction by Virginia's highway planners to make way for Interstate Highway 66. Only intervention by a federal cabinet official and an outright gift of the house by Mrs. Robert Leighey, the owner at the time, saved the house. It was dismantled and moved to Woodlawn Plantation near Mount Vernon and reconstructed in 1964–65. Library of Congress, Prints and Photographs Division.

Falls Church child enjoying a new Raggedy-Ann doll during Christmas 1941. It was a joyless Yuletide for the girl's parents and their friends, seen conversing darkly in the background in companion photographs. The December 7 attack on Pearl Harbor and America's declaration of war against Japan were heavy on many hearts that holiday. Federal Home Administration photo courtesy Library of Congress, Prints and Photographs Division.

CHAPTER XIII

Mobilization and a Second World War

Europe was at war as America, still at peace, celebrated Thanksgiving in 1941. Falls Church's First Church of Christ, Scientist, held a special service in which the text of the day was Psalms 50:14–15—"Offer unto God thanksgiving; and pay thy vows unto the most High; and call upon me in the day of trouble . . ." The Christian Scientists and their fellow townspeople would have been chagrined to learn how quickly they might have opportunity to request Divine help.[1]

The bombing on December 7, 1941, of the U.S. Pacific Fleet in Pearl Harbor, Hawaii caused something of a panic. One Falls Church resident crossing Key Bridge into Washington December 8, the day after Pearl Harbor noticed anti-aircraft guns hastily mounted and manned along the Georgetown shore of the Potomac River.[2]

Preparations for war began immediately in Falls Church and Fairfax County, of which the town was then still a part. The county's draft board resumed physical examinations of all potential draftees.[3]

Consumer rationing and salvage efforts became the way of life in the area. Rubber for automobile tires quickly became in short supply as the Japanese assumed control of the great rubber plantations of Southeast Asia, and a county tire rationing board was established shortly after the new year.[4] As the rubber shortage became "increasingly acute" the county rationing board obtained the draconian power to order private vehicles needing tire servicing off the roads.[5]

Soon to follow were strict rationing controls for gasoline, shoes, farm machinery (including barbed wire), long-distance telephone service, stoves, fat, sugar, coffee, and processed foods.[6] Even milk became scarce in Virginia during 1943.[7] "Don't be a fat-waster!," Falls Church inhabitants were urged. "Two pounds of waste kitchen fats contain enough glycerine to fire 5 anti-tank guns shells."[8]

The county Red Cross, headquartered in Falls Church, established a visible presence early in the war, running frequent and highly successful campaigns to collect "life-saving plasma for the Army and Navy," usually in Falls Church Presbyterian Church.[9] The Falls Church branch of the Red Cross' County Canteen Corps served breakfasts to Fairfax County men inducted into the armed services.[10]

War hysteria prompted Falls Church's town council to enact protective measures quickly. The town council chartered a civilian defense committee which was to assist in managing the after-effects of an enemy attack on Washington, including policing, traffic control, directing refugees, and reporting sabotage or espionage.[11]

Air raid wardens were appointed and Fairfax County's air raid warden headquarters were established in the Falls Church Police Station. By 1943 Falls Church's aircraft observation post, at Oakwood Cemetery, was staffed 24 hours a day, 7 days a week, by 350 volunteer observers. Occasionally local air raid

Falls Church enemy aircraft spotters, manning a hilltop in Oakwood Cemetery, were responsible for the sky watch all the way to Washington and were linked by special telephone to a command and control facility. Anti-aircraft guns such as this one were mounted throughout the capital. Only after the war ended did defense officials realize the shells supplied for each gun were the wrong size. Washington Star *photo, copyright* The Washington Post.

wardens assumed collateral duties, such as in July 1942 when they canvassed all homes in the town to encourage each to make "proper preparations" to "fight incendiary bombs."[12]

The Fairfax County Board of Supervisors enacted a blackout ordinance in February 1942[13] and the first total blackout took place in April. Three prisoners attempted to escape the county jail during the twenty-minute blackout.[14] Virginia's governor ordered blackout drills monthly in at-risk areas, including Falls Church,[15] although since Fairfax County coordinated civilian defense with the District of Columbia it did not necessarily take part in blackouts mandated by Richmond.[16] The county's practice record was not good: drills as late as June 1942 earned caustic reports.[17]

News of the allied invasion of enemy-occupied Europe in 1944 was greeted warmly in Falls Church, where churches held commemorative services and rang bells in unison.[18] Advertisers, ever in time with current events, responded by filling local papers with jingoistic language ("How's your invasion going? HIS seems to be doing all right . . . Buy your Invasion Bonds today").[19]

General Dwight D. Eisenhower stayed with his brother, Milton, in the latter's home, now Tallwood, on East Broad Street during part of the war. Eisenhower, who worked eighteen-hour days, later wrote, "I cannot remember ever seeing their house in daylight during all the months I served in Washington." Helen Eisenhower always prepared the general a pot of cocoa when he arrived home as it helped him to go to sleep. During this time many of Dwight's assignments were secret even from his wife, Mamie, but Milton learned his brother was Allied commander heading the invasion of North Africa. On November 8, 1942, the night of the invasion, Milton, Helen, and Mamie Eisenhower and several friends were playing cards in the Eisenhowers' recreation room. Milton, knowing Dwight would announce the invasion by

This 1944 postcard, mailed to friends in the Falls Church firehouse by one of their number serving in the U.S. Army, included the request, "Take care of all the women till I get back." What is more likely is the women took care of themselves; few men of fighting age remained in Falls Church. Courtesy Falls Church Volunteer Fire Department.

radio at 9 p.m., kept the radio on during the card game. After the invasion announcement and the little group heard General Eisenhower's personal statement, Mamie was silent. Milton relates, "Tears came to her eyes, but for a long time she said nothing . . . 'Milton, I am proud of you for not telling me.'"[20]

Falls Church citizens, meanwhile, were fighting around the globe. One local man based in England wrote that "Every time you write you mention a few more boys who are going into the service. Must be hardly anybody between eight and eighty left." Another, in training in Texas, wrote, "Will you please bake me some cookies or a cake?"[21] Donald M. Moore was cited for bravery on Guadalcanal.[22] Lytton H. Gibson earned the Silver Star in Italy.[23] Charles O. Triebel severely damaged enemy shipping while commanding a submarine, which earned him the Silver Star.[24] Several others earned similar recognition. And Edward R. Pierce of West Falls Church arrested and imprisoned the poet Ezra Pound, who was the spokesman of Italy's Fascist leader Benito Mussolini.[25]

General Dwight D. Eisenhower inspecting American soldiers in England on the eve of their invasion of German-occupied Europe. The general lived with his brother, Milton Eisenhower, in Falls Church during part of the war. The general later could not recall seeing Milton's house once in daylight during World War II. U.S. Army photo.

As the war progressed the sense of immediate physical threat lessened. Local leaders began drafting plans for reabsorbing returning servicemen into the economy after the close of the war.[26] Blackout and air raid regulations were lifted with the fall of the Nazis in Europe,[27] and in June 1945 German prisoners of war began working in Fairfax County agriculture and food processing sites to hasten the delivery of food to U.S. troops in the Pacific. The Germans worked for local farmers until the local prisoner-of-war camp, a branch of a much larger one at Front Royal, closed in November (much to the disappointment of the farmers).[28]

In August it was over. Fairfax County and Falls Church greeted the news surprisingly quietly. Special church services were held, as on "Invasion Day," and sirens were blown, and many businesses and government offices closed the next day.

Twenty-five Falls Church men lost their lives.[29] The world was a very different place but, at last, Falls Church inhabitants were able to honor the Christian Scientists' benediction from that long-ago 1941 Thanksgiving Day service: "Finally, brethren, be of good comfort, be of one mind, live in peace . . ."[30]

Rice House, now known as Tallwood, 708 East Broad Street, circa 1890. This home, built in 1870 on a large farm, was known as the Rice home from 1890 to 1943. Dr. Milton Eisenhower, brother of the future president, purchased the home in 1938 and formalized its appearance by removing the front porch, plastering the brick, and painting it white. It was from this former farm that the land on which the homes lining Hillwood Avenue were built. Courtesy Mary Riley Styles Public Library.

Tallwood, 708 East Broad Street, circa 1982. This view shows the improvements made by Milton Eisenhower, who lived here between 1938 and 1943. The home, built in 1870, was named Tallwood by its new owners in 1943. Courtesy Mary Riley Styles Public Library.

American troops invading German-occupied North Africa. Mamie Eisenhower, whose husband, Dwight, commanded the invasion, learned of it by listening to a special radio broadcast while playing cards in the home of her brother-in-law, Milton Eisenhower, in Falls Church. Mrs. Eisenhower often did not know of her husband's activities until they were publicly announced. U.S. Army photo.

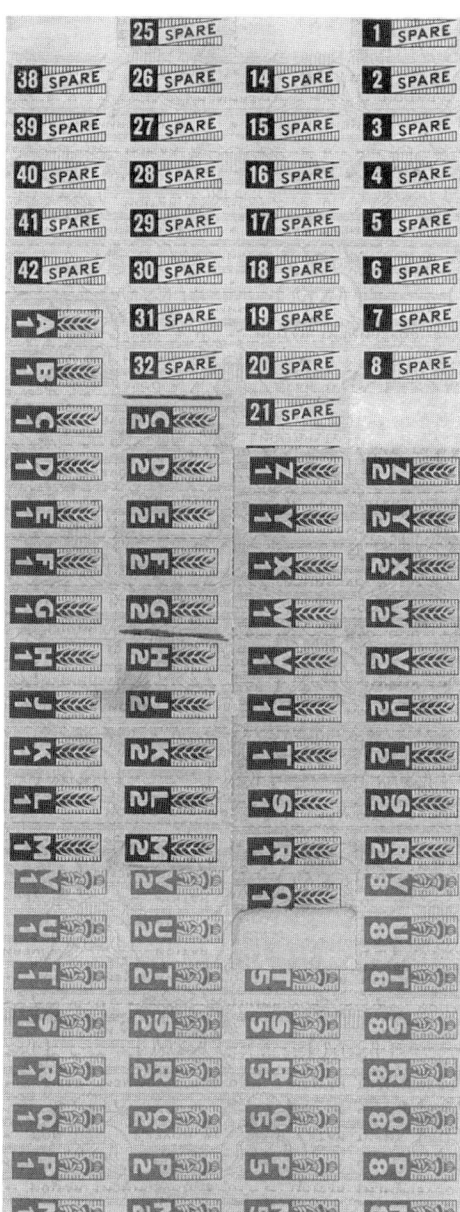

Falls Church resident's ration coupons, circa 1943. The wartime rationing system controlled purchase of foodstuffs, fuel, and consumer goods. Color-coded ration coupons strictly regulated the nature, timing, and amount of purchases. Courtesy Mary Riley Styles Public Library.

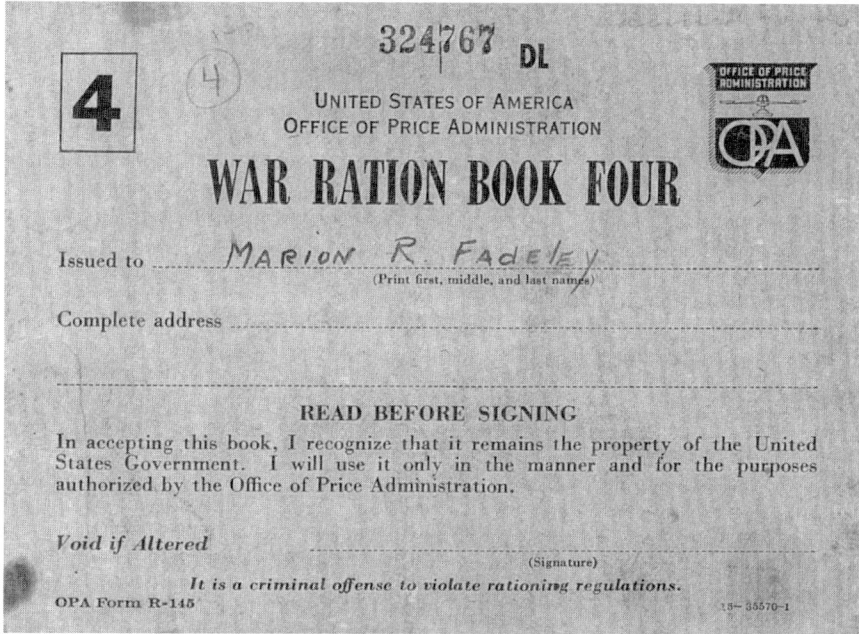

Falls Church's "Bubble Houses," twenty homes built in rolling woodland just outside town at the intersection of West Street and Lee Highway. Each home was formed from concrete sprayed on an inflated balloon. After the concrete set, the balloon was deflated and removed. Rubber shortages during World War II halted development. Demolished, early 1960s. Evening Star *photo, copyright* The Washington Post.

After World War II American industry returned to producing civilian luxury items long in short supply, such as cars. An era of rapidly-increasing prosperity, growth, and consumerism, in which Falls Church would share, was dawning. Falls Church Echo, *July 5, 1946.*

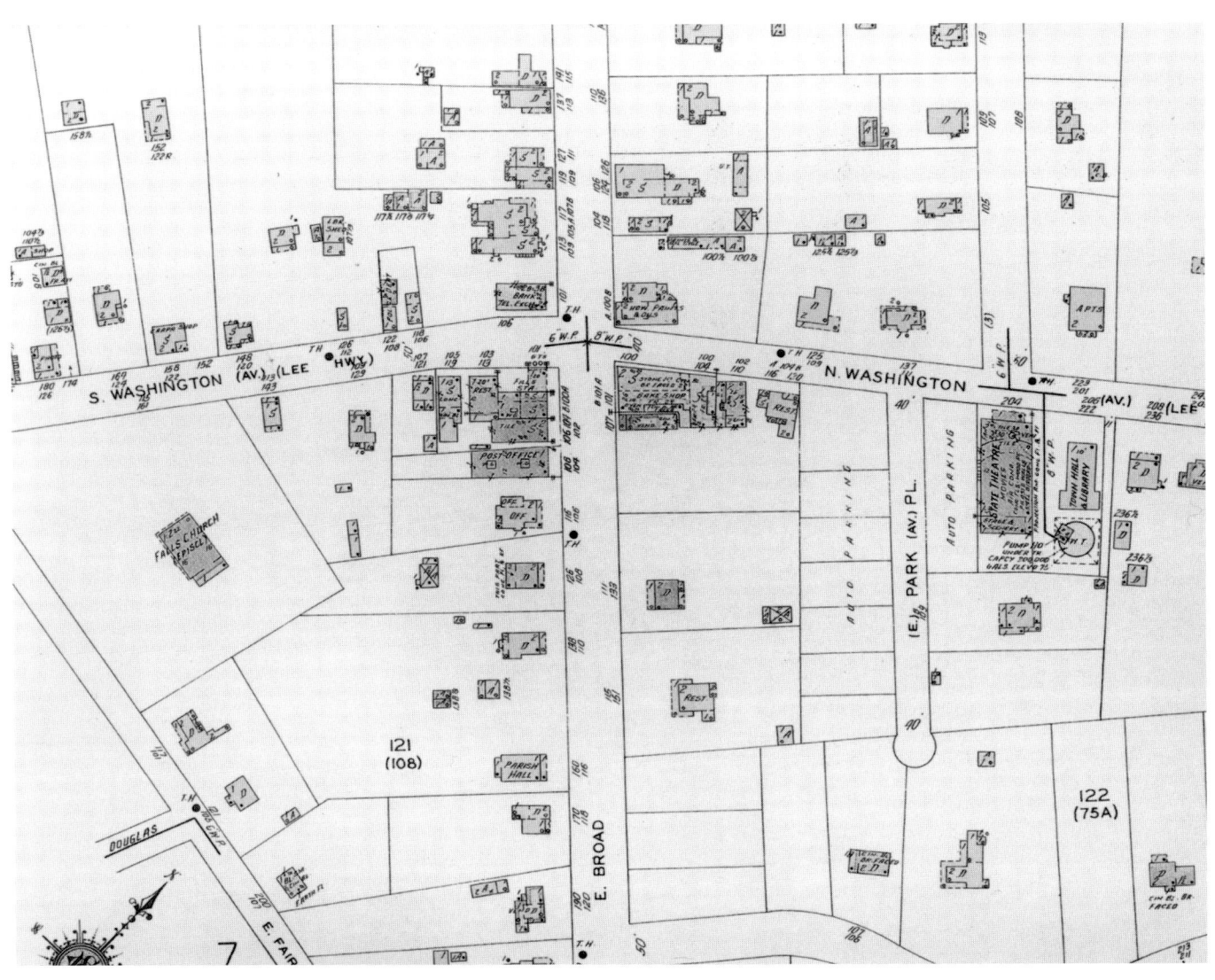

Map of Falls Church, January 1946. Much vacant space remains between buildings; the downtown business core has yet to develop into anything more substantial than a village, and is partially residential; and Washington Street remains almost entirely residential. But rapid growth was just around the corner. Sanborn Map Company, EDR Sanborn, Inc. Used with permission.

CHAPTER XIV

Unparalleled Growth and Prosperity

Post-war prosperity wrought great changes to Falls Church. The fields and farmland which surrounded the town and separated it from other settlements gave way to business development and residential subdivisions and, by the close of the 1950s, they were gone. Seven Corners, one of the region's first suburban malls, opened in 1956. "A quiet little country orchard . . . was transformed overnight into the great Seven Corners Shopping Center,"[1] according to interested observers.

A former slave, Frederick Foote, Sr., had purchased about thirty-nine acres from the Minor family following the Civil War with money he had earned working as a blacksmith for Union troops. The land was owned by his descendants until they sold it for the new shopping center.

An instant success among shoppers, the new commercial complex quickly reduced Falls Church's market territory—that is, the area from which shoppers were drawn to Falls Church—so that it now included only the city and areas west of it. Tyson's Corner, an even larger retail development, which opened on empty farmland to the west in 1966, further reduced Falls Church's market territory to what it is today—the City and immediately adjacent environs.

Meanwhile, Falls Church's business district rapidly expanded to create the commercial "spines" that still exist—North and South Washington Street and West Broad Street. The town's first strip shopping center opened in the 1000 block of West Broad Street (between West Street and the railroad crossing) in 1948. This automobile-oriented strip center, featuring buildings separated from the street by parking lots for cars, proved the prototype for future development in Falls Church, mirroring a nationwide trend. This and other development added enough new businesses to the city to warrant establishment of the Greater Falls Church Chamber of Commerce in 1946.[2]

An unpleasant consequence of the area's newfound reliance on the automobile was the widening of Washington and Broad Streets from two lanes to four and five lanes, which necessitated cutting the shade trees lining both thoroughfares. Citizens objected, but the rapidly increasing population of both the town—and city—which increased from 2,576 in 1940 to 7,535 in 1950, and 10,192 in 1960—as well as in the surrounding areas made the widenings necessary to accommodate all the new cars plying roadways. But this time the state highway department did not replant the trees. West Broad Street remained barren of trees until the 1990s. And Washington Street remains unplanted. The fate of the trees lining these two streets has been a recurring question in town and city life as "growth and progress issues" such as street widenings have caused the trees to be cut and replanted several times.

Infrastructure, in hand with the broader roadways, made physical expansion of the city possible. Donald S. Frady, legendary director of public works, and his staff installed six miles of sidewalks, twenty miles of curbs and gutters, and many thousands of feet of storm drains within ten years of the city's creation in 1948.[3]

With improving roads Falls Church found itself a popular place to live for employees of the expanding federal government in Washington. Several subdivisions sprang up before and after World War II which provided housing for these new citizens. One such area, Virginia Forest, was built amidst a tulip poplar forest on Horseshoe Hill and featured affordable homes of varying floor plans. Virginia Forest remains virtually intact. Falls Church Echo, *circa 1940.*

Civic groups, the equally vital component of any cohesive city, continued to be formed or strengthened in post-war years. The League of Women Voters and several neighborhood groups representing Greenway Downs, Broadmont, and northern Falls Church were active in governmental affairs, and Jaycees, Kiwanis, Lions, Veterans of Foreign Wars, American Legion, and Boy and Girl Scouts all provided fraternal and charitable activities.[4]

During this time Falls Church inhabitants came under the influence of two nonpartisan citizens' organizations rather than of the Republican or Democratic political parties. This was done to comply with the provisions of the Hatch Act, which barred federal employees from being sponsored by national political parties for elective office. Much of Falls Church's population is federally employed. The Hatch Act was recently amended to remove this restriction but Falls Church voters, loyal to the Citizens for a Better City (CBC), the Falls Church Citizens Organization (FCCO), or to the nonpartisan system itself, show no signs of returning to more typical affiliations.

The CBC, the first of the two nonpartisan groups, was formed in 1958 in a successful attempt to endorse and elect to the Council pro-school candidates.[5] The FCCO's formation followed in 1988 largely in response to land use decisions that were not maintaining the character of Falls Church. Since that time the city has generally elected members from divided tickets and independent candidates, including the present council.

Falls Church is unique in this country for the high number of registered voters who participate in elections. In the 1996 national election over 92 percent of registered voters in Falls Church cast ballots. The national average is generally near the fifty percentile.

The Town of Falls Church was separated from the County of Fairfax and became an independent city of the second class by District Court order in 1948. The city's charter was granted by the General Assembly in 1950.

Schools in Falls Church became a top priority. When the new city assumed control of the schools from Fairfax in 1949–50, almost immediately a modernization and rebuilding program was begun with a difference of opinion. To many in the new city it seemed an extravagant use of public monies for capital improvements and for "frills" such as music and art programs. But to the highly educated, mostly federal employees who were driving the modernization push, it seemed a wise use of tax dollars. The pro-modernization side won the argument but only after more than a decade of law suits and protracted, bitter and divisive city elections producing radically different councils as control see-sawed between the two sides.[6]

The city's independence from Fairfax County in 1948 left it without a high school, adequate elementary school space, and with Fairfax County schools within its borders. This somewhat unsettled state of affairs continued for many years, with the Falls Church High School in Falls Church attended by Fairfax County students. Falls Church's own junior-senior high school, which opened in 1952 just across the city boundary on land purchased in the county before the annexation suit was lost, was named after Virginia statesman George Mason, a name chosen from a list which included Old Dominion, Northwestern, Columbia, Falls Church, Thomas Jefferson, MacArthur, and Haycock. The city requested the Fairfax County School Board to change the name of Falls Church High, but it did not. It later was renamed Whittier and was razed in 1997. Mt. Daniel Elementary School, also built on land just outside the city limit, opened in 1952. In 1955 the Oak Street School, renamed Thomas Jefferson Elementary School, was purchased from Fairfax County and the venerable Jefferson Institute, the town's first public school, was closed in 1956 and demolished in 1958. For the first several years after independence Falls Church and Fairfax County exchanged students until each made arrangements to accommodate its own students.[7]

Segregation played a role in Falls Church's history, as it did throughout the state. The Commonwealth of Virginia adopted a "massive resistance" policy toward federally-directed desegregation measures in education until 1959. Falls Church instituted mixed-race education two years later, in 1961, two years behind neighboring Arlington, which instituted it in 1959. Prior to that date the city paid tuition to send its black elementary pupils to Fairfax County's James Lee Elementary School on Annandale Road, and its black high school pupils to school in Manassas.[8]

Separation of the races was also evident in residential areas. Neighborhood covenants in some sections of the city forbade owners from selling their homes to persons "of negro or negroid descent in any degree . . ." These covenants were observed until 1948 when the U.S. Supreme Court ruled them unconstitutional.[9] African-Americans continue to be counted among Falls Church's notable citizens and Tinner Hill, settled by blacks after the Civil War, is home to descendants of those original families today, including the Tinners and the Hendersons.[10]

Seven Corners Shopping Center, when it opened in 1956 on the site of a pastoral crossroads, was the area's first modern automobile-oriented mall and instantly revolutionized the way Northern Virginians shopped. An instant success, it almost as quickly scaled back Falls Church merchants' retail trade territory by one-third. It also became the name for an area which had been known as Fort Buffalo since the Civil War. Evening Star, *October 3, 1956.*

Tyson's Corner, circa World War II. An unassuming country crossroads until 1964, when its development began, Tyson's Corner rapidly eclipsed Seven Corners as the region's retail giant and severely diminished Falls Church merchants' remaining retail trade territory. Courtesy Fairfax County Public Library.

Falls Church Airpark, Arlington Boulevard at Graham Road, 1946. This 3,000-foot runway, which opened in 1946 as the second of its kind in the U.S., served local flying needs until escalating land values doomed it. It first put Falls Church on air maps. Today the nearest airport for private, civilian use is in Manassas. This site is now home of Loehmann's Shopping center. Quentin Porter photo, courtesy Mary Riley Styles Public Library.

It seems humble now, but in 1946 this Falls Church recreation center seemed palatial. It offered, essentially, a place to gather, with none of the amenities of today's Community Center. Quentin Porter photo, courtesy Mary Riley Styles Public Library.

Falls Church switchboard, Chesapeake & Potomac Telephone Company, 1947. Town businessman Merton E. Church brought the fledgling telephone service to the village in 1888. C&P, part of the reknowned Bell Telephone Co., was the only service provider in Falls Church. Quentin Porter photo, courtesy Mary Riley Styles Public Library.

Veterans marching in a Memorial Day parade in downtown Falls Church, 1948. Memorial Day events were especially poignant immediately after World Wars I and II. Quentin Porter photo, courtesy Mary Riley Styles Public Library.

Falls Church's volunteer fire department, 1948. The station is still in use but is being replaced by a new structure which will be large enough to accommodate the greater space requirements of modern fire engine companies. Quentin Porter photo, courtesy Mary Riley Styles Public Library.

Fort Buffalo, now called Seven Corners, in 1948. Only two structures present today are seen. This important intersection of Leesburg Pike, Arlington Boulevard, Wilson Boulevard, Hillwood Avenue, and Sleepy Hollow Road was freed for development only after the descendents of prominent African-American resident Frederick F. Foote convinced a court to invalidate his last will and testament in 1956, which had forbidden them to allow his thirty-three acres to leave the family. Quentin Porter photo, courtesy Mary Riley Styles Public Library.

This cartoon illustrates the massive economic expansion and rise in living standards in which area residents found themselves after World War II. Every driveway soon sported an automobile and every home installed new labor-saving appliances, such as electric clothes washers and dryers and dishwashers, all of which promised Falls Church residents additional leisure time. Falls Church Echo, August 30, 1946.

Snyder's Hardware Store in East Falls Church, 1949. After World War II it was no longer enough to have electricity and running water, but also appliances with which to use them. Shown in this photo are designer kitchen cabinets, hot water heaters, kitchen stoves, freezers, refrigerators, and washing machines. A youthful backlash later developed in the 1960s against the consumerism which these new appliances represented. Quentin Porter photo, courtesy Mary Riley Styles Public Library.

Seven Corners Market at Seven Corners, 1950. The store was a harbinger of things to come: trees behind the building have long since been leveled for additional development. Quentin Porter photo, courtesy Mary Riley Styles Public Library.

In this 1949 view of Falls Church the town center is still ringed by fields and farmland, but not for long. The beginnings of the development which surrounded it in the 1950s may be seen in the upper portions of the photo, in the new residential subdivisions stretching between Lee Highway and Arlington Boulevard. This view looks to the southeast. Quentin Porter photo, courtesy Mary Riley Styles Public Library.

Park Avenue at Little Falls Street, looking toward North Washington Street, circa 1950s. Falls Church remains more a village than a town in this photo. Quentin Porter photo, courtesy Mary Riley Styles Public Library.

West Broad Street, undated photo. This view, facing west from Annandale Road, shows the street as a two-lane road. The "hanging tree," the tree from which, legend has it, John S. Mosby hanged his enemies during the Civil War, stands in the foreground. Courtesy D.C. Public Library.

Progress in this case meant destruction of the trees lining East Broad Street during its widening from two to four lanes, 1952. The trees along South and North Washington Street, cut at the same time, have yet to be replanted. Quentin Porter photo, courtesy Mary Riley Styles Public Library.

Falls Church Public Library, 1951. Then quartered in a frame farmhouse on West Broad Street at North West Street (now the site of a gas station), the library was woefully small, crowded, and inadequate to meet the needs of the growing population it served. City leaders began planning a permanent, spacious home for the collection which would open several years later. Evening Star, *May 3, 1951, courtesy Francis Acosta and Mary Riley Styles Public Library.*

Last passenger train run by the Washington & Old Dominion Railroad, East Falls Church, May 31, 1951. The age of the personal automobile was at hand. E. S. Miller photo. Courtesy Washington & Old Dominion Railroad Regional Park.

Last passenger train run by the Washington & Old Dominion Railroad, 1951. Here a farewell crowd gathers at East Falls Church's station to bid passenger service adieu. The automobile had captured most of the passengers, making the service unprofitable and leaving the town without passenger trains for the first time since 1860, with the exception of a hiatus during the Civil War. Harwood, Rails to the Blue Ridge.

Falls Church Delicatessen, 500 North Washington Street, undated photo. This view demonstrates the variety of foods, and the prices charged for them, in the 1950s. The "product positioning," marketing, and pricing are a far cry from today, but at least one brand remains familiar: Coca-Cola. Quentin Porter photo, courtesy Mary Riley Styles Public Library.

United States Post Office, 1951. Postmasters were important community figures and post offices were the local, usually only, representation of the federal government. Until a few years prior the "three Falls Churches"—East Falls Church, West Falls Church, and the "village"—each had its own post office. Quentin Porter photo, courtesy Mary Riley Styles Public Library.

Falls Church Drug Store, northeast corner of Broad and Washington Streets, 1953. Both streets are two-lane, and the city water tower rises in the background. The water tower was a local landmark for many years, and the city government decorated it with Christmas lights and a star each year. The building was given a third story in the 1980s. Quentin Porter photo, courtesy Mary Riley Styles Public Library.

Fashion show in The Alma Shop in downtown Falls Church, 1954. Women consumers, flush with cash in the post-war years after the privations of the Great Depression and World War II, fueled a national boom in the garment industry which continues today. Quentin Porter photo, courtesy Mary Riley Styles Public Library.

The new, improved Falls Church Recreation Center, 1954. This building even had room in which to gather! But Falls Church did not sport a stable, sizeable environment in which to recreate until 1968 when the Community Center opened. Quentin Porter photo, courtesy Mary Riley Styles Public Library.

Several businesses establishing themselves in Falls Church during its post-war expansion took pride in obtaining for themselves buildings custom-designed by architects. The Falls Church Florist on West Broad Street, which remains in the building represented in this architect's rendering, is one. The building just east of it is another. Courtesy Falls Church Florist.

Architect's rendering of the jet-age Falls Church Coop Center, 502 West Broad Street, 1954. The building is now vacant and slated for demolition and redevelopment. Evening Star *photo, copyright* The Washington Post.

U.S. Army Nike anti-aircraft missiles in launch positions at Lorton, Virginia, 1954. The missile site was one of sixteen ringing Washington. Later the sites housed antiballistic missiles to defend against nuclear attack. The launch site closest to Falls Church was in Pimmit Hills. Had Washington been threatened by atomic attack Falls Church, the population of which was too large to fit into the public bomb shelters available, was to evacuate to Prince William, Stafford, and Rappahannock Counties. Evening Star *photo, copyright* The Washington Post.

The nuclear weapon stand-off which marked the Cold War between the United States and the Union of Soviet Socialist Republics was of direct threat to Falls Church. The town's proximity to Washington would have assured its total destruction had a nuclear attack occurred on the capital. Falls Church Echo, *August 23, 1946.*

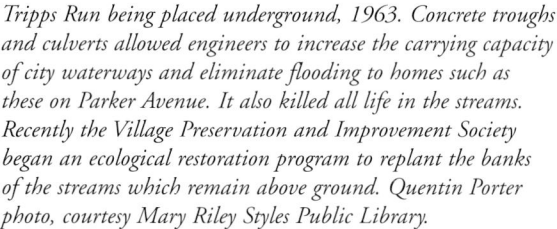

Tripps Run being placed underground, 1963. Concrete troughs and culverts allowed engineers to increase the carrying capacity of city waterways and eliminate flooding to homes such as these on Parker Avenue. It also killed all life in the streams. Recently the Village Preservation and Improvement Society began an ecological restoration program to replant the banks of the streams which remain above ground. Quentin Porter photo, courtesy Mary Riley Styles Public Library.

Four Mile Run experienced frequent and often costly floods until being placed underground or in concrete troughs. In this view, circa 1960s, a Falls Church fireman surveys an East Falls Church automobile dealership swamped by flood waters. Courtesy Falls Church Volunteer Fire Department.

This undated photo shows part of the proud young city's new and emerging infrastructure, in this case the City's first street sweeper. Left to right: C. R. Gray, Donald S. Frady, public works director, and Herman Fink, mayor. Quentin Porter photo, courtesy Mary Riley Styles Public Library.

Demolition of Lynch House, 170 East Broad Street. The city lost a number of historic homes before citizens rallied in opposition in the late 1970s. Historic Falls Church, Inc. was created during this time to assume historic easements to protect properties. George Long photo, courtesy Mary Riley Styles Public Library.

Demolition of the historic Galpin-Hartman home, 424 East Broad Street, 1979. This house had two sixteen by sixteen living rooms and a fourteen by twenty-six dining room. The floors were Georgia pine heartwood. The house appeared to be built on the foundation of a much earlier home. Courtesy Mary Riley Styles Public Library.

Washington & Old Dominion Railroad freight train blocking West Broad Street, 1967. The W&OD, unable to compete with the flexibility of the new interstate highways, and burdened by the need for upgrading its many surface-grade crossings of major throughfares such as this one, ended all service in 1968. T. A. Coons photo. Courtesy Washington & Old Dominion Railroad Regional Park.

Eliminating at-grade crossings such as this one outside Falls Church, a prohibitively expensive proposition, was one of several such needs and considerations prompting the Washington & Old Dominion Railroad to liquidate. Courtesy Falls Church Volunteer Fire Department.

Swan song of the Washington & Old Dominion Railroad, seen here passing through Falls Church, 1968. The railroad was an important factor in Falls Church's growth from its opening in 1860 until its closing in 1968. It was largely supplanted by the new interstate high-speed highways. Its bed now forms the Washington and Old Dominion Railroad Regional Park, operated by a consortium of local governments, including the City of Falls Church. Quentin Porter photo, courtesy Mary Riley Styles Public Library.

Falls Church city councilman Lee M. Rhoads (left), Dr. William S. Hoofnagle, chairman of the Fairfax County Board of Supervisors (center), and Herbert E. Harris II, Fairfax County Board of Supervisors (right), inspecting the new Judiciary Square Metro station, circa 1970. Falls Church received MetroRail service when the Orange Line opened through West Falls Church to Vienna in 1986. Backlick Road station, advertised on the sign in the photo, was instead named Franconia/Springfield. Falls Church was originally planned to be served by a Metro line running under Wilson Boulevard. Courtesy Northern Virginia Transportation Commission.

Architect's rendering of the Northern Virginia Center, a joint undertaking of Virginia Tech and the University of Virginia which opened in 1997. The corner tower and east facade, facing across the county/city boundary into Falls Church's West End, feature many windows and a broken pediment—an architectural tip of the hat to the City. Courtesy the Northern Virginia Center.

Architect's rendering, new fire station, Lee Highway at Four Mile Run. The building is currently under construction behind the existing station, used for more than sixty years. Courtesy Falls Church Volunteer Fire Department.

Virginia Training School for mentally retarded children, 309 West Broad Street, 1904. Miss Mattie A. Gundry opened the school in the former Duryee home in 1899 and operated it until her retirement in 1946. The school was the only one of its kind in the south and became the second largest in the United States. The building was demolished in 1947. Courtesy Mary Riley Styles Public Library.

CHAPTER XV

Reconfirming Village Roots

The powerful forces of a particular brand of prosperity, progress, and modernization, seen in Falls Church and across the country from the 1950s through the 1970s were often disrespectful of history and architecture. In Falls Church, lovely old homes lining North and South Washington Street and Broad Street were razed, as were the I.O.O.F. (International Order of Odd Fellows) Hall, Jefferson Institute, Falls Church Bank, Columbia Baptist Church, and other visual and cultural landmarks in the local streetscape. They were often replaced by architecturally undistinguished structures of predominantly utilitarian design.

But Falls Church, finding itself at the crossroads represented by unbridled change and tempered, selective change, chose the latter. Many jurisdictions did not. In 1962 planners recommended apartment towers for East Broad and North Washington Streets. The City, after measured debate, disagreed. In 1964 planners recommended turning downtown into an "experimental" pedestrian mall. This ambitious plan was in process for ten years and was formally presented in 1974. Apartment and commercial towers were to line the streets. The plan is easy to dismiss now, since it was not undertaken, but numerous other jurisdictions did undertake similar redevelopment schemes. Many features of similar 1970s urban redevelopment plans failed.[1]

But nothing in Falls Church's history threatened it as immediately and physically as the interstate highway network, an outgrowth of the amazing post-war economic prosperity in which it shared.

President Dwight D. Eisenhower announced plans for an interstate highway system in 1956; the Washington area segment called for nine radial corridors and three circumferential highways (beltways) centered on Washington, with five new Potomac River bridges.[2] One such radial corridor, later designated Interstate (or "I") 66, was to link the Shenandoah Valley to the capital.[3]

Falls Church lent its support to this monumental effort. In 1955, fully a year and a half before the Virginia Highway Commission formally proposed I-66, the City Council recommended that the road be built and that the City be on its right of way.[4] Additional details caused the council to rescind its early approval: by 1958 plans called for the new highway to pass through the City of Falls Church along the right of way of the Washington & Old Dominion Railroad.[5] Its eight lanes and associated rights of way would form a corridor 300–500 feet wide. Its interchanges would consume approximately thirty acres each.[6] Over forty homes and forty businesses would be eliminated.[7]

The impact of this proposal—eradicating the entire West End business district and many of the city's historic homes and residential areas—was not lost on the council, which lobbied to have the proposed route shifted. In 1959 the director of the Northern Virginia Planning District Commission assured Falls Church residents that the route would now pass north of the city.[8]

Falls Church's narrow escape proved to be the opening chapter of a complex story. In Arlington, environmentalists, unable to block construction

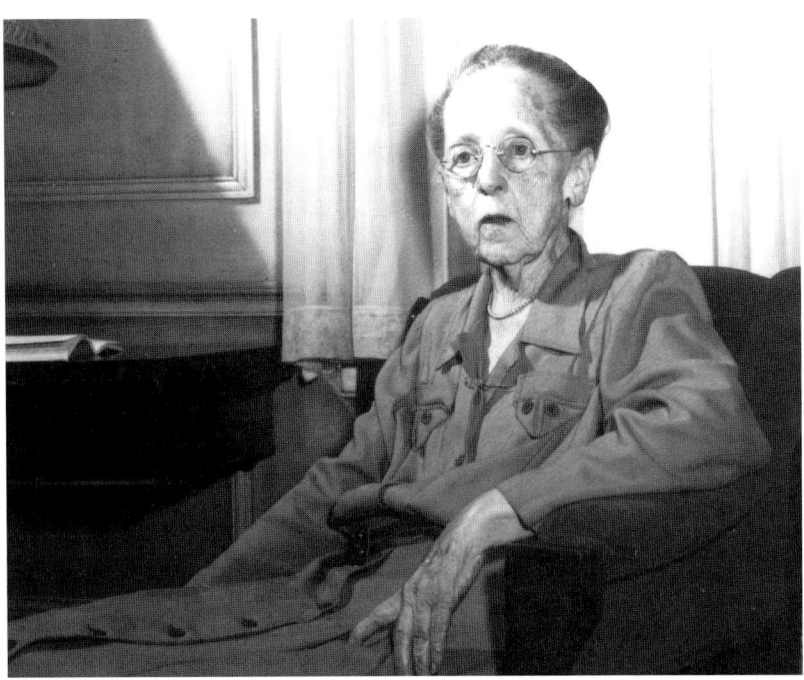

Mattie Gundry, undated photo. Miss Gundry operated her school for the feeble-minded and the Whitehall Sanitorium, also in Falls Church, until she retired in 1946. Gundry was well-regarded in national mental health circles and served as a town councillor in an era before it was common for women to do so. Quentin Porter photo, courtesy Mary Riley Styles Public Library.

entirely, caused the proposed highway, I-66, to be scaled back from eight lanes to four, with portions below grade and with extensive landscaping and sound barriers.[9] In East Falls Church, separated from the rest of Falls Church in 1936, businesses virtually ceased to exist after I-66 made its local appearance. Many residences and its commercial district, which included a movie theater, barber shop, stores, a post office, and doctors offices, were almost entirely sacrificed to make way for the new interstate highway.[10] Falls Church, itself no longer physically threatened by the highway route, was still keenly interested in the issue. City officials viewed the new highway as a bypass around the traffic-choked town. "Perhaps Falls Church's most obvious curse is traffic," said one, heartily endorsing the roadway.[11]

Balancing the needs of automobile transportation against the quality of life increasingly consumed public debate in Falls Church as it adjusted to existence in a rapidly-burgeoning urban area.

Falls Church's downtown became less intimate than before when the streets which intersect there were widened to four and five lanes. Overhead pedestrian walkways were recommended for the intersection of Broad and Washington Streets by a consultant who noted in 1967, "It's worth your life to try to cross there on foot."[12] But Falls Church, through careful street ornamentation and crosswalk treatment, has managed to preserve its downtown as a place where restaurant patrons dine outdoors and residents and visitors interact.

Suburbs, as Gertrude Stein said, are the place where "there is no *there* there."[13] "Falls Church may be a city by name and a metropolitan suburb by locale, but it has the heart and soul of a village," according to one lifelong resident. Villages "are walkable, defined by pedestrians and human scale buildings . . . they are also 'mixed use,' which means that people live, work and shop there," writes another."[14]

Falls Church has been rediscovering its roots as a village for the past several decades. Redefining Broad Street as a pedestrian zone and replanting its long-missing shade trees was the goal of a recent, successful venture in which utility lines were placed underground. Street furniture was added, shrubbery and flowers were installed in curbside planting strips, and trees were planted.[15]

Campus of Mattie Gundry's Virginia Training School, 309 West Broad Street, 1929. Cartographers here have indicated an earlier name for the school and the one by which it was better known locally. EDR Sanborn, Inc. Used with permission.

144

President John F. Kennedy was quick to cable, "Warmest congratulations to Falls Church, Virginia," in 1962 as the city learned that its progressive civic program secured it the All-America City award from the National Municipal League and *Look* magazine. The city showed "noteworthy accomplishments through alert, continuing citizen participation. Such is the only way to make self-government effective," according to contest judges, who praised the city's nonpartisan atmosphere.[16]

One of the most effective protectors of the village legacy has been the Falls Church Village Preservation and Improvement Society (VPIS), the 1965 successor to the 1885–1919 Village Improvement Society. It was a VPIS study which originally suggested replanting trees on Broad Street, and its work in preserving the tree canopy, conserving the stream valleys, and encouraging judicious landscaping using native plant species has been invaluable in preserving the city's natural character. Its popular concerts in Cherry Hill Park and in homes around the city have added immeasurably to the cultural milieu.

"The beautiful historic homes and sites we enjoy today have a way of becoming gas stations, hamburger stands, and high-rises that we must endure tomorrow," wrote Stewart W. Edwards of Historic Falls Church, Inc., a nonprofit corporation formed in 1975 to encourage restoration and administer preservation easements.[17] In 1984 the Council enacted a zoning ordinance designating the entire city as an historic overlay district, giving homes and buildings built in or before 1910 special protection from demolition. Remembrance and preservation of the past are essential ingredients in the life of any village.

Villa Maria Academy, on the campus of St. James Roman Catholic Church, North Spring Street, 1947. The building opened in 1905 and was demolished in 1964. Courtesy Marge Castorina, courtesy Mary Riley Styles Public Library.

St. James Roman Catholic Church campus, North Spring Street, 1946, by which time the church formed a substantial campus. In 1999 St. James's school opened a sleek new gymnasium just north of its classroom building. EDR Sanborn, Inc. Used with permission.

Cupola, St. James Catholic Elementary School, long a fixture of Falls Church's skyline, 1999. Bradley E. Gernand photo.

Madison Elementary School children enjoying a nutritious meal, 1946. After World War II a newly prosperous nation took great measures to feed, clothe, and house its population. Quentin Porter photo, courtesy Mary Riley Styles Public Library.

Falls Church High School's football team, 1946. The high school, located at the intersection of Hillwood Avenue and Cherry Street, was a county school serving Falls Church students until after the new city achieved independence in 1948. Falls Church soon established its own high school, George Mason Junior-Senior High School, which fields a football team known as the Mustangs. The school on this site was later known as Whittier. Quentin Porter photo, courtesy Mary Riley Styles Public Library.

Unidentified baseball player making sporting history, 1946. The bat has broken in mid-swing after hitting the ball, as the facial expressions of the boys in the background will attest. Falls Church High School (later Whittier Intermediate School) is in the background. Quentin Porter photo, courtesy Mary Riley Styles Public Library.

Falls Church Hawks baseball team, circa 1947. Baseball, along with football and basketball remain ongoing traditions in Falls Church and have since been joined by soccer and other less traditional sports. Quentin Porter photo, courtesy Mary Riley Styles Public Library.

Falls Church model airplane club, 1948. Military aviation's role in winning World War II probably sparked the interest of some of these young men. And commercial aviation was uniting the country and world via new and exciting aircraft. Quentin Porter photo, courtesy Mary Riley Styles Public Library.

Falls Church is given its due by the creator of Steve Canyon, a popular and nationally-syndicated newspaper comic strip. Falls Church Echo, *February 3, 1950.*

St. James Catholic Elementary School continues to contribute to the excellent educational choices available to Falls Church students. Here young matriculates of St. James kindergarten class of 1950 pose for a graduation photo. Quentin Porter photo, courtesy Mary Riley Styles Public Library.

Womanless wedding fund-raising event of the Lions Club, circa 1950s. These august and dignified gentlemen bequeathed to present-day Falls Church a club which remains one of the most active of the local fraternal and charitable organizations. Quentin Porter photo, courtesy Mary Riley Styles Public Library.

Sunsinger being lowered into place in the National Memorial Park. Pagan worship of the sun inspired the statue's Swedish sculptor, Carl Milles, who originally was commissioned to produce a work called Astronomer. Wartime shortages of materials intervened, and the artist instead offered Sunsinger. The statue was later placed atop a marble pedestal and stands twenty-five feet high. Evening Star photo, copyright The Washington Post.

Reunion After Death *illustrates the ethereal pageant which is Carl Milles's* Fountain of Faith *statuary ensemble in the National Memorial Park. Here (at bottom) the dead welcome the newly dead to the afterlife which follows. A mother lifts her newborn baby high to the Lord (center); the angel (upper left), perhaps the only figure not representing a formerly living person, listens to the comments of those who visit the fountain. Milles considered the work his greatest sculpture. Courtesy National Memorial Park.*

Honorary Fire Chief Sandy Royston promoting a carnival offered by "her" department. Bob Milnes photo for the Northern Virginia Sun. *Courtesy Falls Church Volunteer Fire Department.*

From this humble tradition—Santa Claus, riding a Falls Church fire engine—has evolved today's yearly and eagerly-anticipated Christmas event: Santa, riding a magnificently-bedecked and resplendent, almost blindingly bright fire engine covered with colorful Christmas lights, blaring cheerful Yuletide carols, traveling every street in Falls Church, throwing candy to excited youngsters. How could Christmas anywhere else be as delightful? Courtesy Falls Church Volunteer Fire Department.

Falls Church celebrates its award as All-America City, 1962. On the right Mayor Charles M. Hailey is assisted by officers Richard Moore and Garland Heatwole, before a crowd of proud residents at the new City Hall. Look *magazine and the National Municipal League issued the young city the award in recognition of its high degree of citizen participation in local affairs, an element of civic life which persists equally strongly today. Courtesy Mary Riley Styles Public Library.*

"Once upon a time there was air you couldn't see," reads one poster. Environmental concerns moved to the forefront of local and national agendas during the 1960s and 70s. These St. James Catholic School students rally in 1965 against pollution, then perceived to be growing unchecked. One handmade sign advertises Earth Day, then a fledgling movement now marked annually both nationally and in Falls Church. Courtesy Mary Riley Styles Public Library.

A plethora of choices confounds this young scholar in the Falls Church Public Library, 1971. Technological advancement has since consigned the library's card catalog, shown here, to the dustbin of history as newer, electronic equivalents have taken its place. The library, which celebrated its 100th year in 1999, averages several hundred visits per day and serves a highly educated population through Internet offerings as well as traditional printed sources. Courtesy Mary Riley Styles Public Library.

Birthday celebrations are not new to Falls Church, which celebrated the centenary of the establishment of the town in 1975. This parade marched east along West Broad Street. Courtesy Mary Riley Styles Public Library.

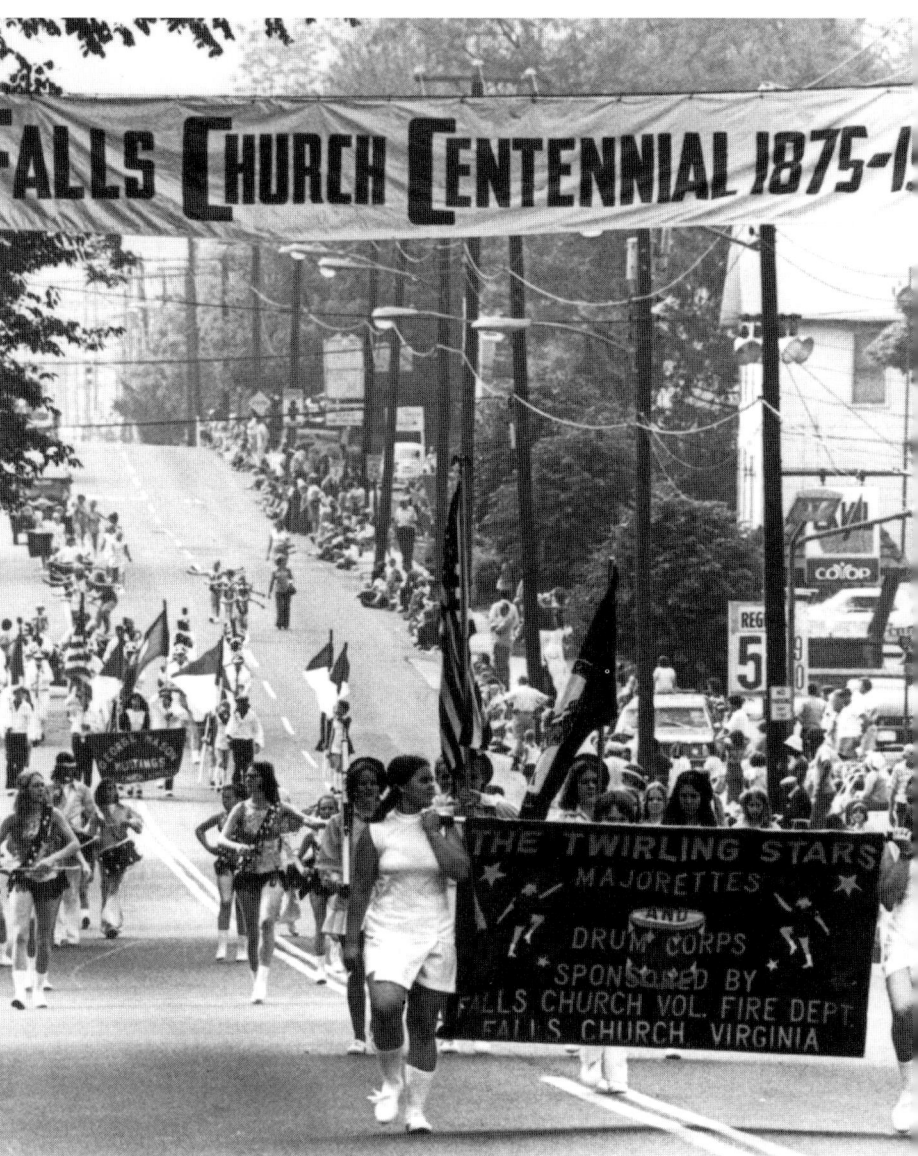

A range of choices confronted Falls Church city leaders, concerned by downtown's anemic retail trade and nightlife, in the 1960s and 70s. In 1974 urban planners recommended closing the downtown intersection of Broad and Washington Streets and converting the area into a Town Square. Traffic was to be rerouted along side streets; existing buildings were to be replaced with mid-rise apartment and commercial blocks. Similar plans undertaken elsewhere soon seemed dated and ultimately failed. This architect's conception looks east along the former Broad Street from Maple Avenue (top), and a courtyard on the former Washington Street (bottom). Courtesy Mary Riley Styles Public Library.

During the 1970s the City of Falls Church emerged as one of the wealthiest jurisdictions per capita in the United States. This may be news to the man in the cartoon, as Falls Church, where housing prices are permanently buoyed by the excellent quality of schools and scant crime, is also one of the most expensive places in which to live. Globe, *August 4, 1977.*

Falls Church's successful opposition to state highway department plans for Interstate 66 to pass through the City was but the opening salvo in a route-selection battle which raged for years. East Falls Church, which seceded from the town in 1936, was now without benefit of city leaders' negotiating prowess and relied on Arlington County for protection from the proposed highway. County officials, however, were forced to weigh that neighborhood's concerns against those of its other neighborhoods. Most of the commercial district of East Falls Church, bulldozed and lying under the modern highway, ceased to exist. Arlington News, *May 3, 1979.*

Falls Church at its tercentenary finds itself fortunate to have a healthy local, home-grown weekly press. Here Falls Church residents read a special election edition of the Falls Church News-Press *in 1992. Falls Church news is also reported to a lesser extent by three dailies, the* Fairfax Journal, Washington Post, *and* Washington Times. Falls Church News-Press, *November 19, 1992.*

Nicholas Benton, publisher of the Falls Church News-Press *and host of a weekly radio show concerning events and governance in Falls Church, interviewing Hap Day, former director of the Greater Falls Church Chamber of Commerce. Courtesy Nicholas Benton.*

Vicki Knickerbocker, general manager of the public access cable television station, Channel 38, with the new DVCAM digital format camcorder in February 2000. Billy Hanger photo, courtesy Falls Church Cable Channel 38.

West Broad Street looking east from Haycock Road, circa 1980. Burgeoning and inefficiently planned growth in post-war years stripped the street of its charm—and trees. The City launched a street renovation and rehabilitation project in the early 1990s which removed utility poles and buried cables underground, bricked sidewalks, planted lush evergreens and trees, and installed street furniture and lighting in keeping with a much earlier day from the street's history. Courtesy John Maier.

Travis Lincoln of the Mustangs' baseball team during a winning game. Athletic prowess marks student life at George Mason Junior-Senior High School, although it is matched by impressive intellectual achievement. Falls Church News-Press, May 16, 1991.

A bell for the Falls Church Episcopal in 1999. This 800-pound bronze bell, cast by the McShane Bell Foundry of Glen Burnie, Maryland in 1895, was found in a disbanded church in Indiana and purchased by Falls Church DAR Regent Caroline H. Bell McGuigan and her husband, Col. William J. McGuigan, Retired. The couple donated the bell to Historic Falls Church. Her Daughters of the American Revolution chapter, named after the church and the town, provided funds to install the bell in the church tower and also to provide an automatic ringer to sound the bell daily during the week, on Sundays and for special events. Courtesy Caroline H. Bell McGuigan and Col. William J. McGuigan.

Columbia Baptist Church, one of Falls Church's historic congregations, has encouraged its growth with a commitment to the increasingly multi-ethnic population of greater Falls Church. In addition to three English-language worship services the church now offers services for Arabic, Hispanic, and Korean congregations. It has begun a Vietnamese-language ministry which it hopes will mature into a full congregation. Maureen Budetti photo, 1999.

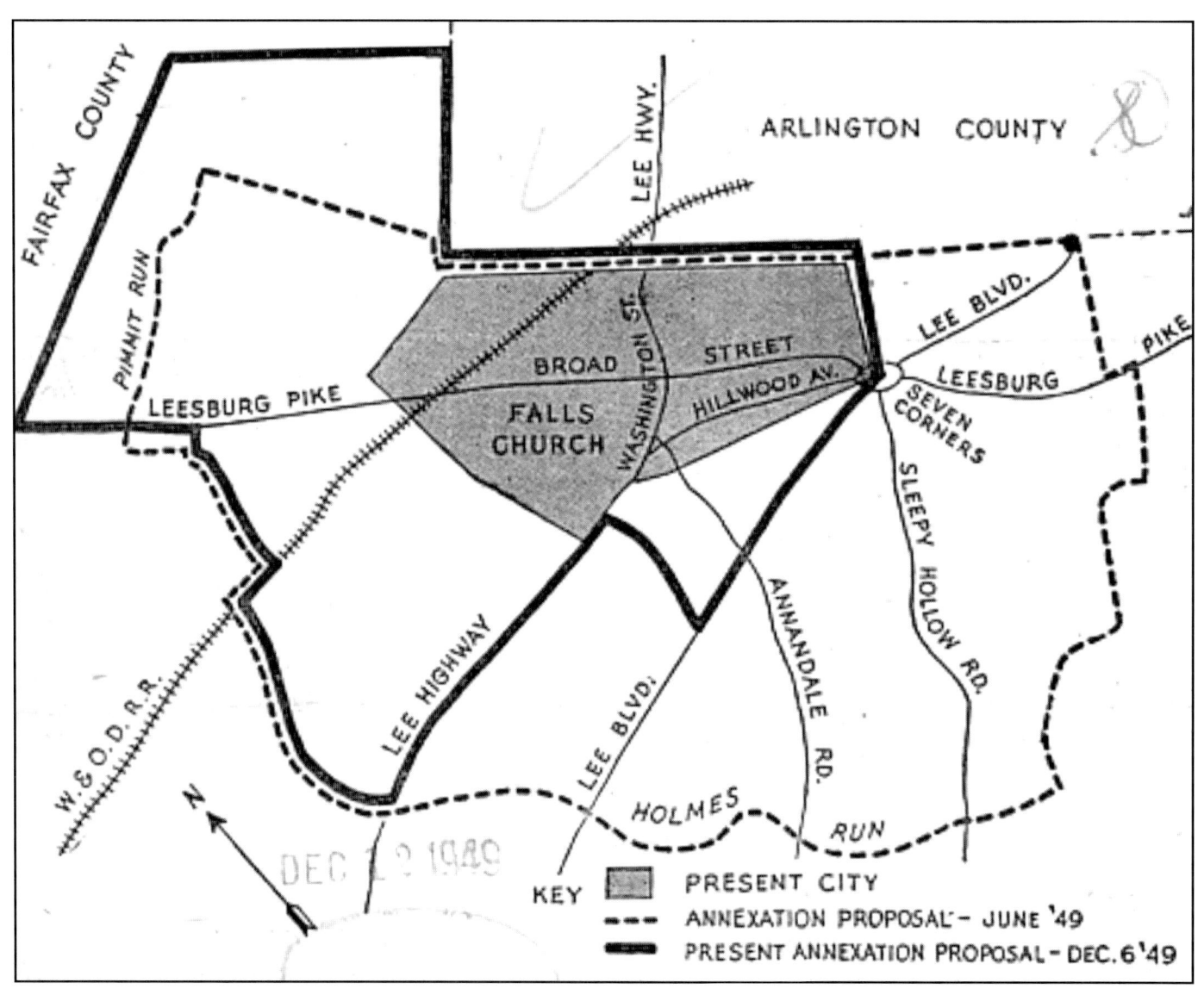

Falls Church was anxious to expand its boundaries to take in additional tax revenue even while still a town. After achieving independence from Fairfax County the young City redoubled its efforts to expand. This map shows two of several such attempts, none of which were ever successful, due to the opposition of the residents in those areas. Within two decades residents of the same areas petitioned the City repeatedly but unsuccessfully for annexation. Evening Star, *December 12, 1949.*

CHAPTER XVI

Of, By, and For the People: Local Government

Effective government involves clear understanding of expectations. There are numerous examples of user-friendly services in practically every Falls Church city government department. Helpful staff members make contacts pleasant even when they include paying taxes.

Joint ventures are shared with neighboring jurisdictions. The city government cooperates with the Arlington County government in providing community-based group homes for court-sponsored programs for teenage boys and girls who need emphasis on personal responsibility, independent judgment, and positive change. Argus House, on Clarendon Boulevard in Arlington, opened in 1976 and Aurora House on South Maple Avenue in Falls Church opened on April 7, 1991. The Friends of Argus and Aurora Houses support extra projects and the Susan L. Olom Scholarship Fund encourages house residents to attend college.[1]

Through the Housing and Human Services Division, programs are provided for families, senior citizens, people with disabilities and residents in crisis. These and other services are available from the city or in cooperation with Arlington or Fairfax counties.[2]

Priorities had been strongly established after the circuit court judge granted Falls Church city of the second class status in 1948 and the General Assembly granted its charter in 1950. The city built two schools: George Mason Junior-Senior High School west of Haycock Road, and Mount Daniel Elementary at the end of Oak Street; both were opened in 1952. The City purchased Oak Street School from Fairfax County in 1955 and renamed it Thomas Jefferson Elementary School. All school buildings had subsequent additions and renovations. The first section of the brick city hall was opened in 1958, as was the first section of the library building.[3] So were schools, government, and the library served.

All of the Falls Church public schools and one private school have been nationally recognized as exemplary learning centers. In 1982–83, George Mason High School received one of the first Excellence in Education awards from the United States Department of Education. Mount Daniel and Thomas Jefferson Elementary Schools received the Excellence in Education award in 1986, and in 1998, George Mason Middle School received a Blue Ribbon award for excellence in education. Also in 1998, the Virginia Tech/University of Virginia Northern Virginia Center on Haycock Road formed a partnership with George Mason High and Middle Schools for a technology learning center.[4] The only private school in Northern Virginia to receive the award that year, St. James Catholic School in Falls Church, was named a Blue Ribbon School for 1998–99 by the U.S. Department of Education. It was one of the Blue Ribbon Schools named nationwide for the school year and was cited for "academic excellence, parental involvement and community support." The school population in 1998–99 at St. James Catholic School, kindergarten through eighth grade, was 625.[5]

Schools have had an important place in the Falls Church community for decades. As Falls Church Public School Superintendent Mary Ellen Shaw wrote in 1999:

> *Since its inception in 1949, the Falls Church City independent school system has produced a concrete measure of its excellence in the form of a continuous stream of well-educated graduates. . . . Buildings have been renovated and new staff hired. New programs have been introduced, Xerox machines, VCRs and computers have replaced purple ditto masters, film strip projectors and typewriters. But one thing has remained the same—the commitment of the community and the staff to provide the best possible education to all of the students in the Falls Church City Public Schools.*[6]

In the initial 1998–99 city budget, the schools' appropriation amounted to $14,246,683, 74.50 percent of the total city budget. Appropriations for school purposes have traditionally represented a high percentage of the annual budget for Falls Church. The public school population for 1998–99 was 1,062 students for kindergarten through eighth grade, and 505 students for ninth through twelfth grades.[7]

The Falls Church Historical Commission, whose members are appointed by the City Council, has an ongoing program supporting historic preservation and providing historical information to city residents and visitors. Special plaques have been placed on many historic structures and historic markers have been erected along the city streets. City maps and publications are available at the City Hall and the Mary Riley Styles Public Library.[8]

Madison Elementary School, 334 North Washington Street, 1946. This sturdy school, built in 1926, was demolished in 1979 after the City consolidated elementary facilities from three schools to two. Quentin Porter photo, courtesy Mary Riley Styles Public Library.

Since the Falls Church Community Center was opened in 1968 under the direction of Ken Burnett, it has filled a large variety of needs for the city and its environs throughout the year and offered numerous opportunities for the constructive use of leisure time. The center, now under director Howard Herman, hosted citizens' groups, health groups, scout groups, athletic clubs, military historians, recyclers, the Victorian Society, and garden clubs, some of the organizations that met in 1999 in the Community Center on a regular basis. Other special events were held in the Community Center's large gymnasium and in Cherry Hill park.[9]

In 1999, the city of Falls Church was named a Tree City USA for the twenty-first year in a row. Under the direction of arborist Shirley Street, the successful program meets four requirements: a community tree board or department, a tree care ordinance, a comprehensive community forestry program, and an Arbor Day observance. National sponsors of the Tree City USA program are the Arbor Day Foundation, the Forest Service, and the Association of State Foresters.[10]

The recycling program in Falls Church began in the 1970s when the city became the first in the region to offer curbside recycling of newspapers to the residents. With the establishment of the "green bin" program in 1990 and the Falls Church Recycling Center in 1991, a wide variety of materials is now collected on a regular basis. Citizen volunteer involvement and youth education programs reaching hundreds of elementary school students have provided opportunities to take part in environmental awareness and action in the community. In recognition of its strong recycling program, Falls Church is one of only nineteen communities across America to be included in an EPA document, *Cutting the Waste Stream in Half: Community Record Setters Show How.* After using open dump sites and a sanitary landfill established by Fairfax County in 1973, Falls Church has relied on Fairfax County for disposal of its solid waste. Nearly all such material collected in the city is now incinerated at the I-95 Energy/Resource Recovery Facility in Lorton.[11]

Vice President Albert Gore issued a National Recycling Challenge on November 16, 1998, asking citizens to renew their commitment to conserve our national resources by recycling. Under the City's Recycling Coordinator, Annette Mills, and with active and enthusiastic citizen participation, Falls Church received the nation's highest rating—67 percent a year later in 1999, forty points above the national average.

As City Manager Louis Z. Johnston, Jr. wrote in 1961:

> *. . . It is on the basis of its contribution to the character of the city as a whole that government should be appraised. It is not for Falls Church to be a great city in the sense of square miles occupied. But Falls Church can be, and is well on its way to becoming, a great city in the sense of offering a fine place in which to live and work. The city is much more than its government: it is homes, churches, organizations dedicated to service, and businesses operated efficiently yet with a strong sense of the public interest; it is the way in which neighbors and even rivals work together in common purpose. But a sense of value and of civic purpose cannot operate without the solid foundation of good government and public service. This is the responsibility of the City Manager, the Superintendent of Schools, and other officials and civil servants. We want all our citizens to understand what we are trying to do; to be frank to suggest ways in which we can serve better or more economically; and to support our effort to make Falls Church the best community in the whole metropolitan area.*[12]

Mayor David Snyder joined elected officials and other well-wishers in front of the Falls Church Community Center the end of March 2000 at the unveiling of the prototype of the new electric buses donated by Virginia Power, for mass transit. News Press photo.

Throughout history, Falls Church has been a crossroads, with its people and that of the region often returning to a common theme of how to maintain and improve the movement of people and freight from one place to another. The Tricentennial year was no different. Representing the City, Mayor David Snyder participated in creating the Northern Virginia 2020 Plan to address the inadequacy of the region's road and transit system in the context of projected dramatic population, job, and motor vehicle growth. Under the Plan, the region will build and widen highways and bridges, maintain and add fifty miles more of subway and thirty-three miles of light rail, expand pedestrian/biking infrastructure and add new technology to the transportation system at a cost of $30 billion. One of the Plan's major new improvements will be a light rail system running through Falls Church, much as the old trolley once did, making the City's businesses more accessible and reducing the reliance on cars and the resulting congestion and pollution.

Early in 2000, the City unveiled its new bus transit system which is a partnership of the City and Federal, State and regional government, Virginia Power and the Metro system. The twenty-two seat electric/diesel hybrid experimental vehicles will link residential and business areas better to the rail stations. In addition to the state-of-the-art technology, the system will operate on different daily schedules to better serve the needs of commuters, school children, senior citizens, employers and employees. Yet again, improving transportation is occupying the minds of the City's leadership and citizens as it has repeatedly throughout the three hundred years of the community's history.

Thomas Jefferson Elementary School, circa 1970s. This school was called the Oak Street School when Fairfax County opened it in 1948; the City renamed it when it assumed control in 1955. Its students have worked with the Village Preservation and Improvement Society to tend to an adjacent butterfly garden and reforest and replant the banks of nearby Tripps Run. Courtesy John Maier.

George Mason Middle School and High School, circa 1970s. The school, which opened in 1952, boasts collegiate-class science laboratories and pupil test scores which are the highest of any area school system. George Mason is situated on land just outside the City limit which Falls Church expected but failed to acquire through numerous annexation attempts during the 1940s and 1950s. Courtesy John Maier.

Mount Daniel Elementary School, undated photo, circa 1990s. This school, which opened in 1952, was built on land in Fairfax County for which the young City had filed an annexation suit, which it lost. The school remains just outside City limits. Courtesy Mary Riley Styles Public Library.

Architect's rendering of the new Falls Church Public Library, circa 1957. Elizabeth M. Styles and Francis H. Styles donated the site, across from their family's farmhouse, Cherry Hill. The library, since named for Mary Riley Styles, mother of Elizabeth and Francis, is built in the Georgian style and complements its architectural progenitor, The Falls Church. The nearby City Hall, built contemporarily, is also Georgian in style. Courtesy Mary Riley Styles Public Library.

City Hall, begun in 1957. Between 1956 and 1974 the city acquired 14.6 acres, once part of Cherry Hill farm, for use as the municipal government center. City Hall, named for Harry E. Wells, was completed with the addition of its east wing in 1982 and is home to the Council Chamber, circuit court, and city administrative offices. Painting by Ken Frye, 1999. Courtesy the artist.

Falls Church's Community Center, completed in 1968. This facility, which includes a gymnasium, meeting rooms, and recreation rooms which were state of the art in 1969, is considered too small to meet the needs of today's community and is to be enlarged. Quentin Porter photo, courtesy Mary Riley Styles Public Library.

"We Wuz Robbed," reads one sign in this 1960s protest by Fairfax County citizens against alleged indifference to their needs by the county government. Originally opposed to annexation by the new City in the 1940s and 1950s, citizens in the county areas adjacent to Falls Church changed their minds as City schools and services swept to regional preeminence. Laws now render annexations into the City difficult and, to date, no such appeals from county areas have been successful. Evening Star, *copyright* The Washington Post.

Groundbreaking of Kaiser-Georgetown (now Kaiser-Permanente) health center, 201 North Washington Street, 1984. Mayor Carol Witte DeLong is shown operating the bulldozer. Mayor DeLong, Falls Church's first woman mayor, served from 1980–88. She is among a distinguished number of women who have served the city as its chief executive, in its council, or in its influential planning commission and other important bodies. Carolyn Cole photo for the Northern Virginia Sun.

Falls Church has two nonpartisan groups, the Citizens for a Better City (CBC) and the Falls Church Citizens Organization (FCCO), rather than having local units of national political parties. Here CBC candidates Bob Tarbert, Merni Fitzgerald, and Robert Perry celebrate their 1992 election to the council. This system evolved to comply with the federal Hatch Act, since repealed, but Falls Church voters show no interest in ending their present system of representation. Courtesy *Falls Church News-Press.*

Dale Warren Dover, first African-American mayor of Falls Church, 1990–92. A former foreign service officer and vice-consul in Tel Aviv and Copenhagen, Dover speaks Hebrew, Mandarin Chinese, Danish, Portuguese, French, and Swahili. And English. Courtesy *City of Falls Church Public Information Office.*

Robert D. "Bob" Hull, representing Falls Church in the House of Delegates in Richmond since 1993. The House of Delegates is the Western Hemisphere's oldest continuous legislative body. Courtesy *Bob Hull.*

Mary Margaret Whipple, representing Falls Church in the Senate of Virginia, framed by the timelessly impressive colonnade designed by Thomas Jefferson. Ms. Whipple has represented Falls Church in Richmond since 1995. Courtesy Mary Margaret Whipple.

City Council of Falls Church during its tricentennial year. Front row, left to right: Mary Ann Capria, Merni Fitzgerald, and Kathy Winkler. Back row, left to right: Samuel Mabry, vice-mayor; David Snyder, mayor; Steven Rogers, and Daniel Gardner. Council was deeply involved in carrying out the festivities. Scott Boatright photo.

Ben Birindelli, chairman of the Falls Church Tricentennial Committee. He is a retired U. S. Navy captain and author of a recently published biography of naval hero Stephen Decatur. Nancy Birindelli photo

CHAPTER XVII

The Falls Church Tricentennial Celebration

In September 1992, the Board of Directors of the Village Preservation and Improvement Society proposed a commemoration of the 300th anniversary in 1999 of the settlement of the community in 1699. This date was selected on the basis of a verbal account of a stone bearing the date "1699" on a chimney in the "Big Chimneys" house which once stood near the present-day intersection of Little Falls Road and Broad Street in Falls Church.

The Falls Church Tricentennial Committee was selected by the City Council in 1993 to develop plans for a year-long celebration in 1999. Committee members appointed were Ben Birindelli, Joyce Cory, Barbara Cram, Ron Crouch, Susan Earman, David Eckert, Merni Fitzgerald, Edna Frady, Rosemary Haynes Jones, John Rodock, Kieran Sharpe, and Maurice Terman. Staff liaisons were Diane Morse, Barbara Gordon, Deane Dierksen, Nancy Birindelli, and Daughters of the American Revolution members Marie Yochim and Doris Katz. During several years of meetings a tentative schedule, month by month, was laid out. In 1998, a Publications Subcommittee signed a contract with the Donning Company of Virginia Beach to produce this pictorial history of the settlement, hamlet, village, town, and city from Indian times through December 31, 1999. Two Falls Church authors, Bradley Gernand and Nan Netherton, were chosen by Donning to research, write, and collect graphics, a process begun in spring 1997.

The Tricentennial Committee deemed it necessary to have a special logo for the observance and a contest was held. The winning design was done by Pat Algie of the City's staff. It was used on numerous banners and printed materials. Additional ideas were developed. More than a dozen cachet envelopes with maps and pictures were authorized by Falls Church Postmaster Joseph Quinones, assisted by his staff person, Patsy Mitchell. These individually illustrated envelopes were designed by artist Barbara Cram and others and specially canceled at different times during the year for stamp collectors and other interested individuals. Over one thousand were sold on December 31, 1999, Tricentennial Eve. This was the first time the U.S. Postal service had produced such a series with special cancellations.

Other souvenirs included ceramic crocks marked with "Falls Church" and the number "300", designed by potter Walt Zotter. Wallets filled with printed play money were negotiable with various local merchants. Golf shirts and pins were also available for sale. Sets of free bookmarks were printed with brief histories of individual schools or churches and made available at the public library. Historic maps of the city were designed, printed, and distributed free to residents and visitors.

Many individuals and groups gave time, talent, and imagination to the planning and implementation of the year's numerous events. In addition to the leadership of the Tricentennial Committee, the following organizations participated: the Historical Commission, the Village Preservation and Improvement Society, the Victorian Society at Falls Church, the Falls Church Public Schools,

Barbara Cram, a D.C. native, was appointed to the Tricentennial Committee by Mayor O'Connor in 1994. She served on the Events and Publicity Committee for the last three years—1997–2000. The popular Tricentennial Commemorative envelope series was designed and produced by her. She also designed the Falls Church Commemorative Crock and Historic Trail Patches. Courtesy of Barbara Cram.

the Tinner Hill Heritage Foundation, the City Manager's office and other City offices, the Library Board, Daughters of the American Revolution, Recreation and Parks, neighborhood groups, the Greater Falls Church Chamber of Commerce, the Economic Development Authority, the Police Department, the American Legion, and Veterans of Foreign Wars veteran's organizations, several civic organizations, and merchants of good will. The efforts of all participants helped to produce memorable shared experiences among the citizens of Falls Church, their children, and guests during the Tricentennial year of 1999.

Festivities began on New Year's Eve, December 31, 1998, an unusually cold and windy night. The "Crossroads in History," Broad and Washington Streets, informally dubbed "Timeless Square"—were transformed into a pedestrian walkway as through traffic was rerouted around the area. Thousands of celebrants, all bundled up, enjoyed music and other entertainment as they visited businesses and churches whose doors had been opened for the occasion, some with historical displays. An outdoor stage was used by music groups. Restaurants and street vendors provided hot and cold drinks and welcome warm food. During the month of January 1999 which followed, both the Falls Church Chamber Orchestra and the U.S. Navy Band presented special concerts in the George Mason High School auditorium.

The January theme of "Crossroads in History" was followed by the February theme of "Government." Two Leadership Round Tables were held, one at George Mason High and the other in the Council Chamber at City Hall. The 50th Anniversary of the City Schools was commemorated with a special music program presented by the fourth and fifth grades, at George Mason High auditorium. At the City's first "Harambee" celebration in February, Black History month was recognized in an appropriate way. It was announced that City Council members had repealed by resolution on February 22, 1999, the segregation ordinance which had been passed by the Town Council in 1915 in an effort to separate races into different residential areas within the corporate limits. A City Hall Open House extended a special invitation to citizens to visit local government offices.

Special recognition of the importance of "Volunteers and Organizations" was given in March honoring the more than sixty active civic and church groups in the City. An organizational Information Fair was held at the Kemper-Macon Ware Masonic Lodge No. 64 in mid-March and included the presentation of a special bust of Virginia colonial statesman George Mason to the city to be placed in front of City Hall. All schools observed one Old Fashioned Day at City schools and the first grades gave a 50th anniversary presentation of the schools musical program at George Mason High.

April was the month to celebrate "Natural and Cultural Resources." The first Falls Church Arbor Day—first in the state of Virginia as well—was held at the Jefferson Institute in 1892. The commemorative observance was held near the old site in Frady Park. The 100th anniversary of the Mary Riley Styles Falls Church Library was celebrated on April 18 with speakers, birthday cakes, balloons, and flowers. A youthful bagpiper and an enthusiastic Barber Shop Quartet performed in appropriate costumes. The Cherry Hill Farm House offered special tours featuring the life of Mary Riley Styles.

"History on Parade" was the theme for May. Civil War Living History groups demonstrated at the Thomas Jefferson School's playing field. And at a dedication of Civil War Trails by the City Council, "Fort Taylor" Park at Seven Corners was officially recognized as a significant location on the Virginia Civil War Trails map. It commemorates the first use of balloons at that site during the Civil War under the direction of Professor Thaddeus Lowe for purposes of military aerial reconnaissance, by the Union, of Confederate positions. Period costumes enhanced a Victorian Ball held at Thomas Jefferson School and a special tea was given at Cherry Hill Farm House. A few days later, the Falls Church Chamber Orchestra presented a concert at George Mason High. In addition to other selections, a special work commissioned and written in honor of the Tricentennial by composer Thomas Schouber was given its inaugural performance. The final public event of the month was the annual Memorial Day Parade, the 3-K Fun Run, and all-day activities in the City Hall-Cherry Hill Complex. Falls Church civic leader Louis Olom was designated the Grand Marshal of the parade.

The theme chosen by the Tricentennial committee for June was "Celebration of People." The Tinner Hill Street Festival celebrated the African-American community and their cultural activities. Also, a large crowd was in attendance that month to honor Deane Dierksen at her retirement party at Cherry Hill for her service to the community as director of the Mary Riley Styles Public Library of Falls Church. An elaborate reenactment of an actual Victorian wedding was held by the Victorian Society at the Abbott house with almost one hundred "guests" in costumes of the period. Music was played and elaborate refreshments were served under the ancient shade trees on the lawn. Later that month, school affiliations were remembered with reunions and picnics for both the George Mason High School alumni and the public school staff with several teachers attending who taught at Madison School in 1949. A large reunion for the classes in the 1960s was held at the State Theater and an all-class picnic at Cherry Hill Park was held on Saturday, June 26.

A broad definition of "Recreational Pursuits" served as July's central theme. On July 4, The Falls Church (Episcopal) held a special colonial church service followed by an audience participation in the reading aloud by many individuals of the original wording of the Fairfax Resolves, the Virginia Declaration of Rights, the Declaration of Independence, and the Federal Bill of Rights. A fireworks show was given that evening at George Mason High's athletic field. During July and part of August, outdoor evening concerts sponsored by the Village Preservation and Improvement Society were held in Cherry Hill Park behind the old barn. The audiences, many of them families with children, brought blankets and chairs or sat on the grass under the trees to enjoy the "music in the air." A special program was held in July commemorating one of two District of Columbia Jurisdiction Stones located on Falls Church's borders. The No. 9 Boundary Stone near Van Buren Street had been declared a National Registered Landmark in 1980 and was named after the black mathematician and astronomer, Benjamin Banneker, who assisted Andrew Ellicott in laying out the entire ten-mile-square encompassing land in Maryland, the District of Columbia, and Virginia. The other stone is the West Cornerstone located at the joining of Arlington County, Fairfax County, and the City of Falls Church on Meridian Street. This stone has been recently named, by agreement of the three jurisdictions, in honor of Andrew Ellicott, chief surveyor of the ten-mile-square of the Federal District in 1791 and 1792. Isaac Crossman park on Four Mile Run was also dedicated that day.

"Happy Birthday, Falls Church!" was the Tricentennial theme in August. A well-attended public concert with the Falls Church Chamber Orchestra and Irish dancers and a ceremonial cutting of the cake were held in Cherry Hill Park. On the fifteenth, a dedication of the supposed site of the "Big Chimneys" was followed by a "Church and Tavern Day in 1763" a week later presented by Falls Church City and organized by the Historical Commission. A meeting of the Truro Parish Vestry was recreated around the old Anglican church and there were many purveyors, artisans, and colonial period reenactors. Gingerbread and root beer were served and George Washington himself made an appearance in an appropriate costume. Gathering and mingling among the visitors were story tellers, musicians, dance masters, tobacco farmers, leather workers, gunsmiths, weavers, wood crafters, blacksmiths, herbalists, quilters, sampler makers, embroiderers, and Native American traders.

In September, following the traditional summer vacations, students returned to school and business people geared up for their fall and holiday activities. The month's theme was "City Schools and Businesses." The quilters took their Bill of Rights quilt to a Council meeting to have it rededicated and arranged to have it permanently mounted on display in the Council Chamber. Open House was held at one of the community's oldest businesses, Brown's Hardware. An all-day Falls Church Fall Festival was held in Cherry Hill Park on the eighteenth. The Falls Church Chamber Orchestra held its third Tricentennial concert at George Mason High the following day. The month ended with the meaningful dedication of Tinner Hill Memorial Arch in a pocket-park at the corner of South Washington Street and Tinner Hill. It was the culmination of persistent efforts by members of the Tinner Hill Memorial Foundation, the Falls Church City Council, elected government representatives, other individuals, merchants, and the National Association for the Advancement of Colored People. A matching grant from the Commonwealth of Virginia, obtained largely through the efforts of Falls Church's Delegate Robert Hull, helped to fund the building of the pink marble arch. This structure was to commemorate the founding of the first rural chapter of the NAACP in the United States. The chapter was organized in 1915 in the Town of Falls Church. Land on Tinner Hill has been set aside by Falls Church and Fairfax County for a future cultural heritage center.

The October theme was "Homes and Hearth." A two-day Private Homes Tour of eleven buildings and one garden was held the first weekend in October, sponsored by VPIS and the Victorian Society. The following weekend there was a well-attended Farm Day at Cherry Hill Park. An exhibit of Victorian clothing took place at Cherry Hill. A Family Sock Hop dance was held at George Mason High. Cherry Hill Farm House was the location for literary evenings of readings to commemorate the 100th anniversary of the founding of the Falls Church Library.

"Places of Worship" was the major theme in November. An ecumenical religious service was held on Veterans' Day, November 11 at which time a Veterans' Honor Roll Plaque was unveiled with lists of names of all of the community's service people who lost their lives in the nation's wars. Information for this plaque was painstakingly collected by a number of dedicated community activists. An annual tradition was repeated during Thanksgiving week—the showing of the classic 1946 film, "It's a Wonderful Life," starring James Stewart, at the Community Center. Local schools received close attention in a November symposium entitled "The Future of Education."

"The City of the Future" was December's theme and a leadership Round Table on the subject was held on December 7 in the newly remodeled State Theater. Entertainment began early in the evening with the classic rock and roll sounds of the David Elliott Band. Then a panel of experts on the local economy, design and development trends, the environment, demographics and government voiced their opinions on the future of Falls Church over the next century. A Holiday Ball was held at the Community Center on December 11 and on New Year's Eve, 1999, a closing ceremony of the Tricentennial Year was held in "Timeless Square" at the City's main crossroads with merriment and music. All that remained to be completed in the formal observance were two things. One was the dedication of a new plaque by the Village Preservation and Improvement Society in the President's Garden under the W & OD Bike Trail Bridge in the West End of the City off Broad Street naming and honoring past presidents of the Society. The other task was to work with collecting certain objects for a Time Capsule commemorating the Tricentennial Year. The kindergarten students in the class of 2012 were asked to participate with the preserving of the capsule at Mount Daniel Elementary School and marking it with a plaque directing that it be opened in the year 2050.

There are more than forty memorials, plaques, and historical markers which have at different times been placed throughout the City of Falls Church. Some of the parks and streets have special names. They commemorate people, events, buildings, and early sites of importance in the growth and development of the community. A current list may be seen in the Local History Room of the Mary Riley Styles Library of Falls Church.

Saying Hello to 2050: Students of Mount Daniel Elementary School pose in front of a time capsule and a scroll atop it which will go inside it bearing their handprints. The time capsule will be opened in fifty years—when the students are about the same age as Falls Church Mayor David Snyder (second from left). Nancy Birindelli, of the school administration, is far left; Mount Daniel principal Kathy Halayko is far right; and Falls Church school superintendent Mary Ellen Shaw is in the back row. Falls Church News-Press *photo.*

Bust of George Mason, author of Virginia's Declaration of Rights and father of the U.S. Bill of Rights, dedicated by Kemper-Ware Masonic Lodge of Falls Church in honor of the City's tricentennial, March 14, 1999. Nancy Birindelli photo.

Tinner Hill Monument. Dedicated in June 1999 by the Tinner Hill Heritage Foundation to honor the contributions of Falls Church's African-American community, longtime residents of the hill. The Tinner family in particular was known for its fine stone masonry; hence the arch. Plaques at the arch's base note the founding of the nation's first rural chapter of the National Association for the Advancement of Colored People (NAACP)—right in Falls Church. Scott Boatright photo.

United States Postal Service aerogramme, released to honor the Falls Church's tricentennial year. The design commemorates Falls Church's role in making military history during the Civil War, when it hosted the first aerial military reconnaisance.

A number of fine homes opened to the public for special tricentennial tours during 1999. One such lovely home was Falcon's Nest on South West Street, which has been owned by the Lanier family for many years. Courtesy William and Norma Lanier.

Dedication of the Veteran's Memorial in front of the Community Center. The memorial is ringed by handsome plaques. At far left is J. Benson Birindelli, chair of the City's Tricentennial Commission. Included in the photo are Maurice J. Terman and Ed Strait of the City's historical commission, who researched the names of Falls Church's fighting sons and daughters installed on the plaques. Nancy Birindelli photo.

The Falls Church Chamber Orchestra was founded in 1996 by French horn musician Eric D. Moore with the help of long-time friend Megan O'Leary. A native of the Falls Church area, he plays with the United States Navy Band as well as with four local symphony orchestras. The Chamber Orchestra performs at least three concerts in the City annually and is composed of professional musicians from throughout the Washington, D.C. metropolitan area. Courtesy of Eric Moore.

The Future of Falls Church was the topic at hand December 7, 1999, discussed by a panel of regional leaders, researchers, and thinkers in the newly renovated and reopened State Theater. And the Falls Church of tomorrow? A vibrant, dynamic community possessing the talent and will to position itself successfully for the next one hundred years. Panelists from left to right were: Martin Ogle, chief naturalist, Northern Virginia Regional Park Authority; Michael Rogers, Washington Metropolitan Council of Government; Maes Van Zee, Northern Virginia Planning District Commission; Amy Liu, Brookings Institution; Nicholas Benton, Falls Church News-Press; *Tom Black, Lincoln Institute; David Eckert, City Tree Commission; Helen Reineke-Wilt, City Planning Department; Carol Jackson, City Housing Corporation; and Brian Gradle, moderator. Joel Hardi photo, courtesy* Falls Church News-Press.

Transit used on the resurvey of the Washington & Old Dominion Railroad through Falls Church, circa early 1900s. This transit is shown with its original finish, three spirit levels, quarter circle vertical vernier, thirty-inch horizontal circle, and adjusting pins. Courtesy of its owner, Sidney O. Dewberry.

CHAPTER XVIII

The Way We Were; The Way We Are

Cherry Hill Farm, 312 Park Avenue. Fred Degnan photo.

Three-panel view of events of the Civil War. The bottom two concern Falls Church and the ring of hills north and east of it. Frank Leslie's Illustrated News, *October 26, 1861.*

Civil War Thanksgiving at Cherry Hill Farm. Reenactment, circa 1990s. Frank D'Aquila photo.

East Falls Church railroad station, circa 1900. Carolyn Grosse Gawarecki, artist. Courtesy Falls Church Community Center.

Watercolor painting of President William McKinley reviewing U.S. troops at Camp Alger, the huge Spanish-American War encampment outside Falls Church. Courtesy of D.C. Public Library.

"There's No Place Like Home." The 1939 classic movie "The Wizard of Oz" provided the Halloween costume theme for these Falls Church residents. Left to right: Kyle Nette ("the Cowardly Lion"), Jill Maier ("Dorothy"), Drew Maier ("the Tin Man"), and Alex Nette ("the Scarecrow"). Halloween and Easter have recently joined Christmas as major local decoration holidays. Janice C. Nette photo.

Flower girls in Victorian wedding reenactment at Falls Church's historic Abbott House, 600 Abbott Lane. Frank D'Aquila photo.

Easter egg hunt, and the Easter bunny, at Cherry Hill Farm. Mary Clare Gubbins photo.

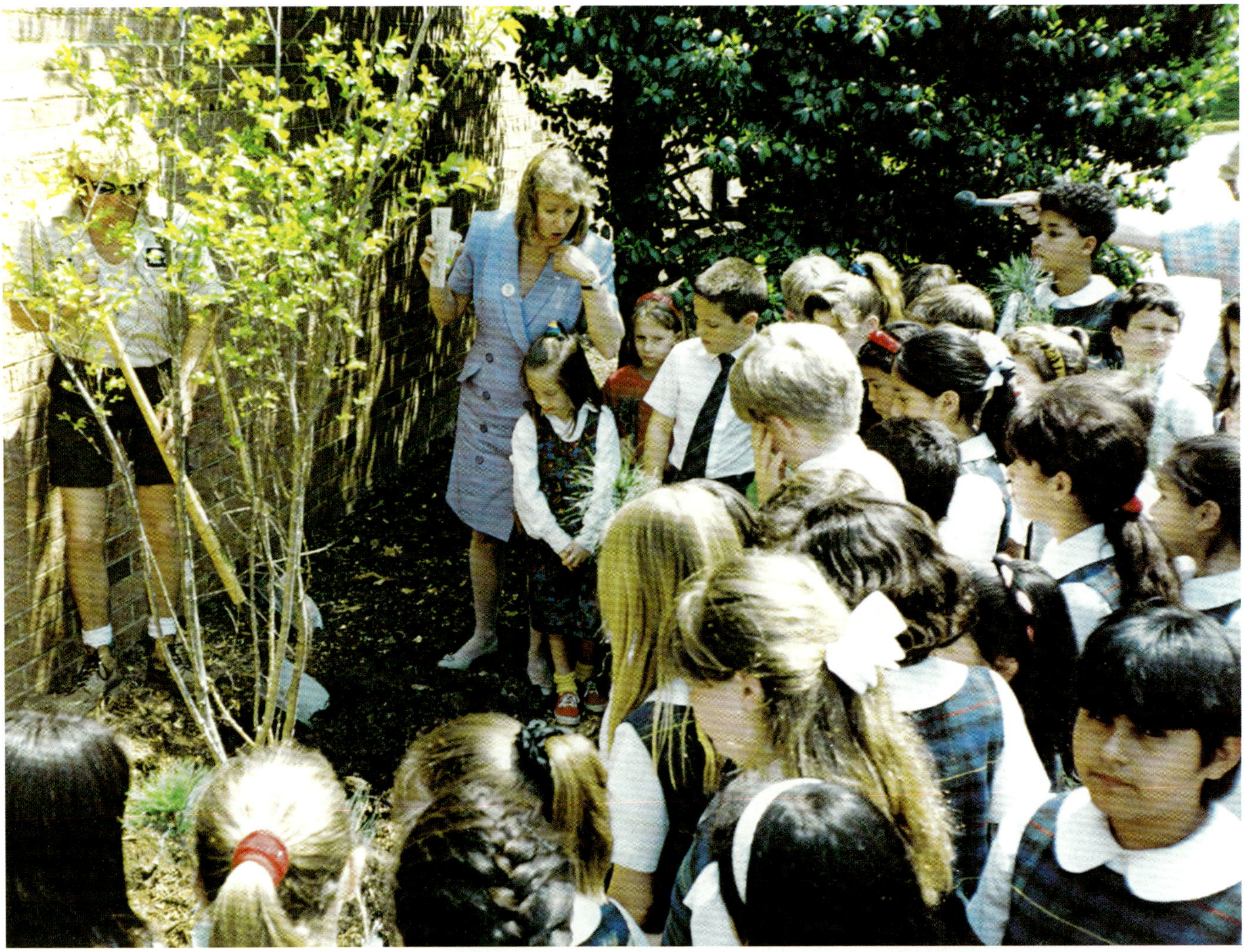

Arbor Day tree-planting at the Falls Church Community Center. Brian DePoorter photo.

Annual three-kilometer ("3K") Memorial Day Fun Run, sponsored by Don Beyer Volvo in Falls Church. The tee-shirts, shown here, are always popular. Courtesy Falls Church Community Center.

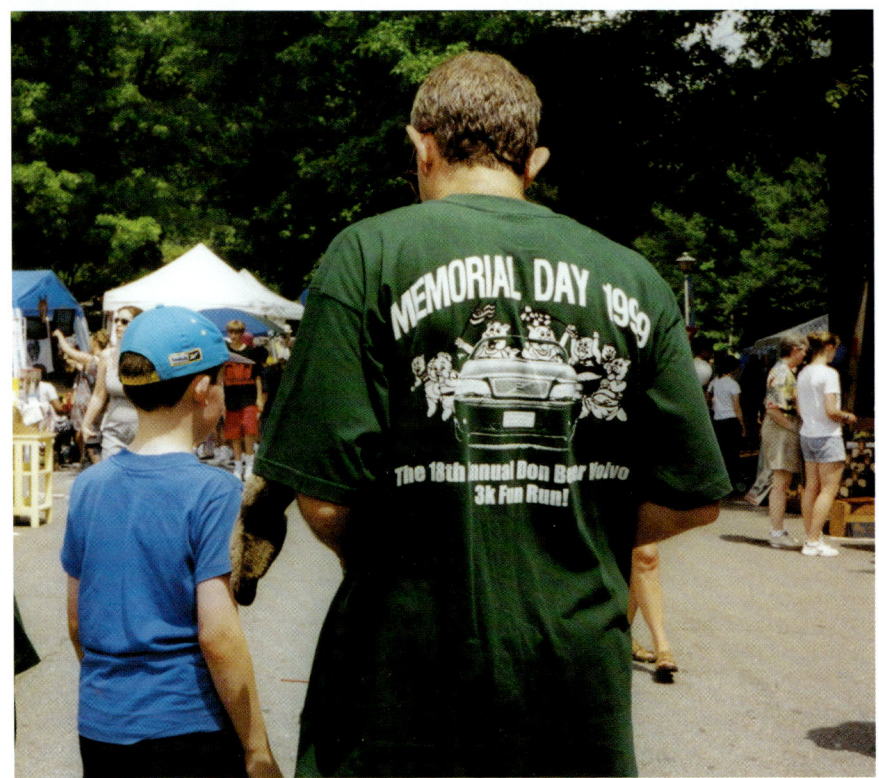

Sculpture, Don Beyer Volvo Motor Company, erected by the Beyer family to commemorate their origin on a pig farm in McLean, Virginia. Sculpture by Richard Beyer. Maureen Budetti photo.

Falls Church Volunteer Fire Department and historic "Old Tom" fire engine, Memorial Day parade on Park Avenue. Linda Treacy photo.

West Broad Street after its renovation and replanting in the 1990s. Nancy Schick photo.

The Falls Church Lions Club, and Falls Church community spirit, making a difference at the Child Development Center for handicapped children, 111 North Cherry Street. Barry Buschow photo.

Weekly Saturday morning farmer's market, City Hall. Howard Herman photo.

Weekly Thursday evening summer concert at Cherry Hill Farm, sponsored by the Village Preservation and Improvement Society. The annual concerts are attended by several hundred Falls Church residents who sprawl comfortably on blankets or in portable chairs. Albert Howlett photo.

Ceramic story tiles alcove, Mary Riley Styles Public Library, 120 North Virginia Avenue. Created and presented by the children of Mount Daniel and Thomas Jefferson elementary schools in celebration of the renovation of the library and in memory of Betty Parish Avery "who loved art, loved books and loved children." Nancy Birindelli photo.

Dedication of the Washington & Old Dominion Railroad Regional Park bridge over West Broad Street, 1992. Walter Mess of Falls Church, fourth from right, helped organize and has been chairman of the Regional Park Authority since it was formed in the 1950s. Courtesy Washington & Old Dominion Railroad Regional Park.

Paul Whitney, Falls Church's "Officer Friendly," showing school children the police department, 1993. Whitney serves in the department's community outreach and Officer Friendly programs. Courtesy Falls Church Police Department.

Royal Victorian Ball, featuring members of the Victorian Society at Falls Church, 1997. Frank D'Aquila photo.

West Broad Street viewed from the corner of North Washington Street, 1998. Falls Church Planning Office photo.

Eden Center on Wilson Boulevard, at Falls Church's eastern tip, the largest Vietnamese shopping center on the East Coast, 1999. The flag of the former Republic of (South) Vietnam flies daily from the flagstaff of this expatriate outpost. Maureen Budetti photo.

An inviting hammock on a beautiful spring afternoon in a lovely Falls Church garden. Maureen Budetti photo.

Appendix A
Mayors and Councilmen of Falls Church Since 1875
*Persons who have served as Mayor

*Dr. J. J. Moran	1875–1876 1877–1878 1882–1883	*G. W. Hawxhurst	1898–1900 1904–1907 1909–1913	*T. A. Williams	1907–1909
Isaac Crossman	1875 1877–1878	W. H. Nowlan	1898–1899 1905–1906	Unverzagt	1907–1909
George B. Ives	1875–1877 1878–1884	*H. L. Turner	1898–1899 1900–1902	Hodgson	1907–1908
Joseph E. Birch	1875–1877 1878–1880 1882	W. E. Parker	1898–1900 1905–1907	Carroll V. Shreve	1908–1914 1915–1919 1922–1924
*T. T. Fowler	1875–1877 1878–1879	*W. M. Ellison	1898–1904 1907–1913	H. R. Thompson	1908–1909
J. J. Carter	1875–1876	J. C. DePutron	1898–1901	A. H. Barbor	1909–1913
Dr. Louis E. Gott	1875–1876 1881	*J. D. Payne	1898–1899 1905–1907 1910–1912	Mandley T. Rust	1909–1911 1949–1950
Wells Forbes	1875–1877 1878–1879	A. M. Smith	1898–1900	H. E. Brown	1910–1911 1913–1914
*Seth Osborn(e)	1876–1877 1878–1879 1882	M. E. Church	1899	*Harry A. Fellows	1910–1914 1920–1926
E. F. Crocker	1876	Dr. T. C. Quick	1899–1902	W. T. Westcott	1912–1917 1926–1930
H. D. Weeks	1876–1878	J. B. (D) Gould	1899–1902 1905–1906 1907–1915	Reginald Munson	1913–1915
Joseph S. Riley	1876–1878 1881	J. N. Gibson	1899–1903 1907–1910	P. B. Nourse	1913–1918
B. W. Pond	1877–1878	*M. M. Erwin	1900 1907–1908	*J. G. Herndon	1914–1916
J.G.W. Brenner	1877–1878 1898	*George N. Lester	1900–1901 1903–1905	R. L. Harmon	1914–1915
Charles Perrigo	1877–1878	Tyer	1900–1901	Samuel H. Styles	1914–1918 1924–1926
S. D. Tripp	1878–1879	J. E. Jacobs	1900–1903	*John F. Bethune	1915–1917 1923–1927 1928–1930
George M. Thompson	1878–1882	J. H. Wells	1901–1904	*S. S. Luttrell	1916–1918
*L. S. Abbott	1879–1880	C. F. Newman	1901–1904	Albert B. Piggott	1916–1920
William Shreve	1879–1881	*C. C. Walters	1901–1904 1906–1907	W. H. Lynch	1917–1919 1920–1924
George W. Mankin	1879–1881	E. J. Northrup	1902	C. W. Lee	1917–1919
John C. H. Brown	1879–1880	E. I. Crump	1902–1904	*J. Edward Thomas	1918–1920
*William A. Duncan	1880–1882	Peter Nobin	1902–1904	Dr. J. R. Smallwood	1918–1922
Frederick F. Foote, Jr.	1880–1889	S. E. Thompson	1902–1905	W. H. Rogers	1918–1920
W. Nathan Lynch	1880–1881 1898–1900 1905–1907 1909–1910 1915–1916	George A. Brunner (Brenner)	1904–1905	Julius H. Parmelee	1919–1920 1929–1935
		H. C. Birge	1903–1904 1905–1909	W. H. Erwin	1919–1921
*William P. Graham	1881	E. A. Kimball	1904–1907	B. F. Elliott	1919–1921 1932–1938
L. A. Crump	1881–1882	Thomas Hillier	1904–1906	E. J. Glasson	1920–1921
Clarke Crossman	1882	John W. Garner	1907	W. T. Parrott	1920–1921 1924–1926 1930–1934
Levi Parker	1882	Billingsley	1907–1910	Charles E. Gage	1921–1922 1928–1938
L.J.B. Gardiner	1882–1883 1898			J. C. Hoskins	1921–1925

193

Name	Years
Harry M. Keyser	1922–1926, 1934–1935
Miss Mattie Gundry	1922–1927
Mrs. P. H. Smyth	1922–1923
Barron Fredricks	1925–1927
R. E. Kendrick	1926–1928
*L. P. Daniel	1926–1928, 1930–1940
*Harmon B. Green	1926–1927
*R. C. L. Moncure, Jr.	1927–1928
Henry Knowles	1927–1929
Clarence M. Sale	1927–1929
Philip M. Talbott	1928–1930
Milton E. Roberts	1928–1934
Clarence W. Boyd	1929–1930
Frank L. Birch	1930–1932
J. V. Turner	1930–1934
W. S. Brown	1934–1936
T. F. Probey	1934–1939
Joseph G. Smith	1935–1939
R. E. Ankers	1935–1939
C. W. Crossman	1936–1938
Paul W. Ferris	1938–1940
R. S. Keyser	1938–1942
C. L. Shotwell	1938–1940
*Charles E. Kellogg	1939–1942, 1951–1959
Charles A. Pendleton	1939–1943
Lawrence E. Laing	1939–1943
*Burns N. Gibson	1940–1943
Ada E. Fowler	1940–1946
J. Harry McCarthy	1940–1944, 1946–1951
W. B. Follin	1942–1948
*Martin E. Haertel	1943–1946
Archie T. Munson	1943–1950
Sherman M. Wells	1943–1951
Fred C. Hess	1943–1944
Foster Wood	1944–1946
Karl L. Anderson	1944–1946, 1950–1951
*Fenner Hazelgrove	1946–1948
Sargeant White	1946–1948
James E. Durant	1946–1948, 1949–1953
John C. McRae	1947–1951
Mrs. Merrill Lee Chanel	1948
Mr. Case	1948
*Albert Orme	1948–1951
John Eakin	1948–1949
Samuel J. Dennis	1948–1949, 1961–1969
Lee M. Rhoads	1948–1951, 1961–1976
Samuel E. McCrary	1949–1953
D. Kemper Grille	1949–1950
Mrs. Jenness Wirt Myer	1949–1951
Carl H. Hink	1950
Kermit Overby	1950–1951
W. David Brewer	1951
W. Raymond Taylor	1951–1959
Margaret C. King	1951–1953
W. Alvin Tasker	1951–1953
Francis A. Wagner	1951–1953
Donald G. Benn	1953–1955
*Herman L. Fink	1953–1957
*M. Eldon Colby	1953–1955
Grant G. Hilliker	1953–1957
Charles C. Seymour	1953–1961
*Thomas A. O'Halloran	1955–1957
Jewell H. Pederson	1955–1957, 1967–1969
Charles Hock	1956–1957
G. Galt Braedy	1957–1961
William H. Harnsbarger	1957–1961
*Charles M. Hailey	1957–1971
Charles J. Hedetniemi, Sr.	1959–1967
Everett D. Johnston	1959–1963
Harold Silverstein	1961–1969, 1974–1978
Thomas R. Jones	1961–1965
Ardith Cronin	1963
*Thomas G. Eastham	1963–1971
John R. Blowers	1965–1969
Mrs. Edna Clark	1969–1974
James H. Lynch	1969–1974
*Louis H. Blair	1969–1974
Jimmie H. Singleton	1969–1974
Paul R. Brockman	1971–1976
*Harold L. Miller	1971–1980
*Mrs. Carol E. DeLong	1974–1990
John M. Enright	1974–1978
Edward B. Strait	1974–1978, 1980–1988
James E. Dougherty	1976–1980
Robert L. Hubbell	1978–1986
Gary D. Knight	1978–1990
Mrs. Nancy Stock	1978–1982
John D. Scanlan	1976–1979
Dr. W. John Cameron	1979–1988
John C. Gannon	1980–1982
Elizabeth L. Cesnik	1982–1984
J. Roger Wollenberg	1982–1988
*Elizabeth A. Blystone	1984–1990
Elizabeth L. Havlik	1986–1900
Susanne Bachtel	1988–1992
Cynthia Garner	1988–1992
James M. Slattery	1988–1992
*Dale Warren Dover	1990–1994
E. D. David Minton	1990–1994
*Brian M. O'Connor	1990–1994
Phillip J. Thomas	1990–1994
Robert Perry	1992–1996
*Jeffrey J. Tarbert	1992–1996
Mary C. "Merni" Fitzgerald	1992–2000
H. Alan Brangman	1994–1998
Jane C. Scully	1994–1998
Kieran Sharpe	1994–1998
*David F. Snyder	1994–2002
Mary Ann Capria	1996–2000
Samuel A. Mabry	1996–2000
Stephen A. Rogers	1998–2002
Daniel E. Gardner	1998–2002
Kathie Winckler	1998–2002

Source: Mary Catherine Gallagher and Elizabeth-Anne Shawen, City Clerks, June 1999

Appendix B
Postmasters of Falls Church

Originally in Fairfax County, Virginia, the post office was officially established on June 11, 1849.
The postmaster appointed on that date declined the position and never served.

Name	Position	Date Appointed
Simon J. Groot	Postmaster	06/22/1849
Charles A. Orton	Postmaster	10/10/1859
William A. Moore	Postmaster	04/05/1860
W. E. Moore	Postmaster	09/24/1861
George B. Ives	Postmaster	04/18/1862
Edward J. Birch	Postmaster	04/22/1872
Albert E. Lounsbury	Postmaster	06/27/1881
Charles E. Mankin	Postmaster	08/27/1885
Edwin F. Crocker	Postmaster	06/20/1889
Samuel R. Newlon	Postmaster	05/31/1893
Edwin F. Crocker	Postmaster	05/07/1897
George W. Hawxhurst	Postmaster	09/07/1906
Vanderbelt Quick	Postmaster	07/13/1907
Ozias B. Livingston	Postmaster	02/25/1909
Emmet W. Skinner	Postmaster	02/26/1915
Miss Ruth C. Mankin	Postmaster	05/09/1919
Mrs. Virginia T. Quick	Postmaster	06/05/1924
Virginia Austin	Acting Postmaster	06/23/1928
Byron Austin	Postmaster	12/20/1928
Clarence M. Sale	Acting Postmaster	07/01/1933
Clarence M. Sale	Postmaster	03/22/1934
B. Frank May	Acting Postmaster	03/31/1945
B. Frank May	Postmaster	03/02/1946
Walter H. Sealock	Acting Postmaster	12/31/1953
Walter H. Sealock	Postmaster	03/09/1955
William Edwin Scheid	Acting Postmaster	12/07/1962
William Edwin Scheid	Postmaster	07/26/1963
L. B. Rothgeb	Officer-In-Charge	01/07/1972
Norman J. Bond	Officer-In-Charge	06/30/1972
William H. Grubb, Jr.	Officer-In-Charge	11/24/1972
William H. Grubb, Jr.	Postmaster	03/17/1973
Elmer O. Etters	Officer-In-Charge	04/20/1979
John C. McCullough	Postmaster	07/28/1979
Richard F. Nye	Officer-In-Charge	08/29/1980
Ralph J. Duncan	Postmaster	11/29/1980
Clair Wayne Galentine	Postmaster	08/03/1985
Lydia A. Harper	Postmaster	06/30/1990
Paris R. Washington	Officer-In-Charge	00/00/1993
Mabel Gerea Hayman	Postmaster	03/06/1993
Joseph J. Quinones	Postmaster	11/08/1997
Lawrence T. McCarthy	Postmaster	03/27/1999

Source: United States Postal Service Historian Corporate Information Services, Washington, D.C., June 1999

Appendix C
Chiefs of Police of Falls Church

Town Sergeant prior to 1948	Elliott H. Howe
May 1948–November 1959	
November 1959–June 30, 1968	George E. Simpson
July 1, 1968–July 16, 1968	Milton J. Robertson
July 17, 1968–March 1973	Robert T. Wheeler
March 1973–January 1974	Ralph L. Adams
January 1974–February 1979	John E. Drass
February 1979–February 1994	Stanley K. Johnson
February 1994–June 1994	Timothy M. Toureau
June 1994–present	Robert T. Murray

Source: Linda Briscoe, Falls Church, Virginia, June 18, 1999

Appendix D
City Managers of Falls Church

City Manager	Term
Roy Braden	c. 1949
W. R. Woodbury	October 1, 1950–January 28, 1957
Lewis Z. Johnston, Jr.	June 1, 1957–November 1, 1963
Harry E. Wells	March 1, 1964–October 15, 1983
Anthony H. Griffin	October 15, 1983–August 25, 1989
John V. Doane	April 27, 1990–August 10, 1992
David R. Lasso	February 2, 1993–October 4, 1996
Hector A. Rivera	May 1, 1997–August 20, 1999
Willie Best (acting)	August 20, 1999–May 31, 2000
Daniel E. McKeever	June 1, 2000

Source: Elizabeth-Anne Shawen, City Clerk, June 1999; Kathleen Buschow, City Clerk, January 2000

Appendix E
Boards and Commissions of Falls Church and Dates of Establishment

Falls Church residents serve on boards and commissions in an advisory capacity to the City Council whose members appoint them.

Architectural Advisory Board (Code Sec. 2.4, October 14, 1968)

Historic Architectural Review Board (Code 38–39, Ord. 1072, 1388 and 1465, May 29, 1984)

Cable TV Access Corporation (Articles of Incorporation, 1983)

City Employees Review Board (Ord. 934, Chap. 25.50, August 4, 1980)

Board of Equalization (State Code Sec. 58–895, April 9, 1951)

Girls' Home Citizens Advisory Committee (Res. 91–4, March 11, 1991)

Historical Commission (Res. June 28, 1965)

Housing Commission (Ord. 709, 1041, November 10, 1975)

Human Services Advisory Council (Res. 91–18, October 28, 1991)

Industrial Development Authority (Chap. 39, July 13, 1981)

Library Board of Trustees (Code Sec. 17.1, Ord. 800, December 12, 1977)

Planning Commission (Charter Sec. 17.02, 1952)

Private School and Day Care Facility Board (Code Sec. 28.2, March 10, 1972)

Public Safety and Human Relations Advisory Commission (Res. 88–26, May 25, 1970)

Recreation and Parks Advisory Board (Charter Sec. 16.06, Ord. 974, 1950)

Recycling and Litter Prevention Council (Res. 89–35, 90–5, September 25, 1989)

Retirement Board (Chap. 25, Sec. 25–63, Ord. 1097, October 23, 1967)

Senior Citizens Commission (Res. 76–3, January 26, 1976)

Transportation, Citizens Advisory Committee (Res. 82–3, Res. 83–8, November 12, 1976)

Tree Commission (Ord. 811, Chap. 35, Sec. 8, March 27, 1978)

Women, Commission for (Res. 76–42, 80–51, 82–48, 89–4, August 30, 1976)

Zoning Appeals, Board of (Charter Sec. 17.15, 1954)

Regional Boards and Commissions

Community Development Citizens Advisory Committee

Fairfax Area Disability Services Board (Sec. 51–5–47 Virginia Code)

Fairfax Commission on Aging

Fairfax-Falls Church Community Services Board (JR May 1969)

Health Systems Agency of Northern Virginia (Agreement)

Metropolitan Washington Council of Governments

Northern Virginia Community College (Agreement)

Northern Virginia Juvenile Detention Home Commission (Res. January 1955)

Northern Virginia Planning District Commission (Agreement)

Northern Virginia Regional Park Authority (concurrent Res.)

Northern Virginia Transportation Commission

Private Industry Council Job Training Partnership Act

Woodburn Community Mental Health Center Board

Source: Elizabeth-Anne Shawen, City Clerk, June 1999

Appendix F
Village Improvement Society and Village Preservation and Improvement Society Presidents

Village Improvement Society, 1885–1919

    W. H. Doolittle
    Rev. David Hoge Riddle
    Rev. Benjamin W. Pond
    Samuel V. Proudfit
    Ambrose E. Rowell
    Elida C. Hough
    George A. L. Merrifield
    Albert P. Eastman
    Levi B. parker
    Tunis C. Quick, M.D.
    George W. Hawxhurst
    George B. Fadeley
    Merton E. Church
    Rev. Franklin Noble
    Harry Andrew Fellows
    George W. Mankin
    William M. Ellison
    Charles A. Stewart
    Samuel E. Hutton
    Edward T. Fenwick
    John Franklin Bethune
    Henry Knowles

Village Preservation and Improvement Society, 1965–1999

    Mel Hallin Bolster
    Elwood Vickers Street
    Owen T. Jones
    Robert R. Perry
    Richard F. Fralick
    Robert L. Hubble
    Frank B. Avery, Jr.
    Louis T. Olom
    George R. Long
    Edward B. Strait
    Merl Marshall Moore
    Lewis W. Shollenberger, Jr.
    Susanne Bachtel
    Rowland T. Bowers
    Raymond C. Stewart
    Charles Lewis King
    Charles Marshall Moore
    David George Eckert
    Cynthia Garner
    Edwin B. Henderson, II
    John M. Maier

Source: Susanne Bachtel and David Eckert, May 1999

Appendix G
Friends of Cherry Hill Foundation Presidents
(Formed in 1976. Incorporated in 1977.)

Mildred Pope	1977
Merelyn Kaye	1978
Ruby Bolster	1979
Nancy Alsfelder	1980–1983
Audrey Kelley	1984–1986
Betty Hughes Melton	1987–1989
Mary Millspaugh	1990–1991
Shirley Camp	1992–1993
Betsy Johnson	1994
Betty Hughes Melton and Joan Burgess	1998
Maureen Budetti	1999

Source: Diane Morse, Cherry Hill Coordinator, June 1999

A list of current community organizations and local churches is available in the Local History Room at the Mary Styles Public Library.

End Notes

Introduction
1. Maurice Terman. "Stepping Stones on the Trail Through Falls Church History." Unpublished paper, 1995, p. 1.
2. Information provided by Shirley Street, arborist for the City of Falls Church. It was printed in a program for a Professor Thaddeus Lowe Civil War balloon marker ceremony on May 16, 1999. The original event took place at Fort Taylor (Seven Corners) on June 24–25, 1861.
3. Interviews with archaeologists Michael Johnson and Martha Williams, January 27, 1999.
4. Reverend Joseph Hodge Alves and Mr. Harold Spelman. *Near the Falls*. Falls Church, Va.: The Falls Church, 1969, pp. 3–4.

Chapter I. Buffalo Trails and Indian Paths
1. Stephen R. Potter, *Commoners, Tribute and Chiefs: The Development of Algonquian Culture in the Potomac River Valley*. Charlottesville and London: University Press of Virginia, 1993, pp. 1, 4, 9, 11.
2. Captain John Smith. *The Generall Historie of Virginia, New England and the Summer Isles*. London: Printed by I. D. and I. H. for Michael Sparkes, 1624, pp. 20–40, 55–77.
3. Potter, *Commoners*, p. 11.
4. Ibid., pp. 48–102; archaeologist Martha Williams, consultant to the City of Falls Church, interview with Nan Netherton, January 27, 1999.
5. Henry Fleet's writings quoted in Fairfax Harrison, *Landmarks of Old Prince William*. Berryville, Va.: Chesapeake Book Bo., 1964, pp. 143, 148.
6. Donald M. Sweig, in Nan Netherton, Donald M. Sweig, Janice Artemel, Patricia Hickin and Patrick Reed, *Fairfax County, Virginia: A History*. Fairfax, Va.: Fairfax County Board of Supervisors, 1978, pp. 5–6.
7. Melvin Lee Steadman, Jr. *Falls Church, Virginia: By Fence and Fireside*. Falls Church, Va.: Falls Church Public Library, 1964, pp. iii, x.
8. Harrison, *Landmarks*, pp. 148, 480.
9. Ibid., p. 399.
10. Ibid., pp. 147–148.
11. Ibid., p. 405.

Chapter II. A Church "At The Cross Roads Near Michael Reagan's"
1. Alves and Spelman. *Near the Falls*, p. 3.
2. Ibid.
3. Ibid., p. 7; Harrison, *Landmarks*, pp. 285–287.
4. Alves and Spelman. *Near the Falls*, pp. 3, 8–11, 98–99.
5. Ibid., pp. 97–98.
6. Sweig in Netherton, et al., *Fairfax County*, p. 6.
7. Martha Beggs Orth, *The House That John Built*. Arlington, Va.: Privately published, 1993, pp. 1–3; Calder Loth, *Virginia Landmarks Register*, Third Edition. Charlottesville: University Press of Virginia, 1987, p. 37.
8. Orth, *House That John Built*, p. 5.
9. Ross Netherton. *Braddock's Campaign and the Potomac Route to the West*. Falls Church, Va.: Higher Education Publications, Inc., 1989 reprint, pp. 1–2.
10. Ibid., pp. 3–5.
11. Lee McCardell. *Ill-Starred General: Braddock of the Coldstream Guards*. Pittsburgh: University of Pennsylvania Press, 1958, pp. 166.
12. Isabel M. Calder, ed. *Colonial Captivities, Marches and Journeys*. "The Journal of Charlotte Browne, matron of the general hospital with the English Forces in America, 1754–1756." New York, 1935; Fairfax Harrison, "With Braddock's Army: Mrs. Browne's Diary in Virginia and Maryland." *Virginia Magazine of History and Biography*, Vol. xxxii, Oct. 1924, No. 4, pp. 310–311.
13. Interview with 83-year-old William Nathan Lynch by Jay Oliver published in his column, "The Solarium," *The Sun*, October 21, 1938.
14. Alves and Spelman. *Near the Falls*, pp. 12–13.
15. Ibid.
16. Janice Artemel. James Wren. An unpublished paper in the Mary Riley Styles Public Library, Local History Room.
17. Fairfax County Court Order Book II, 1765–1768, p. 782.
18. Alves and Spelman. *Near the Falls*, p. 15; John C. Fitzpatrick, A.M. ed. *The Diaries of George Washington, 1748–1799*, Vol. 1, 1748–1770, p. 369, "Ledger A," March 19, 1770.
19. Sweig in Netherton, et al., *Fairfax County*, p. 103.
20. Steadman, *Fence and Fireside*, pp. 441–444.

Chapter III. A War For Independence
1. Emily J. Salmon and Edward D. C. Campbell, Jr., eds., *The Hornbook of Virginia History* (Richmond: The Library of Virginia, 1994), pp. 27–29.
2. Netherton, *Fairfax County*, pp. 102–103; Tony P. Wrenn, *Falls Church: History of a Virginia Village* (Falls Church: Falls Church Historical Commission, 1972), p. 6.
3. Salmon, *Hornbook*, p. 29; Wrenn, *Falls Church*, p. 6.
4. Salmon, *Hornbook*, pp. 29–30.
5. Netherton, *Fairfax County*, pp. 116–117.
6. Wrenn, *Falls Church*, p. 6; Melvin Lee Steadman, Jr., *By Fence and Fireside* (Falls Church: Falls Church Historical Commission, 19, p. 46. The Rev. Edward L. Goodwin, "Washington as a Vestryman," in *Colonial Churches*, Richmond, Virginia: Southern Churchman Co., 1907, pp. 107–121, refers to the Truro Parish Vestry Book and General George Washington's letter to Daniel McCarty, Esq., signifying his resignation as vestryman.
7. Wrenn, *Falls Church*, p. 6.

Chapter IV. A Federal Seat of Government
1. Alves and Spelman. *Near the Falls*. pp. 23–24.
2. Steadman. *Fence and Fireside*, pp. 92–99.
3. *Northern Virginia Sun*, May 3, 1969, p. 3.
4. Junior League of Washington, D.C., ed. Thomas Froncek, *The City of Washington*. New York: Alfred A. Knopf, 1977, pp. 48–49.
5. Arlington County Board Minutes, August 3, 1996; Falls Church City Council Minutes, September 9, 1996; and Fairfax County Board of Supervisors Minutes, November 23, 1998. National Register of Historic Places, February 1, 1991.
6. *Alexandria Gazette*, June 21, 1798.
7. Donald Beekman Myer. *Bridges and the City of Washington*. Washington, D.C.: U.S. Commission of Fine Arts, 1974, pp. v, 1, 3.
8. Dumas Malone. *Jefferson the President: First Term, 1801–1805*, Vol. 4, Boston: Little, Brown and Company, 1970, p. 34.
9. *The Papers of James Madison, Vol. I, 4 March 31-July 1, 1801*. Eds.: Robert J. Brugger, Robert Rhodes Crout, Dru Dowdy, Robert A. Rutland and Jeanne K. Sisson. Charlottesville: University Press of Virginia, 1986, pp. 126–127.
10. Jonathon Lovett map, 1801, Geography and Map Division, Library of Congress.

Chapter V. The War of 1812: Gunpowder and Refugees
1. Benson J. Lossing, *The Pictorial Field Book of the War of 1812* (New York: Harper & Bros., 1868), p. 919.
2. Anthony S. Pitch, *The Burning of Washington: The British Invasion of 1814* (Annapolis: Naval Institute Press, 1998), pp. 39–40; Netherton, et. al., Fairfax County, pp. 224–225.
3. Netherton, et. al., *Fairfax County*, p. 225; Taylor Peck, *Round-Shot to Rockets: A History of the Washington Navy Yard . . .* (Annapolis: United States Naval Institute, 1949), p. 54.
4. Netherton, et. al., *Fairfax County*, pp. 226–227; *American State Papers*, Class V, Military Affairs, pp. 568–569.
5. Ibid., p. 226; and Report of September 10, 1814 by Mordecai Booth on the removal of gunpowder from the Washington Navy Yard, Record Group 45, National Archives and Records Administration.
6. Netherton, et. al., *Fairfax County*, p. 226; Peck, *Round-Shot to Rockets*, pp. 56–57; and Report by Mordecai Booth, September 10, 1814.
7. Lossing, *War of 1812*, p. 935; Netherton, et. al., *Fairfax County*, pp. 226–227.
8. Peck, *Round-Shot to Rockets*, pp. 58–59; Report of Mordecai Booth, September 10, 1814.
9. Peck, *Round-Shot to Rockets*, pp. 58–59; Charles G. Muller, *The Darkest Day: 1814: The Washington-Baltimore Campaign* (Philadelphia: J. B. Lippincott Co., 1963), p. 139; and Report by Mordecai Booth, September 10, 1814.
10. Report by Mordecai Booth, September 10, 1814.
11. Netherton, et. al., *Fairfax County*, pp. 226–227.
12. Lossing, *War of 1812*, p. 933; Pitch, *Burning of Washington*, pp. 124–125.
13. Pitch, *Burning of Washington*, p. 128.
14. Ibid., pp. 128–129.
15. Peck, *Round-Shot to Rockets*, pp. 62–63; Pitch, *Burning of Washington*, pp. 126–127; and Report by Mordecai Booth, September 10, 1814.
16. Pitch, *Burning of Washington*, pp. 127–128; Report by Mordecai Booth, September 10, 1814.
17. Peck, *Round-Shot to Rockets*, pp. 63–65; Pitch, *Burning of Washington*, pp. 172–173; Report by Mordecai Booth, September 10, 1814.

Chapter VI. Internal Improvements
1. Ross Netherton, lecture, "Trails, Rails, and Turnpikes," Falls Church History Symposium, 1995.
2. Ibid.
3. Ibid.
4. Ibid.

5. Benjamin Shreve, typescript, 1934, Benjamin Shreve Papers, Manuscript Division of the Library of Congress, Washington, D.C.; David L. Meyer, lecture, "Village Beginnings: The Role of the Churches (1784–1860)," Falls Church History Symposium, 1995.
6. Ella C. Belz, *Falls Church Presbyterian Church, 1873–1973* (Falls Church: Falls Church Presbyterian Church, 1976), pp. 3–9.
7. Charles A. Stuart, unpublished manuscript, 1937, Virginia Historical Society, Richmond, Va.; Bette Warden, lecture, "James Wren and His Times," Falls Church History Symposium, 1995.
8. Stuart, unpublished manuscript; Augustine Bowyer Williams Papers, manuscript, 1831, Virginia Historical Society, Richmond, Va.
9. Meyer, lecture, 1995.
10. Fairfax Harrison, *A History of the Legal Development of the Railroad System of the Southern Railway Company* (Washington; [publisher unknown], 1901), pp. 532–534; and Netherton, lecture.
11. Bruce McCoy, lecture, "A New Nation and a New Era," Falls Church History Symposium, 1995.
12. Netherton, *Fairfax County*, pp. 153–153, 176–177.
13. *Falls Church, Virginia: Architectural Legacy*, pp. 9–13; C. Richard Bierce, lecture, "The Village Legacy of Architecture," Falls Church History Symposium, 1995; Netherton, lecture, 1995.
14. Netherton, *Fairfax County*, pp. 310–312.

Chapter VII. Balloons and Minie Balls
1. Bowman, *Almanac of the Civil War*, p. 55. *See also* Southern Claims Commission file for Philip H. Minor in Record Group 217, National Archives.
2. Benjamin Franklin Cooling III, *Symbol, Sword, and Shield: Defending Washington During the Civil War* (Hamden, Conn.: Archon Books, 1975), p. 45.
3. James E. Smith, *A Famous Battery and its Campaigns . . .*; Lewis G. Schmidt, *47th Regiment of Pennsylvania Veteran Volunteers*, p. 65. (Washington: Lowdermilk & Co., 1892), pp. 13–15.
4. Betty-Jo Dawkins and Walter E. Bass, *Columbia Baptist Church, Falls Church, Virginia, 1856–1981* (Falls Church: Columbia Baptist Church, 1981), p. 13.
5. Salmon, *Hornbook*, p. 47; Netherton, Fairfax County, p. 337.
6. Journal, June 20, 1861, Samuel Heintzelman Papers, Manuscript Division of the Library of Congress, Washington, D.C.; Smith, A Famous Battery, pp. 13–15.
7. Smith, *A Famous Battery*, pp. 26–27.
8. *The Charleston [S.C.] Mercury*, June 26, 1861; Alfred S. Roe, *The Fifth Regiment, Massachusetts Volunteer Infantry in its Three Tours of Duty . . .* (Boston: Fifth Regiment Veteran Association, 1911), p. 54.
9. Netherton, *Fairfax County*, p. 325.
10. Ibid., p. 343.
11. Harris Andrews, "Life on the Edge: the Falls Church Region During the Civil War," lecture, Falls Church History Symposium; Harrie Webster Papers, Manuscript Division of the Library of Congress, Washington, D.C.
12. James Longstreet, *From Manassas to Appomattox: Memoirs of the Civil War in America* (Philadelphia: J. B. Lippincott Co., 1896), pp. 59–62.
13. Ibid.
14. *Official Records*, series 1, volume 5, p. 183; Haydon, *Aeronautics*, pp. 210–211.
15. Wat Banks Papers, Accession 1571, Box 2, folder 1861, Hargrett Rare Book and Manuscript Library, University of Georgia, Athens, Ga.; F. Stansbury Haydon, *Aeronautics in the Union and Confederate Armies . . .* (Baltimore: The Johns Hopkins Press, 1941), p. 212; Charles H. Banes, *History of the Philadelphia Brigade* (Philadelphia: J. B. Lippincott Co., 1876), p. 20.
16. W. H. Andrews, *Footprints of a Regiment: A Recollection of the 1st Georgia Regulars, 1861–1865* (Marietta, Ga.: Longstreet Press, 1992), pp. 18–19; [Author unknown], *History of the Seventeenth Va. Infantry* (Baltimore: Kelly, Piet & Co., 1870), p. 39.
17. Haydon, *Aeronautics*, p. 211, *n.* 55; *The New York Herald*, January 5, 1862.
18. *The New York Herald*, January 5, 1862; Heintzelman journal, September 29, 1861.
19. John Harrison Mills, *Chronicles of the Twenty-First Regiment, New York State Volunteers* (Buffalo: 21st Regiment Veteran Association of Buffalo, 1887), p. 120; Pound Sterling, *Campfires of the Twenty-Third: Sketches of the Camp Life, Marches and Battles . . .* (New York: Davies & Kent, 1863), p. 35; Joseph Hodge Alves, *Near the Falls: Two Hundred Years of The Falls Church* (Falls Church: The Falls Church, 1969), pp. 37–38.
20. Carl A. Morrell, *Seymour Dexter, Union Army* (Jefferson, N.C.: McFarland & Co., 1996), pp. 59–60.
21. L. P. Brockett, *Woman's Work in the Civil War: A Record of Heroism, Patriotism and Patience* (Boston: R. H. Curran, 1867), pp. 468–470, 741–742; Pardoe-Robinson Papers, U.S. Army Military History Institute, Carlisle Barracks, Pa.
22. Walter Erwin testimony before the Southern Claims Commission, Record Group 217, National Archives and Records Administration.
23. The *Charleston Mercury* reporting a dispatch in the *Philadelphia Inquirer*, September 10, 1862.
24. Frederick Phisterer, *New York in the War of the Rebellion, 1861 to 1865* (Albany: F. B. Lyon Co., 1912), p. 149; Richard N. Scott, ed., *The War of the Rebellion: A Compilation of the Official Records of the Union and Confederate Armies* [hereafter cited as Official Records] (Washington: Government Printing Office, 1881–91), Volume V, pp. 441–442.
25. John Chipman Hoadley, *Memorial of Henry Sanford Gansevoort* (Boston: Franklin Press: Rand, Avery, & Co., 1875), pp. 163–164, 167, 232–233; James J. Williamson, *Mosby's Rangers: A Record of the Operations of the Forty-[?] Battalion of Virginia Cavalry . . .* (New York: Sturgis & Walton Co., 1909), p. 232.
26. Hoadley, *Gansevoort*, pp. 182–183; Phisterer, *New York*, p. 261; Williamson, *Mosby's Rangers*, p. 271; Dawkins, *Columbia Baptist Church*, pp. 325–331.
27. Theodore B. Gates, *The "Ulster Guard" [20th New York State Militia] and the War of the Rebellion* (New York: Benjamin H. Tyrrel, 1879), pp. 160, 166; Brockett, *Woman's Work*, pp. 468–470; Seward R. Osborne, *The Civil War Diaries of Col. Theodore B. Gates, 20th New York State Militia* (Highstown, N.J.: Longstreet House, 1991), p. 12; James Harvey McKee, *Back "In War Times," History of the 144th Regiment, New York Volunteer Infantry* (New York: Horace E. Bailey, 1903), pp. 73, 76; Mills, *Chronicles*, p. 137; C. Van Santvoord, *The One Hundred and Twentieth Regiment, New York State Volunteers* (Rondout, N.Y.: Press of the Kingston Freeman, 1894), p. 28.

Chapter VIII. A Sense of Community
1. Charles A. Stewart, *A Virginia Village*. Falls Church, Va.: Press of J. H. Newell, 1904, pp. 33, 77–84.
2. Patrick Reed in Netherton, et. al., *Fairfax County, Virginia: A History*. Fairfax County, Va.: Board of Supervisors, 1978, pp. 395–397.
3. Announcement. "Rules for Government Schools" dated March 6th, 1871, signed by D. McC. Chichester, Clerk. Mary Riley Styles Library.
4. Ames W. Williams. *Washington & Old Dominion Railroad, 1847–1968*. Washington, D.C.: Capital Traction Quarterly, 1970, p. 27. The day was November 12, 1873.
5. *Virginia Acts of Assembly*, Chap. 316, March 30, 1875. Act of Incorporation and Charter of Town of Falls Church, Fairfax County, Va.
6. Falls Church Town Council Minute Books (TCMB) I, p. 2, April 13, 1875.
7. TCMB, I, pp. 4–5, June 10, 1875.
8. TCMB, I, pp. 5, 7–9, 11, July 1, Aug. 1 and 20, 1875.
9. TCMB, I, July 11, 1876; May 28, Aug. 6, Nov. 12, 1877; April 22, May 27, July 22, 1878; June 28, Aug. 11, Sept. 8, 1879; April 5, May 3, July 1, 1880; Sept. 5, 1881; June 8, July 7, 1882; and June 2, 1884, elected to Council for two-year term.
10. TCMB, I, Aug. 7, p. 49, Nov. 27, p. 62, 1876; May 21, 1877, p. 84.
11. TCMB, I, Oct. 30, 1876, p. 59; Feb. 5, 1877, p. 66.
12. TCMB, I, p. 290, Oct. 2, 1882.
13. TCMB, I, July 17, 1876.
14. TCMB, I, Aug. 19, 1878.
15. TCMB, I, Oct. 6, 1879, p. 192.
16. TCMB, I, Oct. 6, 1879.
17. *Alexandria Gazette*, Oct. 1882.
18. TCMB, I, Feb. 7, 1880; Feb. 7, 1881, pp. 251–252; May 17, 1884.
19. TCMB, I, Dec. 3, 1879, pp. 212–213; Feb. 2, April 5, 1880; Dec. 22, 1881.
20. TCMB, 2, July 20, Oct. 9, 1899.
21. "Brown's Hardware Starts Second Century." Falls Church Historical Commission Annual Report, 1985, pp. 4–5. E. J. Birch was still listed as owner in mercantile records in 1883.
22. Stewart, *Virginia Village*, pp. 16–18.
23. *Virginia Acts of Assembly*, Extra Session, 1887, p. 462, May 21, 1887.
24. Maurice Terman. "Stepping Stones on the Trail Through Falls Church History." Unpublished paper written in 1995, p. 6.
25. *Virginia Acts of Assembly*, Feb. 29, 1888.
26. *Fairfax Herald*, June 12, 1891, p. 3.
27. Stewart, *Virginia Village*, pp. 89–92; Steadman, Falls Church, pp. 284–285.

Chapter IX. The Summer Soldiers of 1898: Falls Church and Camp Alger
1. William C. Cammann, et. al. *The History of Troop "A," New York Cavalry U.S.V. . . , in the Spanish-American War* (New York: R. H. Russell, 1899), p. 34.
2. Noel Garraux Harrison, *City of Canvas: Camp Russell A. Alger and the Spanish-American War* (Falls Church: Falls Church Historical Commission and Fairfax County History Commission, 1988), p. 5.
3. Cammann, *History of Troop "A,"* p. 55; Harrison, *City of Canvas*, p. 78; "Diary of Samual Adams," June 14, 1898, *The Kansas Historical Quarterly*, Winter 1970, p. 409; *Report of the Adjutant General of the State of Missouri, 1897–98*, pp. 36–37, 130–132; and Anthony Fiala, *Troop "C" in Service*, pp. 42–45, 48.
4. Ibid., pp. 46, 66; James Cooper, *Campaign of the First Troop, Philadelphia City Cavalry . . . 1898* (Philadelphia: Hallowell Co., Ltd., 1898), p. 46.
5. Cammann, *History of Troop "A,"* pp. 66–68.
6. Op. cit., pp. 52–54.
7. Frank E. Edwards, *The '98 Campaign of the 6th Massachusetts, U.S.V.* (Boston: Little, Brown & Co., 1899), pp. 34, 38–39.

8. Fiala, *Troop "C" in Service*, pp. 32–34; Edwards, *The '98 Campaign*, p. 26; Cammann, *History of Troop "A,"* pp. 47–49; and Ruby Weedell Waldeck, "Missouri in the Spanish American War," *The Missouri Historical Review*, vol. XXX, 1936, p. 399.
9. Fiala, *Troop "C" in Service*, p. 33; Harrison, *City of Canvas*, p. 30; Netherton, *Fairfax County*, p. 464.
10. "Diary of Samual Adams," July 4, 1898, *The Kansas Historical Quarterly*, p. 413; Cammann, *History of Troop "A,"* p. 69; and letter of Aaron Ward Hartley, July 9, 1898, published in *The Democrat* [Meigs County, Ohio], July 13, 1898.
11. Harrison, *City of Canvas*, p. 74.

Chapter X. Domestic Tranquility
1. TCMB, 2, Dec. 12, 1898, p. 21; Mar. 17, 1899, p. 37; June 26, 1899, p. 41; July 3, 1899, purchase.
2. Stewart, *Virginia Village*, pp. 85–88.
3. Ibid., p. 88.
4. *Fairfax Herald*, Dec. 8, 1899; Steadman, *Falls Church*, pp. 143–144.
5. TCMB, 2. Aug. 7, 1899, p. 48.
6. TCMB, 2. July 30, 1899, p. 44; Aug. 14, 1899, p. 55.
7. TCMB, 2. May 13, 1901, p. 127.
8. TCMB, 2. Nov. 11, 1901, p. 145.
9. Tony P. Wrenn. *Falls Church: History of a Virginia Village*. Falls Church, Va.: Historical Commission of the City of Falls Church, 1972, p. 35; letters from James Thurber to Mrs. Frank Acosta of Falls Church in 1958 and 1959.
10. Noel G. Harrison. Along the Tracks: Northern Fairfax County's First Electric Railway. Unpublished research report prepared for the Falls Church Historical Commission, 1986, p. 12.
11. *Catalogue of Books, Falls Church Library*. Library Association, 1903.
12. Stewart, *Virginia Village*, p. 86.
13. Wrenn, *Falls Church*, pp. 14–15.
14. *Falls Church Handbook*, 1998–1999, p. 19.
15. Charles Alexander Stewart. *Falls Church: A Virginia Village*. Falls Church: 1904, pp. 20–21.
16. Stewart, *Virginia Village*, pp. 21–22.
17. Ibid., p. 32.
18. Margaret K. Castorina. *St. James School, 1906–1981*. Falls Church, Va.: The 75th Anniversary Committee, 1981; Anne Donovan Goodson. A Brief History of St. James Catholic Church. Report prepared for the Falls Church Tricentennial Committee, 1999, p. 3.
19. TCMB, 3, Sept. 10, 1910, p. 45.
20. *Official Program*, Independence Day Celebration, July 4, 1911. Village Improvement Society, p. 6.
21. TCMB, 3. Feb. 12, 1912, p. 111.
22. TCMB, 3. April 8, 1912, p. 114.
23. TCMB, 3. Dec. 14, 1914, p. 216.
24. TCMB, 3. Jan 11, 1915.
25. TCMB, 3, June 28, 1915, Oct. 19, 1915, p. 242.
26. Dr. E. B. Henderson, *History of the Fairfax County Branch of the NAACP*. Fairfax County, Va.: 1965. E. B. Henderson, in addition to working toward interracial understanding, also wrote two books about the Negro in sports in the United States.
27. Richard B. Morris. *Encyclopedia of American History*. New York: Harper & Row, publishers, 1976, pp. 524–535, 679, 773. The 1915 ordinance was finally repealed by resolution of the Falls Church City Council in February 1999, during Black History Month.

Chapter XI. The Great War
1. Edward Grey, First Viscount of Fallodon, *Twenty-Five Years, 1892–1916* (New York: Frederick A. Stokes Co., 1925), vol. 2, p. 20.
2. *Fairfax Herald*, May 25, 1917, p. 2; June 8, 1917, p. 2; June 15, 1917, p. 2.
3. Ibid., June 15, 1917, p. 2; Telegram ca. April 17, 1917, #2475831N, Record Group 94, Records of the Adjutant General's Office, 1890–1917, National Archives and Records Administration.
4. *Fairfax Herald*, Nov. 30, 1917 p. 2; Dec. 7, 1917, p. 3; Dec. 21, 1917, Supplement page 2; Feb. 1, 1918, p. 3; Feb. 8, 1918, p. 3; Feb. 15, 1918, p. 2; Aug. 2, 1918, p. 3; Dec. 13, 1918, p. 3.
5. Ibid., Jan 11, 1918, p. 2; Jan. 25, 1918; Feb. 1, 1918, p. 203; Feb. 8, 1918, p. 2; April 12, 1918, p. 3; May 3, 1918, p. 1.
6. Ibid., Sept. 21, 1917, p. 3; Feb. 22, 1918, p. 2; Mar. 1, 1918, p. 3; Mar. 8, 1918, p. 2; Mar. 22, 1918, p. 3; May 10, 1918, p. 2; June 21, 1918, p. 2; July 6, 1917.
7. Ibid., June 22, 1917, p. 2; Nov. 2, 1917, p. 3; Sept. 27, 1918, p. 3; and Arthur Kyle Davis, ed., *Virginia Communities in War Time* (Richmond: Executive Committee of the Virginia War History Commission, 1917), Source Vol. VII, p. 56.
8. *Fairfax Herald*, Aug. 31, 1917, p. 3; Sept. 7, 1917, p. 3; Oct. 26, 1917, p. 3; Nov. 9, 1917, p. 3; Feb. 8, 1918, p. 3; Mar. 29, 1918, p. 3; April 5, 1918, p. 3; April 19, 1918, p. 3; Aug. 16, 1918, p. 3; Aug. 30, 1918, p. 3; Sept. 6, 1918, p. 3; Dec. 27, 1918, p. 3; and Arthur Kyle Davis, ed., *Virginia War Agencies Selective Service and Volunteers* (Richmond: Executive Committee of the Virginia War History Commission, 1927), p. 323.
9. *The Monitor*, July 12, 1918, p. 1; *Fairfax Herald*, May 18, 1917, p. 2; Nov. 23, 1917, p. 4; May 31, 1918, p. 3; July 5, 1918, p. 3; July 12, 1918, p. 3; Sept. 20, 1918, p. 3; Sept. 27, 1918, p. 3; Nov. 15, 1918, p. 4.
10. U.S. Public Health Service, "Epidemic Influenze [sic] (Spanish Influenza)," Supplement No. 34 (Washington: Government Printing Office, 1918), p. 4; *Fairfax Herald*, Oct. 11, 1918, p. 3; Oct. 25, 1918, p. 3; Nov. 1, 1918, p. 3.
11. Letter, Merton E. Church to Percy B. Tripp, June 14, 1918, Merton E. Church file, Virginia Room, Mary Riley Styles Public Library, Falls Church, Va.

Chapter XII. The Great Depression and Inter-War Years
1. Interview with Tyler M. Birch, March 19, 1979, Virginia Room, Mary Riley Styles Public Library, Falls Church, Va.
2. Editorial, "The Lee Highway," from unidentified and undated Washington, D.C. newspaper. E. Lee Trimble Papers, Box 22. The Library of Virginia, Richmond, Va.
3. Letter drom Dr. S. M. Johnson, general director of the Lee Highway Association to President Warren G. Harding, June 1, 1923. Warren G. Harding Papers, Manuscript Division of the Library of Congress, Washington, D.C.
4. National Highway Association. *Lee Highway: The Backbone Road of the South* (New York: The Association, 1930), p. 1.
5. Letter from the Lee Highway Association to Percy B. Tripp, ca. 1924. Merton E. Church Papers, Box 2. Alderman Library of the University of Virginia, Charlottesville, Va.
6. Ibid., and *Fairfax Herald*, May 18, 1923, p. 5. For information on earlier good roads associations in Falls Church see the *Fairfax Herald*, May 31, 1918, p. 3; June 14, 1918, p. 3; July 19, 1918, p. 3; and Nov. 8, 1918, p. 3.
7. Letter of Merton E. Church to Dr. S. M. Johnson, general director, Lee Highway Association, Sept. 5, 1924. E. Lee Trimble Papers, Box 2, The Library of Virginia, Richmond, Va. According to a notation by Merton E. Church the Falls Church and Fairfax Court House committees paid the Lee Highway Association $3,915 during its first eight years. See the M. E. Church Papers, Box 1, Alderman Library of the University of Virginia, Charlottesville, Va.
8. Letter of Merton E. Church to Dr. S. M. Johnson, Sept. 5, 1924; and *The Washington Post*, Aug. 13, 1922, p. 10.
9. Ibid.
10. Letter of Dr. S. M. Johnson to President Warren G. Harding, June 1, 1923. Warren G. Harding Papers, Manuscript Divison of the Library of Congress, Washington, D.C.
11. *The Washington Post*, April 25, 1931, Lee Memorial Boulevard supplement, p. 3.
12. Ibid., and letter of C. W. Adams to Harry Flood Byrd, governor of Virginia, Aug. 1, 1926. Harry Flood Byrd Papers, Box 41, The Library of Virginia, Richmond, Va.
13. Noel G. Harrison, *Along the Tracks: Northern Fairfax County's First Electric Railway*, report for the Falls Church Historical Commission, 1986, pp. 58–60.
14. Falls Church TCMB, 1920–21.
15. Ibid., Oct. 11, 1920, p. 371; Nov. 8, 1920, p. 372; Jan 10, 1921, p. 375.
16. *The Sun*, Jan. 16, 1936, Jan. 30, 1936, Feb. 6, 1936, March 12, 1936, April 16, 1936, and *Arlington Historical Magazine*, Oct. 1957, vol. I, no. 1, p. 14.
17. Diane Morse, lecture, Falls Church History Symposium.
18. Falls Church Town Council Minute Books, vol. 6, Sept. 4, 1930, p. 5; Oct. 13, 1930, pp. 12–13.
19. Ibid., vol. 6, March 6, 1931, p. 48; June 19, 1931, p. 79.
20. *Falls Church Environmental Services Report*.
21. Op. cit., vol. 2, Aug. 12, 1901, p. 137; July 2, 1902, p. 167, ordinance.
22. Op. cit.
23. *The Sun*, April 16, 1936, May 7, 1936, and June 18, 1937; Arlington County Common Law Order Book 17, pp. 130 and 138.
24. *The Sun*, Dec. 12, 1935, Jan. 23, 1936, and Jan. 30, 1936.
25. *The Sun*, Feb. 6, 1936, May 7, 1936, March 11, 1938, and Aug. 19, 1938.
26. *The Sun*, March 26, 1936; Stephen E. Ambrose and Richard H. Immerman. *Milton S. Eisenhower: Educational Statesman* (Baltimore: The Johns Hopkins University Press, 1983), pp. 52, 58.

Chapter XIII. Mobilization and a Second World War
1. *Fairfax Herald*, Nov. 28, 1941, p. 1.
2. Joe Martin, unpublished paper, "Looking Over My Shoulder: An Autobiography of Joseph B. Martin," p. 40. Joe Oliver Martin Family file, Mary Riley Styles Library, Falls Church, Va.
3. *Fairfax Herald*, Dec. 12, 1941, p. 1.
4. Ibid., Jan. 16, 1942, p. 1.
5. Ibid., Aug. 21, 1942, p. 1.
6. Ibid., July 13, 1942, p. 1; Aug. 7, 1942, p. 1; Oct. 9, 1942, p. 1; Dec. 11 (p. 1) and 25 (p. 1), 1942; Feb. 19, 1943 (p. 1); Jan. 28, 1944, p. 1; and May 5, 1944, p. 1. See also Netherton, *Fairfax County*, p. 623.
7. *Fairfax Herald*, Aug. 27, 1943, p. 1
8. Ibid., Aug. 7, 1942, p. 1.

201

9. Ibid., Sept. 4, 1942, p. 1; [?]; Jan. 15, 1943, p. 1; Feb. 26, 1943, p. 1; April 16, 1943, p. 1; Sept. 24, 1943, p. 1; Nov. 26, 1943, p. 1; Jan. 21, 1944, p. 1; and Sept. 1, 1944, p. 1.
10. Ibid., Nov. 19, 1943, p. 1.
11. Ibid., Dec. 19, 1941, p. 1; *The Sun*, Dec. 12, 1941, p. 1.
12. Martin, unpublished paper, p. 40; *The Sun*, Dec. 19, 1941, Jan. 2, 1942, July 17, 1942, Aug. 7, 1942, Feb. 12, 1943, Mar. 5, 1943.
13. *Fairfax Herald*, Feb. 6, 1942, p. 1.
14. *Fairfax Herald*, Feb. 6, 1942, p. 1.
15. Ibid., May 1, 1942, p. 1.
16. Ibid., Oct. 2, 1942, p. 1; *The Sun*, April 10, 1942.
17. *Falls Church Echo*, June 27, 1942, p. 3; *The Sun*, July 16, 1943, p. 2.
18. *Fairfax Herald*, June 9, 1944, p. 1.
19. *Falls Church Echo*, Aug. 26, 1944, p. 6.
20. Dwight D. Eisenhower, *Crusade in Europe*, p. 24; Milton S. Eisenhower, *The President is Calling* (New York: Doubleday & Co., 1974), pp. 133–134; Ambrose and Immerman, *Milton S. Eisenhower: Educational Statesman* (Baltimore: The Johns Hopkins University Press, 1983), pp. 58, 66–68; personal statement by John Eisenhower to Bradley E. Gernand, July 12, 1998; and Steadman, *By Fence and Fireside*, p. 89.
21. *The Sun*, April 20, 194 [page unknown].
22. *Fairfax Herald*, April 16, 1943, p. 1.
23. Ibid., July 28, 1944, p. 1.
24. Ibid., Sept. 1, 1944, p. 1.
25. *GW Hatchet*, The George Washington University, Washington, D.C., April 7, 1997, p. 13.
26. *Fairfax Herald*, Aug. 4, 1944, p. 1.
27. Ibid., May 18, 1945, p. 1.
28. Ibid., June 8, 1945, p. 1; June 22, 1945, p. 1; and Nov. 23, 1945, p. 1.
29. Ibid., Nov. 16, 1945, pp. 1, 4.
30. Ibid., Nov. 28, 1941, p. 1.

Chapter XIV. Unparalleled Growth and Prosperity
1. *National Capital Area Realtor*, December 1961, p. 3.
2. *Fairfax County Sun-Echo* and *The Standard*, July 3, 1958.
3. Ibid.
4. Ibid.
5. Wayne Dexter. *CBC: Your Hometown Political Party, A History* (Falls Church: Citizens for a Better City, 1993), pp. 4–8; Steve Just, "CBC Offers Its New Year's Resolutions," *Falls Church News-Press*, Jan. 6, 2000.
6. Ibid., Dexter, *CBC*, pp. 2–4; *The Washington Post*, June 3, 8–9, 10–11, 13, 1951; *Washington Star*, June 13, 1951.
7. [Priscilla Reimers,] *Celebrating 40 Years: A History of the Falls Church School System* (Falls Church: Falls Church School System, 1989), pp. 3–9.
8. Ibid., p. 4.
9. Netherton, *Fairfax County*, pp. 578–581; "Schedule A," attached to deeds of ownership in the Virginia Forest section of the City of Falls Church. Copy in Mary Riley Styles Library; Tom Lewis, *Divided Highways: Building the Interstate Highways, Transforming American Life* (New York: Viking, 1997), p. 79.
10. Pamphlet, Tinner Hill Heritage Foundation, ca. 1997.

Chapter XV. Reconfirming Village Roots
1. "Proposed Development Plan, Crossroads Area, Falls Church, Virginia," LBC&W Consultants, Inc., March 1974.
2. Barry Campbell, opinion piece, *The Washington Post*, May 3, 1998, p. C3.
3. Statement by William T. Coleman, Jr., federal secretary of transportation, Aug. 1, 1975, p. 2. Record Group 406, Records of the Federal Highway Administration, Box 27, National Archives and Records Administration.
4. *Evening Star*, Jan. 11, 1955, and *The Washington Post*, Dec. 22, 1982.
5. *Evening Star*, Nov. 29, 1958.
6. Lewis, *Divided Highways*, p. 153; AASHTO Highway Subcommittee on Design, *A Policy on Design Standards*, pp. 4–5; and Moon, *The Interstate Highway System*, p. 18.
7. Op. cit., and same, Feb. 18, 1960.
8. *Washington Star*, Feb. 10, 18, and 24, 1960; and July 24, 1962.
9. Statement by Coleman, pp. 2–12.
10. John F. Iekel, "The Neighborhood That Was: The History of East Falls Church, Virginia," *The Arlington Historical Magazine*, vol. 10, no. 3, Oct. 1995, pp. 37–53.
11. Statement by the Hon. Louis H. Blair on behalf of the City of Falls Church, "Hearings Before the Commission, Virginia Department of Highways, in the Matter of the Results of the Interstate Route 66 Transportation Alternative Study," Dec. 18, 1973, vol. II, pp. II:46–II:51, Record Group 406, Box 24, National Archives and Records Administration.
12. *Washington Star*, Oct. 25, 1967.
13. Lewis, *Divided Highways*, p. 279.

14. Statements by John Maier, president of the Village Preservation and Improvement Society, and Michael Slonim, former chair of the Business Development Commission, *The Village Way*, Village Preservation and Improvement Society, vol. 30, no. 5, Sept. 1997.
15. City of Falls Church, *Adopted Streetscape Plan for West Broad Street*, Aug. 1987.
16. *Fairfax County Sun Echo*, March 29, 1962, and *Look* magazine, April 10, 1962.
17. Stuart W. Edwards, *Preservation Easements in Falls Church* (Falls Church: Historic Falls Church, Inc., 1977), pp. 1–3.

Chapter XVI. By, Of and For the People: Local Government
1. City of Falls Church, Virginia *Annual Report, Services Guide and 1999 Calendar*.
2. Ibid.
3. [Reimers,] *Celebrating 50 Years*, pp. 13, 14, 17, 19, 20, 22, 23, 24, 25, 29, 30, 31; *Ten Years, 1951–1961*. Annual Report of Lewis Z. Johnston, Jr., City Manager, for the year July 1, 1960, to June 30, 1961, p. 3.
4. [Reimers,] *Celebrating 50 Years*, p. 27.
5. Mary Beth Franklin. "St. James Named One of 266 Blue Ribbon Schools in U.S." *Falls Church News-Press*, June 17, 1999, p. 1.
6. Reimers, *Celebrating 50 Years*, p. 5.
7. *Falls Church Adopted City Budget for Fiscal Year 1998–1999*.
8. Monthly Minutes of the Falls Church Historical Commission, Mary Riley Styles Library.
9. Interview with director Howard Herman, Community Center, March 13, 1999.
10. *Falls Church News-Press*, April 22, 1999, p. 9.
11. Annette Mills, Falls Church Recycle Center Summary Report, September 3, 1999.
12. Johnston, *Ten Years*, 1951–1961, p. 3.

A Selected Bibliography

Unpublished Primary Sources

Abbott, L. S. papers. Manuscript Division of the Library of Congress, Washington, D.C. Abbott was an 19th Century Falls Church Farmer.

Adjutant General's Office records, Record Group 94. National Archives and Records Administration, Washington, D.C.

American Institute of Aeronautics and Astronautics records. Manuscript Division of the Library of Congress, Washington, D.C. Contains the papers of Thaddeus S. C. Lowe.

Andrews, Harris. Lecture, "Life on the Edge: the Falls Church Region During the Civil War," Falls Church History Symposium, 199?.

Banks Family Papers. Hargrett Rare Book and Manuscript Library, University of Georgia, AThens, Ga. Wat Banks was a Confederate soldier from Alabama who saw service in Falls Church during the Civil War.

Bierce, C. Richard. Lecture, "The Village Legacy of Architecture," Falls Church History Symposium, 1995.

Birch, Tyler M. Oral History Interview, March 19, 1979. Mary Riley Styles Library, Falls Church, Va.

Booker, James and John. Papers. University of Virginia. Charlottesville, Va. The Booker brothers were Confederate soldiers during the Civil War.

Booth, Mordecai. "Report." National Archives and Records Administration, Washington, D.C. Booth's report on events during the War of 1812 is the single best source of information concerning Falls Church.

Byrd, Harry Flood. Papers. Alderman Library, University of Virginia, Charlottesville, Va.

Church, Merton Elbridge. Papers. Mary Riley Styles Library, Falls Church, Va.

Cockburn, Martin. Papers. Manuscript Division of the Library of Congress, Washington, D.C.

Columbia Baptist Church. Minutes.

Eisenhower, John. Personal statement, 1998.

Fairfax Parish/Christ Church. Records. Virginia Room, Fairfax City Regional Library, Fairfax, Va.

Falls Church Jewish Women's Study Group. Records. Lillian and Albert Small Jewish Museum of the Jewish Historical Society of Greater Washington, Washington, D.C.

Falls Church Presbyterian Church. Minutes.

Falls Church Town and City Council. Minutes. Mary Riley Styles Public Library, Falls Church, Va., and City Hall.

Federal Highway Administration, Record Group 406. National Archives and Records Administration, Washington, D.C.

Green, Charles. Papers. Manuscript Division of the Library of Congress, Washington, D.C.

Harding, Warren G. Papers. Manuscript Division of the Library of Congress, Washington, D.C.

Hartley, Aaron Ward. Letter published in *The Democrat*, Meigs County, Ohio, July 13, 1898.

Hartley, Charles. Letter published in *Tribune-Telegraph*, Meigs County, Ohio, July 27, 1898.

Heintzelman, Samuel Peter. Papers. Manuscript Division of the Library of Congress, Washington, D.C.

Interstate Commerce Commission, Record Group. National Archives and Records Administration, Washington, D.C.

Lawton, Henry War. Papers. Manuscript Division of the Library of Congress, Washington, D.C.

Lowe, Thaddeus S.C. Papers. See American Institute of Aeronautics and Astronautics, Records.

Martin, Joe Oliver. Family Papers. Mary Riley Styles Library, Falls Church, Va.

McCoy, Bruce. Lecture, "A New Nation and a New Era," Falls Church History Symposium, 1995.

Meyer, David L. Lecture, "Village Beginnings: The Role of the Churches (1784–1860)," Falls Church History Symposium, 1995.

Morse, Diane. Lecture, "Civilians Under Siege: The Falls Church Home Front During the Civil War," Falls Church History Symposium, 1996.

Netherton, Ross. Lecture, "Trails, Rails, and Turnpikes," Falls Church History Symposium, 1995.

Pardoe-Robinson Papers. United States Army Military History Institute. Carlisle Barracks, Pa.

Sanborn Fire Insurance Maps. Geography and Map Division of the Library of Congress, Washington, D.C.

Shreve, Benjamin. Papers. Miscellaneous Manscripts Collection. Manuscript Division of the Library of Congress, Washington, D.C.

Southern Claims Commission, Record Group 217. National Archives and Records Administration, Washington, D.C. One of the best sources of information concerning the effects of the Civil War upon Falls Church.

Stuart, Charles A. Unpublished manuscript, "The Falls Church: The Old Colonial Church Near the Falls of the Potomac, 1733–1940." Virginia Historical Society, Richmond, Va. This manuscript offers a complete history of The Falls Church Episcopal from its beginning through 1940.

Trimble, E. Lee. Papers. The Library of Virginia, Richmond, Va.

Truro Parish, Records. Manuscript Division of the Library of Congress, Washington, D.C.

Warden, Bette. Lecture, "James Wren and His Times," Falls Church History Symposium, 1995.

Webster, Harrie. Papers. Naval Historical Foundation Collection. Manuscript Division of the Library of Congress, Washington, D.C. Webster was a resident of Falls Church as the Civil War began.

Williams, Augustine Bowyer. Papers. Virginia Historical Society, Richmond, Va. Bowyer was a Confederate soldier who saw service in Falls Church in the Civil War.

Published Sources

AASHTO Highway Subcommittee of Design. *A Policy on Design Standards*.

Aldous, Joan F. *The Civil War Letters of Albert E. Higley*. Glens Falls, N.Y.: The authors, 1986.

Alexander, Edward Porter. *Military Memoirs of a Confederate*. Bloomington: Indiana University Press, 1962.

Alexandria Gazette. Alexandria, Va.

Alves, Joseph Hodge and Harold Spelman. *Near the Falls: Two Hundred Years of The Falls Church*. Falls Church: The Falls Church Episcopal, 1969.

Ambrose, Stephen E. and Richard H. Immerman. *Milton S. Eisenhower: Educational Statesman*. Baltimore: The Johns Hopkins University Press.

American Automobile Association, et. al. *The Zero Milestone: Marking the Beginning of the National Highways Radiating from Washington . . .* Washington: The Association, 1923.

The Arlington Historical Magazine, vol. I, no. 1 (Oct. 1957).

Bain, Chester W. *A Body Incorporate: The Evolution of City-County Separation in Virginia*. Charlottesville: University Press of Virginia, 1967.

Banes, Charles H. *History of the Philadelphia Brigade*. Philadelphia: J. B. Lippincott & Co., 1876.

Barber, Raymond G. and Gary E. Swinson. eds. *The Civil War Letters of Charles Barber, Private, 104th New York Volunteer Infantry*. Torrance, Calif.: Gary E. Swinson, 1991.

Barnard, J. G. *A Report on the Defenses of Washington*. Washington: Government Printing Office, 1871.

Bates, Samuel P. *History of Pennsylvania Volunteers, 1861–5*. Wilmington, N.C.: Broadfoot Publishing Co., 1993.

Belz, Ella C. *Falls Church Presbyterian Church, 1873–1973*. Falls Church: Falls Church Presbyterian Church, 1976.

Black, Eugene B. *Above the Civil War: The Story of Thaddeus Lowe, Balloonist, Inventor, Railroad Builder*. Berkeley: Howell-North, 1966.

Boatner, Mary Mayo, III. *The Civil War Dictionary*. New York: David McKay Co., 1959.

Boston Young Men's Christian Association. *The Soldiers' Hymn-Book*. New York: Press of the American Tract Society, ca. 1862.

Bowman. *Almanac*.

Brinkley, David. *Washington Goes to War*. New York: Ballentine, 1988.

Brockett, L. P. *Woman's Work in the Civil War: A Record of Heroism, Patriotism and Patience*. Boston: R. H. Curran, 1867.

Bryant, William Cullen and Sydney Howard Gay. *A Popular History of the United States*. New York: Scribner, Armstrong, and Co., 1876.

Byrd, Judith H. and Philip R. Mason, eds. "A Story of the 22d Kansas Volunteer Infantry: From the Diary of Samuel Adams," *The Kansas Historical Quarterly*, (Winter 1970).

Cammann, William C., et. al. *The History of Troop "A," New York Cavalry U.S.V. . . . in the Spanish-American War*. New York: R. H. Russell, 1899.

Camp, Shirley W. *Past Times Around Falls Church: The Change from Plantation to Village and Town, 1729–1875*. Baltimore: Gateway Press, 1997.

Castorina, Margaret R. *St. James School, 1906–1981*. Falls Church, Va.: St. James 75th Anniversary Committee, 1981.

The Charleston Mercury, Charleston, S.C.

Conser, S. L. M. *Virginia After the War: Methodist Episcopal Church in Virginia at the Close of the Civil War*. Indianapolis: Baker-Randolph Litho. & Eng. Co., 1891.

Cooling, Benjamin Franklin, III. *Symbol, Sword, and Shield*. Archon Books, 1975.

Cooling, Benjamin Franklin and Walton H. Owen II. *Mr. Lincoln's Forts: A guide to the Civil War Defenses of Washington*. Shippensburg, Pa.: White Mane Publishing Co., 1988.

Cooper, James. *Campaign of the First Troop, Philadelphia City Cavalry, April 25–November 11, 1898*. Philadelphia: Hallowell Co., Ltd., [1898].

Cowles, Calvin D., comp. *Atlas to Accompany the Official Records of the Union and Confederate Armies*. Washington: Government Printing Office, 1891–95.

Davis, Arthur Kyle, ed. *Virginia Communities in War Time*. Richmond: Executive Committee of the Virginia War History Commission, 1927.

Davis, Arthur Kyle, ed. *Virginia War Agencies Selective Service and Volunteers*. Richmond: Executive Committee of the Virginia War History Commission, 1927.

Davis, Arthur Kyle, ed. *Virginians of Distinguished Service of the World War*. Richmond: Executive Committee of the Virginia War History Commission, 1923.

Dawkins, Betty-Jo and Walter E. Bass. *Columbia Baptist Church, Falls Church, Virginia, 1856–1981*. Falls Church: Columbia Baptist Church, 1981.

Department of Planning. *A Guide to the Development Process*. Falls Church: The Department, 1971.

Department of Planning and Development. *Adopted Streetscape Plan for West Broad Street*. Falls Church: The Department, 1987.

Dexter, Wayne. *CBC: Your Hometown Political Party, A History*. Falls Church: Citizens for a Better City, 1993.

Douglas, H. H. *Falls Church: Places and People*. Falls Church: Falls Church Historical Commission, 1981.

Drickamer, Lee C. and Karen D. *Fort Lyon to Harper's Ferry*. Shippensburg, Pa.: White Mane Publishing Co., 1987.

Dyer, Frederick H. *A Compendium of the War of the Rebellion*. New York: Thomas Yoseloff.

Edward Grey, First Viscount of Fallodon. *Twenty-Five Years, 1892–1916*. New York: Frederick A. Stokes Co., 1925.

Edwards, Frank E. *The '98 Campaign of the 6th Massachusetts, U.S.V.* Boston: Little, Brown, and Co., 1899.

Edwards, Stuart W. *Preservation Easements in Falls Church*. Falls Church: historic Falls Church, Inc., 1977.

Eisenhower, Dwight D. *Crusade in Europe*. Garden City, N.Y.: Doubleday, 1948.

Eisenhower, Milton S. *The President is Calling*. Garden City, N.Y.: Doubleday & Co., 1974.

Ellis, Edward S. *The Youths' History of the United States*. New York: Cassell & Co., Ltd., 1886.

The Evening Star. Washington, D.C. (Later title: *The Washington Star*.)

Falls Church Echo. Falls Church, Va.

Falls Church city government. *Falls Church Environmental Services Report*. Falls Church: City of Falls Church, 1994.

Falls Church Historical Commission. *Falls Church, Virginia: Architectural Inventory*. Falls Church: The Commission, 1969.

Fairfax County Sun Echo. Fairfax, Va.

Fairfax County Sun Echo and The Standard. Fairfax, Va.

Fairfax Herald. Fairfax, Va.

Fiala, Anthony. *Troop "C" in Service*.

Fishel, Edwin C. *The Secret War for the Union*. Boston: Houghton Mifflin Co., 1996.

Fitzpatrick, John C., ed., *The Writings of George Washington*. Washington: Government Printing Office, 1938.

Garreau, Joel. *Edge City: Life on the New Frontier*. New York: Doubleday, 1991.

Gates, Theodore B. *The "Ulster Guard" [20th N.Y. State Militia] and the War of the Rebellion*. New York: Benjamin H. Tyrrel, 1879.

Goode, James M. *The Outdoor Sculpture of Washington, D.C.* Washington: Smithsonian Institution Press, 1974.

GW Hatchet. George Washington University. Washington, D.C.

Hammer and Company Associates. *The Economic Impact of Potential Development in Falls Church*. Washington: The Company, 1962.

Hard, Abner. *History of the Eighth Cavalry Regiment, Illinois Volunteers, During the Great Rebellion*. Aurora, Ill.: The author, 1868.

Harrison, Fairfax. *A History of the Legal Development of the Railroad System of the Southern Railway Company*. Washington: 1901.

Harrison, Fairfax. *Landmarks of Old Prince William*. Berryville, Va.: Chesapeake Book Co., 1964.

Harrison, Noel Garraux. "Along the Tracks: Northern Fairfax County's First Electric Railway." Report for the Falls Church Historical Commission, 1986.

Harrison, Noel Garraux. *City of Canvas: Camp Russell A. Alger and the Spanish-American War*. Falls Church: Falls Church Historical Commission and Fairfax County History Commission, 1988.

Harwood, H. H., Jr. *Rails to the Blue Ridge*. Falls Church: Pioneer America Society, 1969.

Haydon, F. Stansbury. *Aeronautics in the Union and Confederate Armies*. Baltimore: The Johns Hopkins Press, 1941.

Henderson, James H. M. and Betty F. Henderson. *Molder of Men: Portrait of a "Grand Old Man"—Edwin Bancroft Henderson*. New York: Vantage Press, 1985.

Hoadley, John Chipman. *Memorial of Henry Sanford Gansevoort . . .* Boston: Franklin-Press & Rand, Avery, & Co., 1875.

Huffman, James. *Ups and Downs of a Confederate Soldier*. New York: William E. Rudge's Sons, 1940.

Iekel, John F. "The Neighborhood That Was: The History of East Falls Church, Virginia." *The Arlington Historical Magazine*, vol. 10, no. 3 (October 1995).

Jackson, Donald, ed. *The Diaries of George Washington*. Charlottesville: University Press of Virginia

Jewell, Marianne H. Dulin: *From Saddlebags to Satellites: A Story of Faith and Service*. Falls Church: Dulin United Methodist Church, 1969.

Jones, Virgil Carrington. *Ranger Mosby*. McLean, Va.: EPM Publications, Inc., 1972.

Kirk, Hyland Clare. *Heavy Guns and Light: A History of the 4th New York Heavy Artillery*. New York: C. T. Dillingham, 1890.

LBC&W Consultants, Inc. Pamphlet, "Proposed Development Plan, Crossroads Area, Falls Church, Virginia." March 1974.

Lee Highway Association. *Lee Highway: Spanning the Continent from the Nation's Metropolis to the Nation's Capital*. Washington: The Association, 1926.

Lee Highway Association. *Views Along Lee Highway, A Main Street of the Nation*. Washington: The Association, 1923.

Lewis, Tom. *Divided Highways: Building the Interstate Highways, Transforming American Life*. New York: Viking, 1997.

Library of Congress. *Fire Insurance Maps in the Library of Congress*. Washington: The Library, 1981.

Longstreet, James. *From Manassas to Appomattox: Memoirs of the Civil War in America*. Philadelphia: J. B. Lippincott Co., 1896.

Lossing, Benson J. *Our Country: A Household History of the United States for All Readers* . . . New York: Johnson & Bailey.

Lossing, Benson J. *The Pictorial Field Book of the Revolution*. New York: Harper & Bros., 1851.

Lossing Benson J. *The Pictorial Field Book of the War of 1812*. New York: Harper & Bros., 1868.

McKee, James Harvey. *Back "In War Times," A History of the 144th Regiment, New York Volunteer Infantry* . . . Horace E. Bailey, 1903.

Milles, Carl. *Fountain of Faith: A Monument to Life*. Falls Church: National Memorial Park, [1952].

Mills, John Harrison. *Chronicles of Twenty-First Regiment New York State Volunteers* . . . Buffalo: 21st Regiment Veteran Association of Buffalo, 1887.

The Monitor. Rosslyn, Va.

Moon. *The Interstate Highway System*.

Morrell, Carl A. *Seymour Dexter, Union Army*. Jefferson, N.C.: McFarland & Co., 1996.

Morris, Thomas R. and Larry J. Sabato. *Virginia: Government and Politics*. Virginia Chamber of Commerce and Center for Public Service of the University of Virginia, 1990.

Mosby, John S. *The Letters of John S. Mosby*. Carlisle, Pa.: Stuart-Mosby Historical Society, 1986.

Muller, Charles G. *The Darkest Day: 1814: The Washington-Baltimore Campaign*. Philadelphia: J. B. Lippencott, 1963.

Myer, Donald Beckman, AIA. *Bridges and the City of Washington*. Washington: U.S. Commission on Fine Arts, 1974.

National Capital Area Realtor (December 1961).

National Highway Association. *Lee Highway: The Backbone Road of the South*. New York: The Association, 1930.

Nature Conservancy. "Crossing the Fence: Ecoregional Conservation." *Virginia Chapter News* of The Nature Conservancy, (Summer 1997), pp. 1, 8,.

Neely, F. Tennyson. *Neely's Panorama of our New Possessions*. New York: The author, 1898.

Netherton, Nan, Donald Sweig, Janice Artemel, Patricia Hickin, and Patrick Reed. *Fairfax County, Virginia: A History*. Fairfax, Va.: Fairfax County Board of Supervisors, 1978.

Netherton, Ross D. *Braddock's Campaign and the Potomac Route to the West*. (Reprinted from the Winchester-Frederick County Historical Society "Journal," Vol. I.) Falls Church, Va.: Higher Education Publications, Inc., 1989.

The New York Herald. New York, N.Y.

Northern Virginia Regional Planning Commission. *Northern Virginia REgion Community Shelter Program*. Falls Church: The Commission, 1968.

Northern Virginia Sun. Arlington, Va.

Ollier, Edmund. *Cassell's History of the United States*. London: Cassell Petter & Galpin, 1875.

Osborne, Seward R. *The Civil War Diaries of Col. Theodore B. Gates, 20th New York State Militia*. Hightstown, N.J.: Longstreet House, 1991.

Peck, Taylor. *Round-Shot to Rockets: A History of the Washington Navy Yard and U.S. Naval Gun Factory*. Annapolis: United States Naval Institute, 1949.

Phisterer, Frederick. *New York in the War of the Rebellion, 1861 to 1865*. Albany: J. B. Lyon Co., 1912.

Pitch, Anthony S. *The Burning of Washington: The British Invasion of 1814*. Annapolis: Naval Institute Press, 1998.

Planning Commission and Department of Planning. *A Plan for the Central Business District, City of Falls Church, Virginia*. Falls Church: The Commission and Department, 1965.

Planning Commission. *Falls Church Master Plan*. Falls Church: The Commission, 1978.

Pope, Loren. "Twenty-Five Years Later: Still a Love Affair." *Historic Preservation*, Vol. 17, No. 3 (May-June 1965).

Potter, Stephen R. *Commoners, Tribute, and Chiefs: The Development of Algonquian Culture in the Potomac Valley*. Charlottesville: University Press of Virginia, 1993.

Rawlings, James Scott. *Virginia's Colonial Churches: An Architectural Guide*. Richmond: Garrett & Massie, 1963.

Reimers, Priscilla. *Celebrating 40 Years: A History of the Falls Church School System*. Falls Church: Falls Church School System, 1989.

Reimers, Priscilla. *Falls Church City Public Schools: Celebrating 50 Years: A History*. Falls Church, Va.: City Schools Publication Committee, 1999.

Ritchie, Norman L., ed. *Four Years in the First New York Light Artillery: The Papers of David F. Ritchie*. Hamilton, N.Y.: Edmonston Publishing, Inc. 1997.

Ritzenthaler, Mary Lynn, Gerald J. Munoff, and Margery S. Long. *Archives and Manuscripts: Administration of Photographic Collections*. Chicago: Society of American Archivists, 1984.

Roe, Alfred S. *The Fifth Regiment, Massachusetts Volunteer Infantry*. Boston: Fifth Regiment Veteran Association, 1911.

Salmon, Emily J. and Edward D. C. Campbell, Jr., eds. *The Hornbook of Virginia History*. Richmond: The Library of Virginia, 1994.

Schmidt, Lewis G. *A Civil War History of the 47th Regiment of Pennsylvania Veteran Volunteers*. Allentown, Pa.: The author, 1986.

Scott, Robert M. *The War of the Rebellion: A Compilation of the Official Records of the Union and Confederate Armies*. Washington: Government Printing Office, 1881–91.

Smith, James E. *A Famous Battery and Its Campaigns, 1861–64*. Washington: W. H. Lowdermilk & Co., 1892.

Southern Historical Society. *Papers*. New Orleans, La.

Steadman, Melvin Lee, Jr. *Falls Church: By Fence and Fireside*. Falls Church: Falls Church Public Library, 1964.

Sterling, Pound. *Camp Fires of the Twenty-Third: Sketches of the Camp Life, Marches, and Battles of the Twenty-Third Regiment, N.Y.V.* . . . New York: Davies & Kent, 1863.

Stewart, Charles Alexander. *A Virginia Village: Historical Sketch of Falls Church and the Old Colonial Church*. Falls Church: Press of J. H. Newell, 1904.

Stone, Edwin W. *Rhode Island in the Great Rebellion*. Providence: George H. Whitney, 1865.

The Sun. East Falls Church, Va.

Thompson, George Raynor. "Civil War Signals." *Military Affairs*, vol. 18, no. 4 (winter 1954), p. 191.

Thayer, George Burton. *History of Company K, First Connecticut Volunteer Infantry, During the Spanish-American War*. Hartford, Conn.: R. S. Peck & Co., 1899.

Tinner Hill Heritage Foundation. Pamphlet, ca. 1997.

U.S. Army Corps of Engineers. *Washington Aqueduct.* Washington: the Corps, 1970.

U.S. Public Health Service. "Epidemic Influenze (Spanish Influenza)." Supplement No. 34.

Van Santvoord, Cornelius. *The One Hundred and Twentieth Regiment New York State Volunteers.* Rondout, N.Y.: Press of the Kingston Freeman, 1894.

Village Preservation and Improvement Society. "Falls Church: A Virginia Village." *The Village Way,* Vol. 30, No. 5, (September 1997), p. 1.

Village Preservation and Improvement Society. *Falls Church Historical News and Notes.* Falls Church: The Society, 1993.

Village Preservation and Improvement Society. *The Future of the City: Genesis for Progress in Falls Church: North Washington Street.* Falls Church: The Society, 1993.

Virginia Department of Highways. *Hearing Before the Commission, Virginia Department of Highways in the Matter of the Results of the Interstate Route 66 Transportation Alternatives Study.* December 18, 1973.

Waldeck, Ruby Weedell. "Missouri in the Spanish American War." *The Missouri Historical Review,* vol. XXX (1936), p. 399.

The Washington Post. Washington, D.C.

The Washington Star. Washington, D.C. (Earlier title: *Evening Star.*)

Williams, Ames. *The Washington and Old Dominion Railroad.* Springfield, Va.: The Capital Traction Quarterly, 1970.

Williamson, James J. *Mosby's Ranger*s. New York: Sturgis & Walton Co., 1909.

Wistar, Isaac Jones. *Autobiography of Isaac Jones Wistar, 1827–1905.* Philadelphia: Wistar Institute of Anatomy and Biology, 1937.

Wrenn, Tony P. *Cherry Hill Farm: Falls Church, Virginia.* Falls Church: Falls Church Historical Commission, 1971.

Wrenn, Tony P. *Falls Church: History of a Virginia Village.* Falls Church: Falls Church Historical Commission, 1972.

Graphics Collection

Arlington County Public Library. Virginia Room, Central Library. Arlington, Va.

Fairfax County Public Library. Photographic Archive, Virginia Room, Fairfax City Regional Library. Fairfax, Va.

Library of Congress. Geography and Maps Division. Washington, D.C.

Library of Congress. Prints and Photographs Division. Washington, D.C.

Library of Virginia. Photographic Archives. Richmond, Va.

Martin Luther King, Jr. Library of the District of Columbia Public Library. Washingtoniana Division. Washington, D.C.

Mary Riley Styles Public Library. Virginia Room. Falls Church, Va.

National Archives and Records Administration. Still Pictures Branch. Washington, D.C.

Public Information Office, City of Falls Church. Falls Church, Va.

U.S. Army Military History Center. Photographic Archive. Carlisle Barracks, Pa.

Washington & Old Dominion Railroad Regional Park, Northern Virginia Regional Park Authority, Fairfax Station, Va.

Index

(Italicized numbers indicate photographs)

A

Abbott House, 171
Abbott, J.G., *94*
Acosta, Frank, Mrs., 83
Advertisements, *95*
Aerial views, *130*, 132, 133
African-Americans, *16*, 30, 57, 59, 62-63, 67, 83–87, 90, 102, 104–106, 107, 109, 127, 129, 166, 170–171
Airports, *130*
Alexandria, Loudoun & Hampshire Railroad, 42–43, 59
Alexandria, Va., 14, 37
Algie, Pat, 169
All-America City Award (1962), 145, 151
Alma Shop, The 137
American Legion, 128
American Red Cross, 99, 121
Andrews, William A., 48
Annandale Road, 105, 106
Anti-aircraft guns, 121
Anti-aircraft weaponry, 121, *138*
Apollo Room (Williamsburg, Va.), 26
Arab immigrants, *155*
Arbor Day, 62, 66, *184*
Arbors, *60*
Architects' renderings, 137–138, 141, 152, 162
Architects, 23, *119*, *137*
Argus House, 157
Arlington and Fairfax Railway, 104
Arlington Boulevard, 103–104, *113*
Arlington County, Va., 23, 42, 105, *153*, 157
Arlington Memorial Bridge, *113*
Arringdon Hall, *60*, 91
Artifacts, *12*
Artists' renderings, 19, 30, 40, *181*
Asbury, Francis, 31
Automobile garages, *101*, *110*
Automobiles, *95*, 103–104, 108–110, 127
Aviation, *130*, 148

B

Bakeries, *84*
Ball-Sellers House (Arlington, Va.), 23
Balloons, 46–47, *50*, 175
Ballston, Va., 45
Ball, John, 22–23, *23*
Ball, William A., 84
Bands, *81*
Banks, *111*, 143
Banneker Stone, *32*, 171
Banneker, Benjamin, 31
Baptist churches, 40, 45, 49, 62, 63, 93, *155*
Barber shops, *77*
Barton, Clara, 77
Baseball, *147*, 154
"Battle Hymn of the Republic," 56
Bells, *155*
Benton, Nicholas, *153*, 177
Big Chimneys, 13, *18–19*, 84, 169, 171
Birch family, *97*, 108, 119

Birch House, 40
Birch, Frank L., *113*
Birch, John E., 60
Birindelli, J. Benson, *168*, 169, 176
Birindelli, Nancy, 169, 173
Blackburn, Edward, 23
Blackburn, Richard, 21
Black, Tom, *177*
Blood collection drives, 121
Bonnie Brier (home), *73*
Booth, Mordecai, 35, 37
Boundaries, *32*, 33
Boundary stones, 31, *32*, 33, 72, 171
Boy Scouts of America, *107*, 128
Braddock, Edward, 22
Brady, Mathew, 51
Bridges, *112–113*
Broad and Washington streets, *48*, 89, 90, *109*, 110, 111, 126, 133, 136, 152
Broad Street, East, *23*, *40*, 60, 88, 92-94, 96–97, 107, 108, 124, 127, 134
Broad Street, West, 82, 90, 94, *95*, 107, 108, 115, 127, 134, 137, 139, *140*, 142, 145, 154, 186, 191
Broadmont, 128
Broadwater, Charles, 21, 27–28
Browne, Charlotte, 23
Brown, Hugh, 95
Brown, John, 43
Brown, J.C.H., 61
Brown's Hardware Store, *70*, 82, 90, 172
Bubble Houses, *125*
Businesses, *37*, 82, 84, 92, 94, 114

C

Camp Russell A. Alger, 75–81, *76*, 99, 181
Capria, Mary Ann, *167*
Carnivals, *150*
Carter, Joel, 60
Cartoons and caricatures, *28*, 101, 125, 132, 138, 148, 152–152
Catholic churches, 42, 66
Cemeteries, *25*, 149–150
Chain Bridge, *112*
Chaves, Tony, 66, 89, 114
Cherry Hill, *41*, 60, 115, 145, 179, *180*, 188
Chesapeake & Potomac Telephone Company, 131
Child Development Center, 187
Children, *58*, 69, 84, 86, 106–107, 120, 130, 146, 148, 182–184, 189, 190
Christmas, *91*, 120, 150
Church Hill (estate), 31
Church of England, 21, 23, 31, 41
Churches, 21, 24, 30–31, *38*, 40–42, 45, 49, 50, 52-53, 59, 60, 62–64, 66–67, 71, 87, 88, 92–93, 96, 118, 144, 155
Church, Guy Northrop, 69
Church, Merton Elbridge, 63, 69, 85, *96*, 99–100, 103–104, *109–110*, 111
Citizens for a Better City, 128
City Council, *167*
City Hall, 157, *162*, 188

Civil defense, 122, 138
Civil War (1861–1865), 40, 41–57, 180
Cobb, James E., 86
Cockburn, Martin (Admiral), 36
Colbert, J. W., 85
Cold War (1946–1991), 138
Colored Citizens Protective League, 85
Columbia Baptist Church, 40–41, 45, 48–49, *49*, 57, 93, 143, 155
Columbia Street, 90, 93
Confederate Military Telegraph, 47
Connecticut Infantry, 47, 78, *78*
Connell, William, 21
Consumer rationing, 99–101, 121, 125
Coop Center, 138
Cory, Joyce, 169
Cows, *11*
Cram, Barbara, 169, *170*
Crocker, E. Frank, 60
Crossman House, 63
Crossman Methodist Episcopal Church (North), *64*
Crossman, Isaac, 60, 63
Crouch, Ron, 169

D

Dances, *190*
Daniel, L. P., 105, *113*
Darby, Willie May, 64
Daugerrotypes, 42
Daughters of the American Revolution, *155*, 169–170
Day, Hap, 153
DeLong, Carol Witte, *165*
Demolitions, *139*
Demonstrations, *151*, 164
DePutron House, *72*
DePutron family, *58*
DePutron, Maurice Bentley, *11*, 58, 73
Dierksen, Deane, 169, 171
Disasters, *139*
Doctors, 96, 97, *80*
Dodge, Pickering, 84
Dolls, *58*, 120
Don Beyer Volvo Motor Company, *185*
Donald S. Frady Park, 66
Doolittle, W. H., 62
Dover, Dale Warren, *166*
Downtown intersection, *48*, 89, 90, *109*, 110, 111, *114*, 126, 133, 136, 152
Dozier, Bennett, 35
Drug stores, 69, 94, *118*, 136
Dulany, Daniel and Sarah, 35, 37
Dulany, Daniel F., 45
Dulin Methodist Episcopal Church (South), *60*, 71, 96
Duryee House, *70*
Duryee, Schuyler, 62, 70, 83, 142

E

Engravings, 14–16, 18, 22, 23, 26, 28, 34, 36, 47, 49, 55–56
Enterprise (Balloon), 46

207

Environment, *151*, 159
Erwin House, *71*
Erwin, George, 71, *84*
Evans, Edna, *104*

F
Fadeley family, 125
Fadeley, George B., 84
Fadeley, Mac, *98*
Fairfax Chapel, 30–31, 40, 45, 49
Fairfax County, Va., 164
Fairfax Court House (Va.), 49
Fairfax family, 15
Fairfax Parish (Va.), 23
Fairfax Resolves, 27, 171
Fairfax Seminary (Alexandria, Va.), 41
Fairfax, George William, 21
Fairfax, Henry, 42
Fairfax, John, 60
Fairfax, William, 21
Falcon's Nest (home), *175*
Falls Church Bank, *111*, 143
Falls Church Chamber Orchestra, 170–172, *176*
Falls Church Citizens Organization, 128
Falls Church Community Center, 159, *160*, 163
Falls Church Delicatessen, *136*
Falls Church Drug Store, *136*
Falls Church Filling Station, *110*
Falls Church Florist, *137*
Falls Church High School, 128–129, *147*
Falls Church Negro School, 105–106
Falls Church News-Press, 153
Falls Church Police, 121, *190*
Falls Church Presbyterian Church, *66*, 67, 92, 93
Falls Church Public Library. (*See also* Mary Riley Styles Public Library), 84, *135*, 151, 157, 162
Falls Church Telephone Company, 62
Falls Church Temperance Society, 41
Falls Church Volunteer Fire Department, 83, 107, 123, *131*, 139, 141, 150, 185
Falls Church Woman's Club, *64*, 107, 118
Falls Church (Episcopal), The, 24-25, 42, 48-49, *49*, 52, 53, 171
    Abandonment, 41–42
    Bell, 155
    Civil War (1861–1865), 48, 49, *49*, 52–53
    Construction, 23, 25
    Establishment, 21
    Revolution, *24–25*, 28 28
    Tricentennial of City (1999), 171
Falls Church, Va.
    Annexation attempts (ca. 1940s–1950s), 156, 161
    Centennial of town charter (1975), 152
    Establishment (ca. 1699), 13
    Incorporation as town (1875), 60
    Origin of name (ca. 1700s), 15
    Removal of East Falls Church (ca. 1936), 104–105
    Tricentennial (1999), 167–177
Farmer's market, *188*
Farmers, 22
Fashion shows, 137

Fenwick, Edward G., 100
Fink, Herman, *139*
Fire engine companies, 62, 83, 107, *131*, *141*, 185
First Congregational Church, *64*, 118
Fitzgerald, Merni I., *166–167*, 169
Flagg, Edmund, 61
Flags, U.S., *87*, 90, 101
Fleet, Henry, 13
Floods, 138, *139*
Follin, John, 28
Football, *147*
Foote, Frederick Forrest, Jr., 61, *67*, 68
Foote, Frederick Forrest, Sr., 57, 127
Fort Belvoir, Va., 99
Fort Buffalo, Va., 57, 103, 129, 132
Fort Ethan Allen, Va., 47
Fort Ramsay, Va., 56
Fountain of Faith (statuary ensemble), 150
Four Mile Run, 23, *139*
Fowler, T. T., 60
Frady, Donald S., 127, *139*
Frady, Edna, 169
Fraternal organizations, 67, 71, 83, 128, *149*, 187
French and Indian War (1754–1763), 22

G
Galloway Methodist Church, 59, *87*
Galpin-Hartman House, *139*
Galpin, Charles Parker, *74*, 76
Garbage collection, municipal, 107
Gardner, Daniel, *167*
Garland, Ralph and Mabel, 103
Gas lighting, 94
Gas service, municipal, 85
George Mason Jr.-Sr. High School, 129, *154*, 157, *161*
Georgetown Reservoir, *116*
Gernand, Bradley E., 169
Gibson, Burns "Bunny," *108*
Gibson, Lytton H., 123
Gillam, Pete, *90*
Girl Scouts of America, 128
Gooch, Sir William (Colonial Governor), 14
Gordon's Tavern, 39
Gordon, Barbara J., 169
Gott, L. E., 60
Gradle, Brian, *177*
Graffiti, 52, 53
Grant, Ulysses Simpson, 59
Gray, C. R., *139*
Great Depression, 105
Great Falls Diversion Dam, *116*
Greater Falls Church Chamber of Commerce, 127, 170
Green Gables (home), *97*
Greenway Downs, 128
Groot Hall, 92
Gundry Home for the Feeble-Minded, 70
Gundry, Mattie A., *64*, 70, 83, 104, 142, *144*

H
Hailey, Charles M., *151*
Halayko, Kathy, *173*
Halloween, *182*
Hamlin, Hannibal, 46

Hangman's Tree, *134*
Hardware Stores, 70, 82, *133*
Harper's Ferry, Va. (now West Va.), 43
Harris, Herbert E., II, *141*
Hawxhurst, George W., 84
Hayes, George E. C., 86
Heatwole, Garland, *151*
Heintzelman, Samuel, 49
Henderson, Edwin Bancroft, 85, *105,* 129
Henderson, John B., 84
Henderson, Mary Ellen Meriwether, *105*
Herman, Howard, 159
Highland View (home), *61*
Hills, *14,* 44, 54
Hillwood Avenue, 124
Hispanic immigrants, *155*
Historic Falls Church, Inc., 38, 40–41, 139, 145
Historical Commission, 159, 169
Holidays, 77, 83, *86-87*, 90, 91, 97, 101, 119–120, 131, 172, 182–185
Homes, 18, *19*, 23, 38, 40, 41, 61, 63, 64, 68, 71, 72, 73, 88, 90, 91, 97, 104, 108, 119, 124, 125, 128, 139, 175
Hoofnagle, William S., *141*
Hoosier, Harry, 30–31
Hopkins, W. S., 91
Horses, *48*, 52, 54, 63
Horseshoe Hill, *128*
Hospitals, 49–50, 64
Hotels, motels and inns (*See also* Taverns), 39, *114*
Hough, Lawrence and Phil, *98*
Howe, Julia Ward, 56
Hull, Robert D., *166*, 172

I
Ice houses, 91
Immigrants, *111*, 155, 191
Independence Day, 77, 83, *87*, 90, 101
Independent Order of Good Templars, 83
Independent Order of Odd Fellows, 71, 83
Indians of North America, *12*, 13, 14
Inns, 39, 114
Interstate Highway 66, 105, 119, 143–144, *153*
Ives, George B., 60, 61, 68
I.O.O.F. Hall, *71*, 143

J
Jackson, Carol, *177*
James Lee Elementary School, 105, 129
Jaycees, 128
Jefferson Institute, 62, *66*, 107, 129, 143
Jefferson, Thomas, *33*, 39
Johnston, Louis Z., Jr., 159
Jones, Rosemary Haynes, 169

K
Kaiser-Georgetown Medical Center, *165*
Kansas Infantry, *78*, 81
Katz, Doris, 169
Kemper-Macon Ware Lodge, *174*
Kiwanis, 128
Knickerbocker, Vicki, *154*
Korean immigrants, *155*

L

Ladies Aid Society, *67*
Land grants & patents (colonial), *17*
Lanier, William, 175
Lawton House, *41*, 47
Lawton, Henry Ware, 41
League of Women Voters, 128
Lee Highway, 75, 103–104, 107, *109–110*
Leesburg Pike, 14, 23, *33*, 39, 40
Leesburg, Va., 60
Lewinsville, Va., 47
Libraries, *135*, 151, 162, 170, 172, 189
Lincoln Avenue, 97
Lincoln, Travis, *154*
Lindsay's Tavern, 39
Lions Club, 128, *149*, 187
Little Falls of the Potomac River, 13, *15*
Little Falls Street, *112*
Little, Charles, 28
Liu, Amy, *177*
Longstreet, James, 41, 47–48
Lorton, Va., *138*
Love, James, 60
Love, Richard, Mrs., 36
Lowe, Thaddeus S.C., 46–47, *50*, 170, 175
Lynch House, *139*
Lynch, William Henry Greenburg, *42*
Lynch, William Nathan, family, *88*

M

Mabry, Samuel, *167*
Madison Elementary School, 107, *146*, 158
Madison, Dolley P., *36*, 37
Madison, James, *36*, 37
Maier, Drew and Jill, *182*
Maier, John, 160–161
Maps, 14, 15, 17, 20-22, 33, 44, 54, *65*, 117, 126, 144
Markets, *94*
Mary Riley Styles Public Library. (*See also* Falls Church Public Library), 158, 172, 189
Masarch, Wendelyn, *111*
Masonic Lodge, 83
Mason, George, 21, 25, 27-28, *29;* bust, 170, *174*
Mayors, *65*, 113, 139, 151, 160, 165-166
Mayo, William, 21
McCarty, Denis, 21
McClellan, George, 55
McGroarty, Stephen P., 100
McKinley, William, 76, *181*
McTear's Tavern, 39
Memorial Day, *131*, 184, 185
Mercer, Kathleen C., *112*
Merrifield, George A.C., 61
Mess, Walter, *189*
Methodist churches 30-31, 40, 45, 49, 60, 64, 71, *87*, 96
MetroRail, *141*
Middle Turnpike. (*See also* Leesburg Turnpike), 14, 39
Midway Plaisance, 76
Milles, Carl, 149–150
Mills, *92*
Ministers and clergy, 30, 40, 57, *63*
Minor's Hill, 50
Minor's Tavern, 39
Minor, George, 35, 37
Minor, Philip H., 45
Missiles, *138*
Mitchell, Patsy, 169
Model airplanes, *148*
Moore, Donald M., 123
Moore, Eric D., *176*
Moore, Richard, 151
Moran, John J., 60, *65*
Morgan, Henry J., *40*
Morrison, Robert, 62
Morse, Diane, 169
Mosby, John Singleton, 50–51, 57, 134
Mother's Day, *119*
Motorcycles, *108*
Mount Daniel Elementary School, 129, 157, *161*, 173, *173*
Mount Hope (home), *38*, 183
Municipal buildings, *118*, 130, 135, 137, 157, 162, 163
Munson's Hill, 47, 49–50, 56
Munson, D. D., 63

N

NAACP (National Association for the Advancement of Colored People), 85
National Memorial Park, *149–150*
Netherton, Nan, 169
Nette, Alex and Kyle, *182*
New York Cavalry Regiment (13th), 49, 50-51, 52, 53, 55, 56, 57, *77, 80*
Newspapers, 153
Northern Neck Proprietary, 13, *15*, 21
Northern Virginia Regional Parks Authority, *159*
Northrup, E. J., 62

O

Oak Street, North, 92
Oakwood Cemetery, 30, 31, 40, 121
Ogle, Martin, *177*
Olom, Louis, 171
Olom, Sue T., *157*
Osborne, Seth, 63
Oxen, *90*

P

Parades, 83, *131*, 152, 171, 185
Parish, Betty, *189*
Park Avenue, *134*
Parker Avenue, *138*
Parks, 66, 113, *188*, 189
Pearl Harbor, Hawaii - Attack on (1941), 69
Pearson, Simon, 25
Pennsylvania Infantry, 75
Perkins' Hill, 50
Perry, Robert, *166*
Physicians, *80*
Pierce, Edward R., 123
Pierpont, Francis Harrison, 45
Pigs (statuary), *185*
Pimmit Hills, 138
Pioneers, *18*
Police stations, *118*, 121
Politics and governance, 128, *166*
Pope-Leighey House, *119*
Post offices, *38*, 85, 94, 136
Postcards, 64, 66, 89, 123
Potomac Fruit Growers Association, 83
Potomac River, *15*
Pound, Ezra, 123
Powell, George W., *63*
Powell, Y. W., 85
Powhatan, *14*
Presbyterian churches, *38*, 40, 50, *66-67*, 92
Presidents, U.S. 33, 36, 59, 76, *96*, 181
Protestant Episcopal Church in Virginia, 31
Protests, public, *151*, 164
Public works, 85, 105-107, *116*, 127, *138*, 139

Q

Quaker Oats Company, *95*
Quarry Inn, *114*
Quick, T. C., *96*
Quinones, Joseph, 169

R

Racial segregation, 85–86, 129
Railroad crossings, *140*
Railroad stations, *73*, 78, 86, 94, 108, 115, 135, 181
Railroads, 42-43, 59, 78, 94, *95*, 104, 108, 115, 135, 140–141, 178
Raleigh Tavern (Williamsburg, Va.), 26
Read, John, 51, 57
Reagan, Michael, 21
Realty firms, *109*
Recreation centers, *130*, 137, 159, 163
Recycling of consumer goods, 159
Red Cross, 99, 121
Reed, Walter, 77
Republican Party, *68*
Restaurants, *114*
Revolution (American) (1776–1783), 26–27, *28–29*
Rhoads, Lee M., *141*
Rhode Island Infantry, 76
Rice House, *124*
Riley, Joseph Harvey, 84, *115*
Riley, Joseph S., 60–61
Roads, 13-14, *16*, 22-23, 33, 39, 40, 103–104, 109–110, 113, 119, 143–144, 153
Roberts Park, 113
Roberts, Milton E., *113*
Rodock, John, 169
Rogers, Michael, *177*
Rogers, Steven, *167*
Rokeby (home), 36
Rollins House, 68
Rosslyn Mill, *92*
Royston, Sandy, *150*
Rust/Bonnell/Douglas House, *91*

S

Sandburg, Carl, 77
Santa Claus, *150*
Schools, 59, 61-62, 66, 70, *105–106*, 107, 128-129, 141–142, 144-148, 154, 157, 158, 159, 160-161, 173
Schouber, Thomas, 171
Scott, America Virginia, *48*
Scott, Artemisia, *48*
Second Baptist Church, 59, *62–63*
Service stations, *101*, 110

Seven Corners, 57, 103, 127, *129*, 132, 133, *133*, 191
Sewall, Sabilla, 42
Sewerage, municipal, 106–107
Shadow Lawn, *64*
Sharpe, Kieran, 169
Shaw, Mary Ellen, 159, *173*
Shepard House, *108*
Sherwood subdivision, 63
Shopping centers, 127, *129*
Signs, *37*, *94*
Simmons, G. W., 85
Simms, Charles, 28
Smallwood, John, 97
Smith, John [Captain], 13, *14*
Smyth, Mrs. P. H., 104
Snyder's Hardware Store, *133*
Snyder, David, 160, *160*, 167, 173
Soldiers
    Civil War (1861-1865), 41, 45–57, *46*, 180
    French and Indian War (1754–1763), 22
    Revolution (1776–1783), 28
    Spanish-American War (1898), 76, *76*, 77, 78, 80, 81
    War of 1812 (1812–1814), 35
    World War I (1917–1918), *98*
    World War II (1939–1945), 69, 124
South Falls Church, 57, 62, *63*, 65, 84
Spanish-American War (1898), 74–81, 181
Spanish Influenza, 100
Spofford and Church Drug Store, *69*
Sports, *147*, 154
Spring Street, North, 88, 144–145
Stables, 52
Stambaugh, Ralph, 100
Star Tavern, 40, *48*
State Theater, 107, *115*, 177
Statuary, *149-150*, 185
Steeples, 64
Stereopticon images, *77*, 88
"Steve Canyon" (syndicated newspaper feature), 148
Stewart, Charles Alexander, 84
Stonemasons, *102*
Stone structures, 31, *32*, *33*, 66, 88, 93, 111
Storms, 55
Strait, Ed, *176*
Streams, *14*, 16, 138–139
Street lamps, 85, *94*, 104
Stuart, James Ewart Buell ("J.E.B."), 47
Styles, Elizabeth Morgan, *86*, 162
Styles, Francis Holmes, *86*, 162
Styles, Mary Elizabeth Riley, *112*, 162
St. Clair, Sir John, 22
St. James Elementary School, 85, *144*, 146, 148, 151, 157
St. James Roman Catholic Church, 42, 85, *66*, 88, 144–145
Subdivisions, 63, *128*
Sunsinger (statuary), 149
Sypher, Jay H., *112*

T

Taft, William Howard, *96*
Talbot, T. M., 63
Tallwood (home), 107, 122–123, *124*
Tarbert, Bob, *166*

Taverner, Walter L., 100
Taverns, *37*, 39, 46, 48
Taylor's Hill, *46*
Taylor's Tavern, 45, *46*
Taylor, Summerfield, *94*
Telegraphs, 62–63, 69, 96
Telephones, 62, 69, *131*
Television Channel 38, *154*
Temperance movement, 41, 76
Terman, Maurice J., 169, *176*
Thanksgiving (holiday), 172
Thomas Jefferson Elementary School, 129, 157, *160*
Thomas, George W., 57
Thompson, G. M., 61
Thompson, William Blaine, *94*
Thurber, James, 83, 90
Time capsules, *173*
Tiner, J. B., 85
Tingey, Thomas, 35, *37*
Tinner Hill, *104*, 107, 129
Tinner Hill Heritage Foundation, Inc., 170
Tinner Hill Memorial Arch, 172, *174*
Tinner, Charles, *104*
Tinner, Frank, *104*
Tinner, Joseph B., *102*
Tobacco farming, 14, *16*
Toll gates, *40*
Toys, *58*, 88, 120
Trammell, Milcah, *25*
Tree City USA (award), 159
Trees, 62, 93, 107, *115*, 127, 134, 145, 159, 170, 184
Tricentennial Committee, 169
Triebel, Charles O., 123
Tripps Run, *138*, 160
Truro Parish (Va.), *20*, 21, 23
Tyler, Daniel, 45–46
Tyson's Corner, Va., 23, 51, 127, *129*

U

Underwood Street, North, *119*
United Daughters of the Confederacy, 83
United States Navy Band, 170
United States Sanitary Commission, 49
Upton's Hill, 47, 50, 55, 56
Urban planning, 143, *152*
USS *Maine* (battleship), *74*, 76

V

Valentine's Day, *97*
Van Zee, Maes, *177*
Veterans, 128, *131*, 170, 172, *176*, *176*
Vice-presidents, U.S., 46
Victorian Society at Falls Church, The, 159, 169, 171-172, 190
Vietnamese immigrants, *155*, 191
Villa Maria Academy, *145*
Village Improvement Society. (*See also* Village Preservation and Improvement Society), 104, 145
Village Preservation and Improvement Society. (*See also* Village Improvement Society), 14, 62, 83, 93, 99, 101, *138*, 145, 160, 169, 172, 173, 188
Virginia - Secession from Union (1861), 45
Virginia Forest (neighborhood), *128*

Virginia Militia, 60th Regiment (ca. War of 1812), 35
Virginia State Audubon Society, 84
Virginia Tech-University of Virginia Northern Virginia Center, *141*, 157
Virginia Training School, 70, 83, *142*

W

Walden Court, *73*
Walnut Hill (home), 42, *175*
War Camp Recreation Society, 99
War of 1812 (1812–1814), *34*, 35-37
Ware's Drug Store, *118*
Warner, John, 21
Washington-Virginia Railway, 104
Washington Aqueduct, 106, *116*
Washington House, *64*
Washington Navy Yard, 34–35
Washington Street, North, 64, 89, 90-91, 96, 115, 118, 127
Washington Street, South, *109*, 118
Washington & Old Dominion Railroad Regional Park, 173, 189, *189*
Washington & Old Dominion Railroad, 59, *95*, 135, 140, 143, 178
Washington, Augustine, 21
Washington, D.C.
    Boundaries (1790–1846), 32, 33, 72
    Destruction (1814), 34, 36
    Founding (1790–1800), 31
    World War II (1939–1949), 121–122
Washington, George, 21, 22, 25, 27-28
Water towers, *91*, 115, 136,
Water works, 106, *116*
Waterways, *138*, 145, 160
Weddings, *108*, 149, 183
Wells family, *110*
Wells, Claude, *110*
Wells, Harry E., *110*, 114, 162
West End, *73*, 108, 115, 140, 141, 143
West Falls Church, *73*, 104–105, 108, 115
West Street, 91, 175
West, John, 21, 27
WFAX-AM radio, *153*
Whipple, Mary Margaret, *167*
Whitehall Sanitarium, *64*, 144
Whitney, Paul, *190*
Whittier Elementary School, 129, *147*
Williamsburg, Va., 26
Williams, Nancy, *40*
Wilson Boulevard, 39, 56, 141
Wilt-Reineke, Helen, *177*
Windmills, 68
Winkler, Kathy, *167*
"Wizard of Oz" (movie), *182*
Womanless weddings, 149
Women, 49, 67, *165*
Woodbrook (home), 68
Wood, Leonard, 91
World War I (1917–1918), 98–101
World War II (1939–1945), 69, 120–125, 132
Wren's Tavern, 35–37, *37*, 39
Wren, James, 21, 23, 25, 28
Wright, Frank Lloyd, 119

Y
YMCA (Young Men's Christian Association), 99
Yochim, Marie, 169

Z
Zotter, Walt, 169

Sources

A
Acevedo, Marjorie McElroy, 110
Acosta, Francis, 135
Allison, Joseph, 38
Anderson, James E., 92
Arlington News, 153

B
Barrett, Bier, 41
Barrett, William Edmund, 24, 40, 71, 111
Birindelli, Nancy, 168, 173, 174, 176, 189
Boatright, Scott, 167, 174
Brady, Mathew, 46, 51
Bray, Robin, 37
Briggs, Lee, 25, 87, 104
Brown, Hugh, 82, 95
Budetti, Maureen, 155, 185, 191–192
Buschow, Barry, 187

C
Cammann, William C., 80
Carter-Bailey Studio, 108
Castorina, Marge, 145
Century Collection of Civil War Art, 56
Chaves, Tony, 64, 66, 89, 114
Cole, Carolyn, 165
Coons, T. A., 140
Copley, Joe, Mrs., 71
Corbett, V. P., 44

D
D'Aquila, Frank, 180, 183, 190
Degnan, Fred, 179
DePoorter, Brian, 184
Dewberry, Sidney O., 178
District of Columbia Public Library, 134, 181

E
Evening Star, 113, 122, 125, 129, 135, 138, 149, 156, 164

F
Fairfax County Public Library, 129
Falls Church Cable Channel 38, 154
Falls Church Community Center, 181, 184
Falls Church Echo, 125, 128, 132, 138, 148
Falls Church News-Press, 153, 154, 160, 166, 173, 177
Falls Church Planning Office, 191
Falls Church Police Department, 190
Falls Church Public Information Office, 166
Falls Church Volunteer Fire Department, 123, 140–141, 150
Federal Highway Administration, 16
Federal Home Administration, 120
Fenwick, Eleanor, 72, 87
Fowx, Egbert Guy, 65

Fox, Clarence, Sr., Mrs., 108
Frank Leslie's Illustrated New York Magazine, 48
Frank Leslie's Illustrated News, 180
Frank Leslie's Pictorial History of the American Civil War, 47, 55
Frye, Ken, 162

G
Galkin family, 94
Galleher, George, 61
Garner, Wally, 90
Gawarecki, Carolyn Grosse, 181
George Studio, 119
George Washington's Office Museum, 28
Gernand, Bradley E., 146
Globe, 152
Gubbins, Mary Clare, 183
Gunston Hall Plantation, Board of Regents, 29
G. W. Davis Studio, 67

H
Harper's Weekly, 48–49
Hartman, Clarence, 76, 93
Harwood, H. H., Jr., 43, 135
Henderson, James, 105
Herman, Howard, 188
Hildebrand, Ruth Mankin, 96
Hopkins Atlas, 65
Houdon, Jean Antoine, 29
Howlett, Albert, 188
Hull, Robert D., 166

J
Johnson, Michael, 12

K
Kansas State Historical Society, 78, 81

L
Library of Congress
    Geography and Map Division, 15, 20
    Prints and Photographs Division, 34, 46, 55, 74, 76–77, 101, 119–120
Long, George, 139
Lossing, Benson, 16, 18, 22, 26
Lovett, Jonathon, 33

M
Maier, John, 154, 160–161
Mary Riley Styles Public Library, 32, 33, 37, 38, 40, 41–42, 54, 57, 60, 63–73, 76, 78, 82, 84–88, 90–98, 101, 108, 109, 110, 115, 118, 119, 124, 125, 130, 131–132, 133, 134–135, 136, 137–138, 139, 140, 142, 144, 145–149, 151–152, 161, 163, 170
McGuigan, William J., Mrs., 155
Miller, E. S., 135
Mitchell, Beth, 17
Mount Vernon Ladies' Association, 29

N
National Archives and Records Administration, 15, 51–52, 55, 80
National Memorial Park, 150
Nette, Janice C., 182
New York Illustrated News, 50

New York State Library, 44
Ninde, Julian, Jr., Mrs., 119
Northern Virginia Sun, 150
Northern Virginia Transportation Commission, 141

P
Parrott, Harold, 112
Pictorial War Record, 54–55
Piggott, Willard, 42, 88
Porter, Quentin, 32, 71, 115, 130–134, 136–140, 144, 146–149, 158, 163
Prior, Erle, 19

R
Rakeman, Carl, 16
Rosenthal, Albert, 29

S
Sanborn Map Company, 126, 144
Schick, Nancy, 186
Smith, Malcolm, 118
Spangler, Michael L., 113
Speakman, Kay, 11, 58, 72–73
Stewart, Elizabeth Tabb, 40

T
Terman, Maurice J., 33
Thompson, Myron, Mrs., 85
Titbull, Dexter, 86
Treacy, Linda, 185

U
United States Army Corps of Engineers, 116
United States Army Military History Institute, 52
United States Army, 123–124
University of Virginia - Alderman Library, 60, 91

V
Vanderhoof, Charles A., 56
Village Preservation and Improvement Society, 14

W
Wagner's Complete Map of District of Columbia..., 117
Warner, John, 15
Washington & Old Dominion Railroad Regional Park, 115, 189
Wells, Harry E., 114
Wendelin, Rudolph, 23
Whipple, Mary Margaret, 167
Williams, Barbara, 57, 62–63, 68, 90, 104–107, 111
Williams, J.L.B., 108

Y
Yochim, Marie, 18

Bradley E. Gernand is a native of Antlers, Oklahoma, a small town in the beautiful but rugged Kiamichi Mountains of the Choctaw Nation. His childhood spent among the Choctaw prompted his early interest in history. He has served as archivist in the National Archives and is now a senior archivist in the Library of Congress, and is a U.S. Navy officer in the reserve. He holds degrees from the University of Oklahoma.

Gernand moved to Falls Church in 1990, where he serves on the library board of trustees and has served on the historical commission and Falls Church Jaycees. He is the next-door neighbor of Robert Pogorzelski Matthews, a lifelong resident of Falls Church, who graciously tended to Gernand's many outdoor chores, without being asked, to provide the coauthor additional time in which to work on this book—"the embodiment of what makes Falls Church unique among places," according to Gernand.

Nan Netherton was born in Chicago, Illinois and raised in a tiny village called Ozone in the Tennessee mountains. She and her husband Ross and their children settled in the Falls Church area in 1951.

Deeply interested in history during her academic years, she valued the opportunities which brought her to Northern Virginia. Historian for ten years in the Fairfax County Office of Comprehensive Planning, she has written, been coauthor or has been senior editor of more than 35 published monographs and books on Northern Virginia's rich local history.

Nan served for several years on the board of directors of the Friends of Cherry Hill Foundation. She holds academic degrees from the University of Chicago and George Mason University.